MARINES

PAGE 1: During the island-hopping campaign in the Pacific, Marine snipers use cover of damaged coconut trees to pick off Japanese naval infantry in pillboxes.

THIS PAGE: A Marine Rifleman from Company H, 2nd Battalion, 5th Marines, leaps across a break in a rice paddy in Quang Tin Province, August 15, 1966.

MARINES
An Illustrated History
The U.S. Marine Corps from 1775 to the 21st Century

Chester G. Hearn

ZENITH PRESS

Project manager: Ray Bonds
Design: Mark Tennent/Compendium Design
Maps: Mike Marino
Diagrams: Mark Franklin
Photo research: Anne and Rolf Lang

Acknowledgments
Thanks to all those who helped by providing photographs for this book. Most of the images come from the Library of Congress (LoC), National Archives (NA), Department of Defense, Defense Visual Information Center (DVIC), or Marine Historical Center (MHC) many via Ray Bonds' private collection (RB). Specifics are as follows:
Pages 1-6: NA. 7: top NA, bottom LoC. 8-9: DVIC. 10-29: LoC. 30: RB. 31-33: LoC. 34: NA. 35: left LoC, right NA. 36-38: LoC. 39-40: NA. 41: top DVIC, bottom NA. 42: LoC. 43 NA. 44: NA. 45: left LoC, right NA. 47-48: NA. 49: right LoC, rest NA. 50-51: LoC. 52-53: NA. 54: top LoC, rest NA. 55: LoC. 56: top left LoC, rest MHC. 57: LoC. 58: MHC. 59: NA. 60: LoC. 61: left Loc, right top MHC, right bottom NA. 62-63: NA. 64: RB. 65: MHC. 66: NA. 67: MHC. 68: LoC. 69-70: MHC. 71: top left NA, top right Compendium, bottom right MHC. 72-73: bottom left MHC, rest NA. 74-109: NA. 110: NA. 112: left NA, right MHC. 113-121: NA. 122-123: bottom left MHC, rest NA. 124-125: NA. 126-127: RB. 128-129: top left RB, rest MHC. 130-131: bottom left MHC, rest NA. 132: top MHC, bottom NA. 133-145: NA. 146-147: DVIC. 148: top right DVIC, rest NA. 149: NA. 150-187: DVIC.

RIGHT: Marine artillerymen fire a 75mm pack howitzer to stem a Japanese counterattack at Gloucester, New Britain, December 1943.

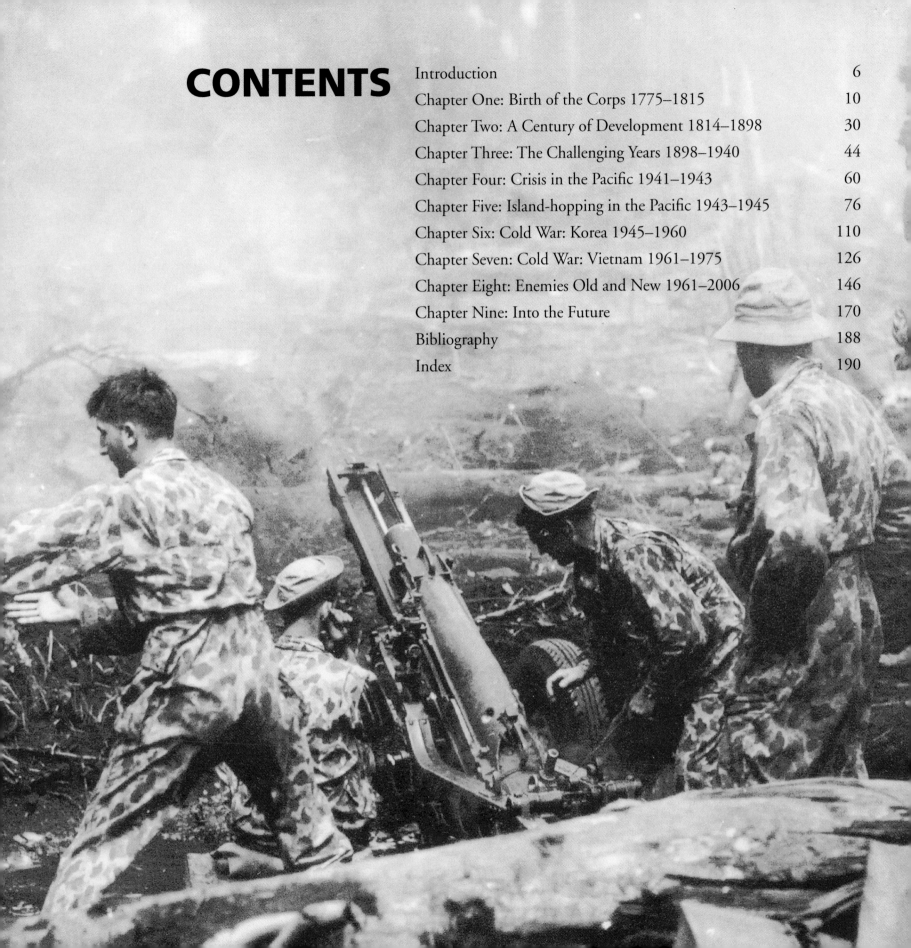

CONTENTS

INTRODUCTION

FAR RIGHT, TOP: Whatever the call, at land or sea, the U.S. Marine has put his hard training to good use and without faltering has served under the harshest of conditions wherever required around the world.

FAR RIGHT, BOTTOM: Marines have always had to recruit hard after near-decimation of the Corps by service rivals and politicians. Here, Joe Rosenthal's famous flag-raising photo on Iwo Jima was the basis of a painting by Sgt. Tom Lovell to stir the spirit of young men.

RIGHT: Since the first amphibious assault on Providence Island in the Bahamas in 1776, the U.S. Marine Corps has been preparing itself for assaulting enemy beaches (shown here moving inland at Socorro in support of Philippine Constabulary against Colorum guerrillas, January 1924), but nothing quite compared with the shock of going to war in the Pacific.

The history of the United States Marine Corps is all about tenacity and how a handful of bedraggled and unappreciated ships' guards known as Continental marines grew from a sprinkling of untrained officers and men more than 230 years ago to become in the 21st century a superb, multi-functional, ready-response force combining ground, air, and sea power. The transformation has never been smooth. Besides fighting on distant shores or quelling disturbances at home, Marine Corps commandants, especially during peacetime, had to adroitly battle penurious politicians and interservice rivals who tried on several occasions to emasculate the Corps. The constant struggle for survival made Marines unlike the men and women in any of the other services. They fought for their niche at home and abroad, and turned every crisis into an opportunity to prove their worth. The constant pressure to be the best created a special bond—a fellowship of valor—that made Marines the most determined fighters on earth. Leathernecks know it as *esprit de corps*—their spirit, their Corps—and they have made it their own because they believe they are the best.

The Marine Corps has always been the smallest of America's armed services. Even when it has filled its ranks with manpower from the wartime draft, the Corps maintained its elitist image by characterizing all marines—men and women, including reservists—as volunteers. The tradition of being the "select few" traced back to the 19th century when Marine officers stressed military appearance, strict obedience to orders, marksmanship, and disciplined behavior to distinguish the Corps from the bluejackets and naval officers with whom they served.

Finding themselves often on the chopping block during the 20th century, Marines knew they must develop skills that differentiated them from the other services. After the Spanish/American War the Corps concentrated on amphibious doctrine—thereby displacing bluejackets—and superior combat effectiveness, as opposed to the more conservative policies of the regular army. The conversion to a new battle doctrine may have saved the Corps because even Theodore Roosevelt, Harry S. Truman, and Dwight D. Eisenhower, being army and navy men, questioned the expense and rationality of retaining marines as a fighting force. From his World War II headquarters in Europe, Eisenhower never paid much attention to the 475,000 men and women Marines who defeated the Japanese during the war in the Pacific. To three respected presidents it was not enough that Marines had distinguished themselves as the most ferocious and determined fighters when they spearheaded the attacks at Belleau Wood and Mont Blanc Ridge during World War I and forever engraved their immortal combat history on the blood-drenched islands and atolls of the Pacific during World War II.

Perhaps the greatest threat to the survival of the Marine Corps occurred after World War II when the Army Air Force, then a part of the U.S. Army, attempted to convince the government that large navies and ground troops would no longer be necessary, the airmen's theory

being that all wars would be nuclear and require a vast fleet of strategic bombers in place of ground troops. In 1947 the air corps, with Truman's approval, succeeded in extracting itself from army control and became the U.S. Air Force, but failed to change the role of the navy and the Marine Corps. Three years later the 1st Marine Division came to the rescue of South Korea and spearheaded a conventional ground war that had not been anticipated by military policy makers.

Marines take an interest in anything new. They were among the first to grasp the importance of air power and the first to urge the development of the helicopter. Air power and the flexibility of helicopters fit neatly into the Corps' concept of ready-response for

ENLIST NOW
U.S. MARINE CORPS

ABOVE: With terrorism spreading, Marines have become more involved in military operations in urban territory (MOUT), which is the reason that the 3rd Battalion, 2nd Marines, began assault training on the MOUT facility at Camp LeJeune, North Carolina. The kneeling Marine is armed with an M16A2 assault rifle, while his buddy has an M240G medium machine gun.

their ever-changing amphibious assault doctrine. Today, with their own ships, aircraft, and special operations capability, Marines have become the most versatile, self-sufficient, all-encompassing, ready-response warriors on the planet. Leathernecks enjoy elitism because they have earned it.

Despite the efforts of past presidents, politicians, and air proponents to diminish the role of the Corps, the Marines have never relinquished a major function or suffered one being stripped away by interservice rivalry. They still serve as detachments on capital ships and act as security guards at naval shore installations. But today they are no longer pegged as infantrymen because they have become experts in every element of

warfighting and peacekeeping. Among other duties, they are uniquely trained in amphibious warfare and organized into highly mobile attack groups operating from specially designed ships. Marines fly fighter-bombers, helicopters, and surveillance planes, and operate from amphibious assault vessels. Unlike members of the old Corps, they are equipped with the very best weapons and equipment, including the latest instrumentation for pinpoint targeting and delivery of guided missiles, bombs, bullets, and artillery shells.

Since Korea, warfighting has drastically changed. The enemy no longer wears uniforms. Like the Viet Cong, they blend into the civilian population. In Afghanistan and Somalia, a good guy could not be

distinguished from a bad guy. Terrorism has made the situation worse because Islamic militants bent on destroying western civilization are no longer confined to a country but are everywhere. Marines are continuously modifying their doctrine to respond to the evolving global war on terrorism.

At the beginning of the 21st century, Commandant General James L. Jones, Jr., and his planners looked into the future and designed *Marine Corps Strategy 21.*

The new doctrine addresses every aspect of warfighting, peacekeeping, humanitarian tasks, and rapid response to emergencies. It provides the "vision, goals, and aims to support the development of future combat capabilities." The new strategy also provides

the tools to accomplish the tasks, and none of these tasks is more important than defeating terrorism before the enemy strikes.

General Michael W. Hagee, the 33rd Commandant of the Marine Corps, charged "each and every marine" to join him "in this challenging journey into the twenty-first century. Our tasks are before us," he said. "We will win the current battles and be ready to defeat our nation's future foes. Let us proceed with boldness, intellect, and confidence in each other, as we continue to forge the legacy of our great Corps and strive to take our rightful place in that 'long line' of Marines that have acquitted themselves with the greatest distinction, winning new honors on each occasion."

ABOVE: After completing combat training exercises in June 2005, a convoy of Marine Amphibious Assault Vehicles (AAV7A1) operated by the 3rd Amphibious Assault Battalion moves along the shore of the Pacific Missile Range Facility at Oahu, Hawaii.

BIRTH OF THE CORPS 1775–1815

RIGHT: An odd assortment of Continental Marines with a smattering of state Marines join Ethan Allen's Green Mountain Boys during May 1775 to assist in the capture of Fort Ticonderoga on Lake Champlain.

"We are engaged in a good cause, and are fighting the Lord's battles.
John Trevett,
Continental
Marine, Journal of John Trevett"

Marines can be traced back to 480 B.C., when 6,000 sword- and spear-carrying Greeks dressed in bronze armor became a decisive factor in the naval battle of Salamis during the Persian War. Then, in the 3rd century B.C., during the Punic Wars, the Romans and Carthaginians frequently had 500 warships at sea, manned by as many as 150,000 sailors and Marines. After the tactics proved successful, Roman ships continued to carry Marines, and the practice persisted through centuries to become firmly implanted in the navies of Europe.

In 1740 the British went to war against Spain and raised a regiment of 3,000 American colonists. Virginia's lieutenant governor, Colonel William Gooch, took command of the unit, soon to become known as "Gooch's marines." In April 1741 the colonel led his regiment against the forts at Cartagena, Colombia, where his men suffered heavy casualties and retired. In August, Gooch's marines assaulted and captured Walthenham Bay (now Guantánamo Bay, Cuba), but disease riddled the unit. Only 10 percent of the men survived the six-month campaign.

During the Seven Years' War (1756–1763), American marines serving on British warships performed new roles. They toughened sailors to their duties and enforced ship discipline. When engaged in battle at sea, they climbed aloft as sharpshooters and grenadiers, and when fighting ships closed they led the boarding parties. Then as now, marines spearheaded the attacks.

The Outbreak of War (1775)

On April 19, 1775, British Major John Pitcairn's marines accompanied by foot soldiers from Boston, Massachusetts, skirmished with colonial militia at Lexington and Concord. The action raised the curtain on the American Revolution (1775–1783) and trouble soon followed.

On May 9, a small colonial munitions-seeking expedition led by Ethan Allen and Colonel Benedict Arnold captured Fort Ticonderoga on Lake Champlain. A few days later the Continental Congress received word that the rag-tag American garrison needed "men and money" to hold the fort. Eight "well spirited and equipped" Connecticut state marines accompanied a relief expedition organized at Hartford. Those nameless eight men are still extolled by the U.S. Marine Corps as the "Original Eight." Later, another state unit with marines arrived from Albany, New York, to serve on boats and garrison the fort. Colonel Arnold took one look at the motley lot and described them as "the refuse of every regiment."

LEFT: Very few Continental Marines experienced the dubious pleasure of receiving uniforms, which were stitched from the cheapest material, seldom fit, and after a few weeks of wearing began to shred.

The Continental Marines

In August 1775, General George Washington armed two fishing schooners to prey on British commerce. He pulled fishermen from his infantry and made them marines. By the end of October, three types of marines were fighting for independence: army marines under Washington, state navy marines, and privateering marines. Washington eventually commissioned eleven schooners, and by 1777 his seaborne marines had captured fifty-five prizes before becoming Continental Marines.

Much like British marines (formally organized in 1664), Continental Marines served the navy, not the army. In November 1775, the Marine Committee, formed by the Continental Congress, met at Tun Tavern on King Street in Philadelphia. While sipping ale, the committee drafted the "Rules and Regulations of the Navy of the United Colonies." Part of the program included the creation of a Continental fleet of eight ships and two battalions of "American Marines." On November 10, pressed by John Adams of Massachusetts and the Marine Committee, the Continental Congress halfheartedly authorized:

> ". . . two Battalions of Marines be raised consisting of one Colonel, two Lieutenant Colonels, two Majors & Officers as usual in other regiments, that they consist of an

equal number of privates with other battalions . . . and are good seamen, or so acquainted with maritime affairs to be able to serve to advantage by sea, when required."

Although another ten months elapsed before Congress formed the United States of America, Marines honor November 10, 1775, as the birth date of its Corps.

RIGHT: Thirty-one-year-old Captain Samuel Nicholas of Philadelphia, owner of a prosperous tavern, became the Marine Corps' first commandant on November 28, 1775. He served six years and remained the senior officer in the Continental Marines throughout the Revolution.

Samuel Nicholas Takes Command

The act providing for "American Marines" clearly stated that a colonel would be in charge of the unit, but the clerk of the Continental Congress had no blank commission forms for signing on Marines. He did have blanks for officers of the Continental Navy, so he made 31-year-old Samuel Nicholas a "Captain of Marines" in the navy. On November 28, 1775, President John Hancock signed the order and unintentionally made Nicholas the first officer in the Continental Navy.

Nicholas's selection as Captain of Marines occurred because of his family's close association with Robert Morris, an influential Philadelphia maritime shipper.

Nicholas was the son of a Philadelphia blacksmith, and his maritime experience extended no farther than having served as supercargo on Morris's ships. He was better known as an innkeeper with a passion for shooting ducks on the Schuylkill and Delaware rivers.

Tun Tavern, owned by Robert Mullan, became Nicholas's recruiting center. The patriotic tune "Drum, Fife, and Colours," augmented by liberal servings of grog, helped fill the ranks. Sobering reality occurred after the recruit learned he would be paid a paltry six-and-two-thirds dollars a month. His natty green and white uniform, if he ever received one, would be of the cheapest fabric. His daily navy ration was a pound of bread; a pound of beef or pork; a pound of potatoes or turnips or a half pint of peas; and a half pint of rum—supplemented at times with butter, cheese, and pudding. It rapidly deteriorated at sea.

Although Congress originally intended to field two Marine battalions, it never happened. Nicholas recruited enough men for the navy's first expedition, a raid on New Providence Island in the Bahamas on February 17, 1776. He also succeeded in raising

Public Notice

On Board the *Boston*   April 11, 1778
Wanted, for the use and service of the
Marines belonging to this ship:

40 green coats faced with white
40 white waistcoats, and 40 white breeches
The buttons of the whole to be plain white.
Coats to be open-sleeved, and a belt for
every waistcoat.

In behalf of the Captain of Marines,
William Jennison
Lieutenant of Marines

enough men to serve on the new frigates being built at Philadelphia, and in December 1776 his Marines helped Washington cross the Delaware River.

Nicholas commanded the "American Marines" from November 28, 1775, to August 25, 1781, but he spent most of his time assisting his patron, Robert Morris, who was Agent of Marine and responsible for juggling the frugal funds of the fledgling navy. In 1781 Nicholas embarked on his final adventure working for Morris. Through 350 miles of Tory-infested territory, he escorted from Newport, Rhode Island, to Philadelphia an ox cart filled with a million silver crowns loaned by King Louis XIV of France.

Although Nicholas never commanded more than a small battalion of men, today's Marine Corps justifiably regard him as its first commandant.

Marines at War

Following the Providence Island assault, Nicholas became the first major of the "American Marines." Although historians called the expedition "the first fight in the records of the Regular Navy," Marines marked it as the first in the Corps' long history of successful amphibious operations. There was never another like it during the eight-year Revolution. Nor did Nicholas control all the Marines that fought in the war. Thousands served on privateers and in navies organized by the states. On October 11, 1776, Nicholas was attending to business in Philadelphia when Brigadier General Benedict Arnold's Marines fought off a British fleet of fifty-three boats near Valcour Island, which stopped the enemy's advance down Lake Champlain. The action became strategically important because it

ABOVE: During Commodore Esek Hopkins's expedition to the Bahamas in March 1776, Captain Samuel Nicholas led his battalion of Marines ashore on New Providence Island, capturing two forts and the capital of Nassau.

The New Providence Expedition

During the winter of 1776, Captain Nicholas prepared 268 Marines for their first expedition, an eight-ship foray into the Bahamas under the command of former sea captain Commodore Esek Hopkins of Rhode Island. After distributing four companies of Marines throughout the squadron, Nicholas joined Hopkins on the 24-gun flagship *Alfred*.

On February 17, the Continental squadron followed the winter ice down the Delaware River and on March 1 rendezvoused off Great Abaco Island in the Bahamas. Hopkins expected to find 600 barrels of gunpowder at Nassau, on New Providence Island, and formed a landing party of Marines to assault two British forts. The strategy required that Nicholas land on the east side of the island, capture Fort Montague, then march west along the coast and capture Fort Nassau while Hopkins stood offshore and blockaded the harbor.

On Sunday afternoon, March 3, American Marines performed their first amphibious operation. They rowed ashore in whaleboats and landed two miles southeast of Fort Montague. Marine Lieutenant John Trevett led his company to the fort, which surrendered after ineffectively firing a few 18-pound shot. Nicholas spent the night at Montague and at daybreak marched to the outskirts of Nassau. He demanded and received the keys to Fort Nassau and hauled down the British colors.

The spoils fell far short of everyone's expectations. Because Nicholas had dallied overnight at Fort Montague, and because Hopkins failed to adequately blockade the harbor, the British governor waited until nightfall and shipped most of Nassau's gunpowder to Florida. Nicholas located only 24 casks of powder but collected 46 cannon, 12 artillery pieces, 15 mortars, and several tons of shot.

On March 17 Hopkins sailed for home with the plunder, along with three American ships recaptured from the British, and three prisoners, including the governor. During the voyage Hopkins grossly mishandled an engagement with the British frigate *Glasgow*. The action took the lives of seven Marines, including Second Lieutenant John Fitzpatrick, who earned the unfortunate distinction of becoming the first Marine to die in combat.

ABOVE: Homeward bound from the Bahamas, Nicholas's Marines engaged in a second battle on April 6 between the Alfred and the HMS Glasgow. In a confused night action, Lieutenant John Fitzpatrick became the first Marine officer killed in action.

led to the defeat of British General John Burgoyne at Saratoga, New York, the following summer.

In 1776 the British drove Washington's army out of Long Island and Manhattan and began pushing the Continentals across New Jersey. When Philadelphia became threatened, Congress fled to Baltimore. Major Nicholas remained behind and pulled 131 Marines off the ships in the Delaware River. On December 2 he formed a battalion and offered his services to Washington.

On Christmas Eve, Marines crossed the ice-littered Delaware and struck the Hessian garrison at Trenton. The unexpected assault attracted the attention of Lord Cornwallis, who moved to box Washington's small force between the Delaware and the Atlantic Ocean. Instead, Washington took his force, and with the help from Nicholas's Marines, slipped eastward over a disused road and defeated the British force at Princeton. The Marines' first land campaign ended with Washington flanking British communications and forcing Cornwallis to evacuate lower New Jersey.

Marines also appeared as a riverine force when 27-year-old Captain James Willing raised thirty-five men and on January 10, 1778, started out from Fort Pitt, Pennsylvania, in an old boat he appropriately named the *Rattletrap*. Willing raided British posts and captured several ships while sailing down the Ohio and Mississippi rivers. Lieutenant Robert George aided the operation by scouting ahead in a canoe. By the time Willing reached New Orleans, his company numbered more than a hundred. After defeating a British sloop on Lake Pontchartrain, Willing sent his force back up the Mississippi to fight Indians alongside George Rogers Clark.

During the summer of 1779, Marines participated in one of the most poorly executed expeditions of the war. The British had erected a fort at the mouth of the Castine River in Penobscot Bay, which was then a part of Loyalist Massachusetts but is now in Maine. Commodore Dudley Saltonstall and Massachusetts militia Brigadier General Solomon Lovell plotted to seize the fort. From the frigate *Warren*, Marine Captain John Welsh commanded the fleet's three hundred Marines, half of which belonged to state navies. On July 26, while American warships fired on the fort, Welsh landed his Marines on Nautilus Island and routed the British defenders.

On July 28, Welsh's Marines landed on the mainland peninsula and climbed a steep bluff to the British fort. Accompanied by militia, Marines led the assault and drove the British force into the fort. Lovell soon arrived and organized a siege. When on August 13 a British squadron from New York arrived offshore, Saltonstall panicked, embarked the ground force, fled up the Penobscot River, ran his ships ashore, and set them afire. The American force, including Welsh's Marines, escaped overland. Unlike every other unit in the expedition, Welsh's battalion performed gallantly, marking the first time Marines had landed from the sea in force in the face of enemy fire.

LEFT: Three small companies of Continental Marines get a dose of George Washington's temper when they momentarily falter during the battle of Princeton, New Jersey, on January 3, 1777.

LEFT: After being upbraided by General Washington, Marines reorganize under the leadership of Captain Nicholas, fix bayonets, and with drums beating, lead the charge on the British flank and score a major victory.

FAR LEFT: With chunks of ice floating down the Delaware, Marines pole General Washington across the river on Christmas night, 1776, and launch a brilliant morning surprise attack on the British garrison at Trenton.

LEFT: During the abortive battle of Penobscot Bay, Marine Captain John Welsh and his company fiercely attack and overrun the British position on Bagaduce Peninsula, but suffer seventy casualties.

John Paul Jones's Marines

During late 1777 Captain John Paul Jones, commanding the *Ranger*, sailed into France with a complement of Lieutenant Samuel Wallingford's Marines. In April 1778 the *Ranger* returned to sea to terrorize British shipping in the Irish Sea. One escapade involved a raid on Jones's hometown of Whitehaven, England, where he and Wallingford's Marines spiked the guns at the town's fort, attempted to burn the waterfront, and then crossed Solway Firth to St. Mary's Island, where they seized the residence of the Earl of Selkirk. The operation marked the first purely foreign invasion of England since the Norman Conquest in 1066. Wallingford may have changed his good luck by seizing Selkirk's silver. The following day he fell during a fight with the 20-gun British sloop-of-war *Drake*.

Jones's climactic sea battle occurred on September 23, 1779, while commanding a broken-down French merchantman he renamed *Bonhomme Richard* and four other ships, among them the 36-gun frigate *Alliance*. Marine Lieutenant Edward Stack, a 23-year-old officer from an Irish regiment, had pulled together a force of 137 Marines to serve on the 42-gun *Richard*. Captain Matthew Parke commanded Marines on the *Alliance*, but her French captain later proved to be worthless in battle.

While sailing off the east coast of Scotland, Jones encountered the 50-gun *Serapis*, the 20-gun *Countess of Scarborough*, and forty-one British merchantmen. Off England's Flamborough Head, Jones attacked the *Serapis* and would have been whipped if the two vessels had not collided and become entangled. When Captain Richard Pearson of the *Serapis* shouted, "Has your ship struck?" Jones replied, "I have not yet begun to fight!"

At this critical point, Stack's Marines took charge of the battle. They hooked onto the *Serapis* with grapples and brought the vessels abeam, Jones shouting from the steerage, "Well done, my brave lads. We have got her now!"

Captain Pearson struggled to break from the deadly embrace, but every time a British sailor showed on deck Marine sharpshooters in the tops greeted him with a hail of musket fire. Every

time British gun crews tried to man the 18-pounders, Stack's Marines swept them from the deck.

Jones had problems with several French officers who wanted to surrender, but the Marines stood firm. They played a decisive role in saving the day but not the shattered old ship. The *Bonhomme Richard* eventually sank, but not until after Jones had taken possession of the *Serapis* and transferred his men to the prize.

TOP: Time came when it no longer seemed possible for the Bonhomme Richard to stay afloat, but John Paul Jones refused to surrender. Above the firing of Marines, he shouted to the captain of the HMS Serapis: "I have not yet begun to fight."

ABOVE: While cruising in the Irish Sea in April 1777, Marine Lieutenant Samuel Wallingford went ashore at Whitehaven with John Paul Jones and a boatload of Marines, thus invading English soil for the first time since 1066.

The New Republic

On April 11, 1783, the Treaty of Paris brought an end to the Revolution. The Continental Congress abolished the American Marines and the Continental Navy. Samuel Nicholas became an innkeeper again, and congressional shortsightedness soon became challenged by more expensive problems.

In 1789 the first U.S. Congress assembled in New York to begin the task of governing. Because the Royal Navy no longer protected American commerce in the Mediterranean, Barbary pirates captured merchantmen and demanded tribute. Having no money, Congress refused to meet the terms. Shipping losses mounted, and five years passed while legislators realized that rebuilding a navy might be cheaper than paying tribute. On March 1794, Congress authorized six frigates but failed to provide the funds. Two years passed before Congress appropriated enough money to build three of the frigates: the *United States*, the *Constellation*, and the *Constitution*. On July 1, 1797, as an afterthought, Congress authorized 167 Marines: 5 lieutenants, 8 sergeants, 8 corporals, 3 drummers, 3 fifers, and 140 privates. A Marine Corps had not been officially organized, so the men became part of the navy's crew.

The U.S. Marine Corps

On April 9, 1798, Secretary of War James McHenry recommended that an organization of Marines be formally established. Congressman Samuel Sewall of Massachusetts put the wheels of lawmaking in motion and sponsored a bill calling for "a battalion to be called the Marine Corps." The Senate, finding themselves upstaged by the House, increased the size of the Corps to a regiment. The bill passed on July 11, 1798, placing the Corps directly under the chief executive. Until President John Adams decided whether Marines should belong to the army or the navy, the regiment would exist as "Presidential Troops." By pushing the

musicians moved with it, thereby ensuring that the president would always have his band. After Thomas Jefferson defeated Adams for the presidency in 1800, the band played for Jefferson's inauguration. By 1804, when ill health forced Burrows to resign, the band had become the "President's Own."

The Quasi-French War

During Burrows's administration, French privateers began menacing American merchantmen on the high seas at the same time that Barbary corsairs were doing likewise in the Mediterranean. Without a navy, the United States could neither go to war nor defend its merchant fleet. On July 13, 1798, Secretary of the Navy Stoddert explained the situation best when he wrote Captain John Barry, "Congress will break-up on Monday, without a declaration of war against France. We shall not on that account be the less at war, against their armed vessels."

During the undeclared war with France, Marines served aboard American ships and participated in every engagement afloat and ashore. In 1799, Lieutenant Bartholomew Clinch's Marines on the USS

legislation through Congress, Sewall earned the rightful title of "Father of the Marine Corps."

The Corps of 1798 consisted of 33 officers and 848 enlisted men, including musicians. Its mission, according to recently appointed Secretary of the Navy Benjamin Stoddert, was to be "of amphibious nature," with duty at sea, duty in forts, and "any duty on shore, as the President, at his discretion, shall direct." On signing the bill into law, President Adams appointed William Ward Burrows, Major, Commandant of the Marine Corps.

A Charleston, South Carolina, businessman and veteran of the Revolution, Burrows wasted no time selecting outstanding officers to bring the Corps to strength. Although privates received four dollars less per month than ordinary sailors, they voiced no complaints. Burrows took advantage of having drummers and fifers authorized and organized the U.S. Marine Band by the simple expedient of assessing every officer ten dollars. When the government moved from Philadelphia to Washington, D.C., Burrows and his

Organization and Pay of the Marine Corps—1798

Major	$50 and 4 rations
Captain	$40 and 3 rations
First lieutenant	$30 and 3 rations
Second lieutenant	$25 and 2 rations
Sergeant major	$10
Drum major: fife major	$9
Sergeant	$9
Corporal	$8
Fifers and drummers	$7
Privates	$6

his adventurous Marines sailed into Puerto Plata on the north coast of Santo Domingo and captured the local fort, spiked the cannon, and sailed away.

During the Quasi-French War, which ended in February 1801, Marines contributed to the capture of eighty-five French ships, including two frigates, against the U.S. Navy's loss of one.

The Barbary Wars

The undeclared war with France had barely ended when on May 14, 1801, Yusef Caramanli, the pasha of Tripoli, declared war on the United States in an effort to extract greater payments of tribute. The declaration scotched President Jefferson's plans to downsize the navy and the Marine Corps. By then, the Barbary States had extorted $2,000,000 from the United States, enough to build a formidable navy. Stoddert hurriedly assembled a four-ship squadron and sent Commodore Richard Dale with the frigates *President, Essex,* and *Philadelphia* and the schooner *Enterprise* to the Mediterranean. With too few ships to stop the host of Barbary corsairs sailing out of Morocco, Tunis, Algiers, and Tripoli, Dale called for reinforcements.

On October 31, 1803, while attempting to blockade Tripoli, Captain William Bainbridge accidentally grounded the *Philadelphia* when chasing a corsair running into the harbor. Tripolitans captured the frigate,

ABOVE: Off Puerta Plata, Santo Domingo, during the Quasi-war with France, Captain Daniel Carmick's Marines, after hiding on the sloop Sally, boarded the French privateer Sandwich "like devils," and then entered the harbor and stormed the fort.

RIGHT: Eight Marines joined a night raid led by Lt. Stephen Decatur to burn the USS Philadelphia, captured by Tripolitans on October 31, 1803.

Constellation played a prominent role in capturing the 40-gun French frigate *L'Insurgente.* One year later the same Marines fought a five-hour night action against the 56-gun French frigate *Vengeance* and forced her into Curaçao.

One noteworthy episode during the Quasi-French War occurred on May 11, 1800, when Captain Daniel Carmick, commanding Marines on the *Constitution,* joined forces with sailors on the sloop *Sally* and recaptured the British ship *Sandwich* from the French. Using the *Sandwich* as a "Trojan Horse," Carmick and

refloated her, towed her into port, and imprisoned Bainbridge, his sailors, and forty-four Marines in Yusef's fort. On the night of February 16, 1804, Lieutenant Stephen Decatur stole into the harbor with a complement that included eight Marines and burned the *Philadelphia,* thereby depriving Yusef of his prize.

In an effort to free *Philadelphia*'s crew, American consul William H. Eaton and Marine Lieutenant Presley N. O'Bannon plotted with Hamet Caramanli, the pasha's brother, to overthrow Yusef. The trio organized an expedition of mercenaries in Alexandria,

Egypt, and began a seven-week, 600-mile march across the desert. On April 25, 1805, O'Bannon's Marines and Eaton's squabbling mercenaries stood before the fortress at Derna. Hamet demanded Yusef's surrender, to which the pasha replied, "My head or yours."

On April 26, supported by three navy ships posted offshore, O'Bannon assaulted the fort, planted the American flag on its ramparts, and turned the batteries on the demoralized Tripolitans. In a thoroughly lopsided affair, O'Bannon became the first American to raise the national ensign over a captured fortress in the

ABOVE: After a 600-mile overland desert march from Alexandria, Egypt, Lieutenant Presley O'Bannon's Marines reached Derna on April 25, 1805. On the following afternoon Marines assaulted the fortress and planted the American flag on the ramparts.

ABOVE: During the battle of Lake Erie on September 10, 1813, Marines from the disabled USS Lawrence rowed Captain Oliver Hazard Perry to the USS Niagara, and then joined the fight to defeat England's fresh-water squadron.

BELOW: After all the American militia forces were chased off the Bladensburg battlefield on August 24, 1814, Marines under Captain Samuel Miller stood their ground and delayed the British advance for two crucial hours.

Old World. Had he not done so, *The Marines Hymn* could not have included the stanza: "To the shores of Tripoli." The episode marked the beginning of the end of Barbary depredations in the Mediterranean.

The War of 1812

On June 1, 1812, when President James Madison asked Congress to declare war on Great Britain, most of the ten officers and 483 enlisted men of the Marine Corps were at sea. Madison gambled that part of Canada could be seized by American forces because the British were warring with France and hopefully too distracted to fight on two fronts. Madison expected the fighting to be at sea, although the United States had only three first-class frigates (*President*, *United States*, and *Constitution*), but he believed that privateers would make up the deficit in commissioned fighting ships. To some degree, Madison was correct. It was not long before the 44-gun *Constitution* whipped the HMS *Guerrière* off Boston, the 44-gun *United States* seized the HMS *Macedonian* in the mid-Atlantic, and the

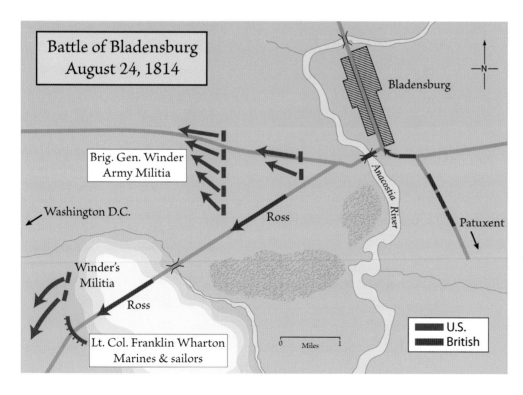

Battle of Bladensburg
August 24, 1814

Bladensburg

Brig. Gen. Winder
Army Militia

Washington D.C.

Ross

Anacostia River

Patuxent

Winder's
Militia

Ross

Lt. Col. Franklin Wharton
Marines & sailors

0   Miles   1

U.S.
British

Constitution sank the HMS *Java* off Brazil. Marines participated in all the actions.

One adventure involved Marine Lieutenant John M. Gamble, who in 1813 sailed into the Pacific on the 32-gun frigate *Essex* with Captain David Porter. In June, the *Essex* captured the 10-gun British whaler *Greenwich*. Because Porter had run out of navy officers to use as prize-masters, he put Gamble in charge of the ship and provided him with a crew of fourteen men.

On July 14 Gamble stumbled across the 22-gun British privateer *Seringapatam,* which had been terrorizing American whalers. He maneuvered the *Greenwich* according to the best principles of naval tactics and forced the stronger *Seringapatam* to strike. Gamble became the only Marine officer in the history of the Corps ever to command a ship.

Not all naval actions occurred on the high seas. On September 10, 1813, Captain Oliver Hazard Perry defeated a British freshwater squadron on Lake Erie. Having been provided with only a few Marines, 28-year-old Perry used them to train army volunteers as sharpshooters. One year later Master Commandant Thomas McDonough defeated another British freshwater squadron on Lake Champlain. With only 1,500 regulars and Marines and 3,000 militia, he defeated the British squadron and forced 11,000 British soldiers commanded by Major General George Prevost to withdraw to Canada.

In April 1814, the war quickly shifted to land operations after Napoleon abdicated and Britain's Peninsular War veterans became available for operations

ABOVE LEFT: After taking position beside ditches, Marines fought the final battle of the war among the bayous of New Orleans on January 8, 1815, and distinguished themselves while serving under General Andrew Jackson.

ABOVE: First Lieutenant John Brooks, Jr., son of the governor of Massachusetts, urged his Marines to keep firing from the tops of the USS Wasp as the ship came abeam of the HMS Reindeer.

LEFT: With a pair of cannon, 114 Marines, and a handful of sailors, Captain Samuel Miller's battalion held off 4,000 British regulars during the battle of Bladensburg. Miller claimed the first blast from an 18-pounder "completely cleared the road."

ABOVE: Surrounded by batteries operated by leathernecks, General Andrew Jackson sits astride a white horse, watching as Captain David Carmick's Marine artillery repulses British General Sir Edward Pakenham's final effort to capture New Orleans on January 8, 1915.

December 24, 1814, the United States and Great Britain signed the Treaty of Ghent, a simple instrument reverting to prewar status quo. Fifteen days later, on the fog-drenched morning of January 8, 1815, British Major General Sir Edward M. Pakenham attacked New Orleans with a force of 7,500 battle-hardened veterans. General Andrew Jackson waited in a well-designed defensive position organized around regulars, militia, Jean Lafitte's pirates, and 300 Marines under the command of Major Daniel Carmick.

The battle began when British columns, weighted down with heavy packs and carrying scaling ladders, marched over a narrow strip of land and into a hail of American musket and cannon fire. Marines were everywhere: some with the Creoles, some with artillery on the left, and some fighting shoulder-to-shoulder with army regulars. Despite brave assaults by the British, by noon the battlefield grew silent. More than 2,500 British lay dead or wounded, among them General Pakenham. Congress passed a resolution of thanks "for the valor and good conduct of Major Daniel Carmick, of the officers, non-commissioned officers, and Marines under his command."

in America. The first campaign began on August 19, when British General Robert Ross landed unopposed on Maryland's Patuxent River and marched on Washington, D.C. Five days later the British reached Bladensburg, a few miles outside the capital, where 6,000 local militiamen fled at the first sound of musket fire. Only 114 Marines under Captain Samuel Miller and a handful of sailors under the command of Commodore Joshua Barney stood their ground. Having nothing more than muskets and a single 18-pounder, the men under Miller and Barney delayed the British advance for two hours and inflicted 250 casualties. The British pressed into Washington, burned the White House, but left the Marine Barracks untouched. On September 12, Ross's veterans mounted an unsuccessful attack on Baltimore and re-embarked after being repulsed.

The British campaign to capture New Orleans developed into the most bizarre battle of the war. On

The Question of Commandants

Had Carmick not eventually died of wounds received at New Orleans, he might have become one of the Marine Corps' great commandants. Major Franklin Wharton, who held the post, had fled from Washington during the battle of Bladensburg to save the Marine payroll, he said. Marines accused him of cowardice. Tried in 1817, Wharton was acquitted but not exonerated. In 1819 Major Anthony Gale replaced Wharton but proved to be an incapable, drunken dunderhead who soon fell foul of incoming Secretary of the Navy Smith Thompson. Court-martialed, Gale pleaded not guilty by reason of insanity and was dismissed from the service. Had Archibald Henderson not been selected as the next commandant, the Marine Corps might never have become what it is today.

Marines At Home and Abroad

Henderson kept the Marines busy. Wherever the navy went, Marines went. The commandant put them in Commodore David Porter's squadron to suppress piracy in the Caribbean. In 1832 he used them on the *Lexington* to free captured American whalers held on the Falkland Islands by Argentines. He sent them to the other side of the world to punish Malayan pirates who had murdered the crew of the American merchantman *Friendship*. From 1838 to 1842 a detachment of Marines in each of five ships went on a voyage of exploration that surveyed the coast of Antarctica, skirmished with Chinese at Canton, and made interim stops at the Fijis, Samoa, and the Philippines. When in 1843 Commodore Matthew C. Perry landed a detachment of Marines on Africa's Ivory Coast to suppress the slave trade, a sergeant saved the commodore's life by shooting Ben Krako, the Berribee chief, and paved the way for a settlement.

Henderson also used Marines to quell domestic problems. When in 1834 inmates at the Massachusetts

LEFT: During the 1843 suppression of the slave trade in western Africa, Commodore Matthew C. Perry takes a detachment of Marines ashore at Liberia. His life is saved when a Marine sergeant shoots Ben Crack-O, chief of the Berribees.

Archibald Henderson

On October 17, 1820, a fiery and ambitious redhead, 38-year-old Archibald Henderson, became the fifth commandant of the Marine Corps. Born in Colchester, Virginia, in 1783, he grew up near the present-day Marine base at Quantico. In 1806 he joined the Marine Corps as an officer, served with distinction on the *Constellation* during the War of 1812, and for bravery received the brevet of major.

Once Henderson became commandant, the future of the Marine Corps began to improve. He compelled all new officers to report to the Marine Barracks for instruction. The program evolved into the Basic School of the future. He made all officers serve at sea, which sometimes resulted in political melodramas if well-connected families complained to the president.

When President Andrew Jackson attempted to merge the Marine Corps into the army, Henderson used friends in Congress to quash the proposal. He preserved the Corps, although the 1834 "Act for the Better Organization of the Marine Corps" provided that the president could assign duties to Marines however he wished. The act also made the Corps a part of the navy department, but not a part of the navy itself.

In May 1836, Jackson exercised his presidential option to deploy the Corps however he wished and sent a two-battalion regiment against the Seminoles and Creeks in Florida and Georgia. Henderson took command of the regiment and brigaded it with the army's 4th Infantry Regiment. Utilizing Indians as scouts, Henderson forced a band of Seminoles to the banks of the Hatchee-Lustee River, and in an action filled with more noise than killing, persuaded Seminole chiefs to relocate to a reservation. For his role during the Seminole Wars Henderson received promotion to brevet brigadier general. Commandants did not normally take to the field, but Henderson would have fought in the Mexican War had he not been sixty-three years old. Though now confined to Washington, he worked assiduously to ensure that the Corps continued to expand its niche in sea-land operations.

On January 6, 1859, after serving as commandant for thirty-nine years, Henderson died in office two years before the outbreak of the Civil War. His annual pay and emoluments of $2,636.16 per annum were a bargain for the United States. His many years of strong and determined leadership probably preserved the Corps after Colonel John Harris, the next commandant, exasperated Secretary of the Navy Gideon Welles with a pathetic performance.

ABOVE LEFT: For many years, the Marine Corps suffered from mediocre leadership from the top. That changed in October 1820 when thirty-eight-year-old Archibald Henderson became commandant and began implementing a doctrine for Marines.

ABOVE: When Seminole Indians in Florida's Everglades resisted deportation from their homeland, Marines searched far up waterways in boats and canoes, often passing within yards of the well-hidden and camouflaged natives sheltered among the spreading roots of cypress trees.

state prison mutinied, Major Robert D. Wainwright and thirty men from the Marine Barracks broke into the prison, faced off against 283 prisoners, and restored order. From 1836 to 1842, one hundred and ninety Marines served on the so-called "Mosquito Fleet," a combination of patrol craft, revenue cutters, barges, and canoes used to chase Seminoles hiding in the swamplands. By 1845, the Marines had learned to fight at sea and in the deserts, cities, swamps, and jungles of the world, but they were still a small, specialized military force trying to find a niche in a growing nation.

The Mexican War

Henderson watched for opportunities, and in 1845, when Congress annexed Texas, he eagerly turned 1st Lieutenant Archibald H. Gillespie over to President James K. Polk for a special mission through Mexican territory to California. Gillespie carried "top secret" instructions to Commodore John D. Sloat, commanding the Pacific Squadron, and Captain John C. Frémont, commanding an armed overland "scientific expedition." On May 9, 1846, when war erupted with Mexico, Sloat and Frémont took possession of California.

ABOVE: When Mexicans attacked a small bluejacket garrison at San Diego in November 1846, Marines— unused to riding horses— disembarked from ships, formed as cavalry, raised the siege, and afterwards hastily relinquished their mounts.

RIGHT: Marines under the command of Commodore Matthew Perry stormed ashore on the Tabasco River during the Mexican War, capturing the town of San Juan Bautista and staging raids on other localities throughout the region.

After General Zachary Taylor's army crossed the Rio Grande into Mexico, Captain Alvin Edson, serving on board Commodore David Conner's Gulf Squadron, organized a 200-man battalion of Marines to open supply bases along the Mexican coast. Edson's force, sprinkled with bluejackets, landed at Frontera and San Juan Bautista and on November 14, 1846, captured Tampico. Two days later Taylor captured Saltillo, which enabled him to draw supplies from Tampico, and on February 22–23, 1847, defeat General Santa Anna at Buena Vista.

ABOVE: While guarding General Winfield Scott's wagon train on the march to Mexico City, Marines turned back a heavy attack on August 20, 1847, when General Santa Anna attempted to stop American forces by destroying the army's supplies.

On March 9, 1847, Commodore Conner put part of General Winfield Scott's army ashore near Veracruz. Commodore Matthew Perry arrived twelve days later with more ships, and relieved Conner. Scott wanted Alvarado captured to protect his flank, so Perry organized an amphibious force of 1,500 men. Captain Alvin Edson took a battalion of Marines and a battery of artillery ashore and on April 1 captured the town. Seventeen days later, Marines and bluejackets captured the fortified town of Tuxpan.

The Mexican War offered other opportunities for Marines who wanted combat duty. When 4,000 army soldiers stopped fighting because their enlistments had expired, Henderson stripped every navy yard of Marines, formed a full regiment of 1,000 Marines, put the unit under the command of Lieutenant Colonel Samuel E. Watson, and sent it to Scott. Henderson set new standards for the Marine Corps, but in 1847 nobody understood the meaning of "rapid response." Perry wanted Marines as badly as Scott did, and frustrated Henderson's effort by disregarding the secretary of the navy's orders and posting all but 357 of Watson's Marines with the Gulf Coast naval brigade.

LEFT: *Marine Major Levi Twiggs insisted that his battalion lead the charge on Chapultepec Castle, and at 8:00 a.m. on September 13, 1847, his leathernecks opened the way for General Quitman's division to seize the fortress.*

BELOW: *The capture of Chapultepec on September 13, 1847, made it possible for Marines to march down both causeways and become the first to fight their way into Mexico City by clearing the entrances at San Cosme and Belen.*

The March to Mexico City

General Scott assigned his share of Marines to an army division led by Franklin Pierce, later to become America's 14th president. On July 16, 1847, the column began marching to Scott's forward base at Puebla. After repulsing six attacks, the Marines arrived in good order and reported to Colonel Watson. Brigadier General John A. Quitman incorporated the battalion into the 4th Army Division and put Watson in charge of an army brigade. Watson assigned the troops to Major Levi Twiggs, a veteran hardened in the Seminole Wars, and two days later 11,000 men began marching toward Mexico City.

The Marines chafed during the battles of Cherubusco, Contreras, and Molino del Rey because Quitman saddled them with guarding Scott's supply train. It soon became clear to Scott that the key to Mexico City led through the fortress of Chapultepec Castle, where 800 defenders looked down upon the

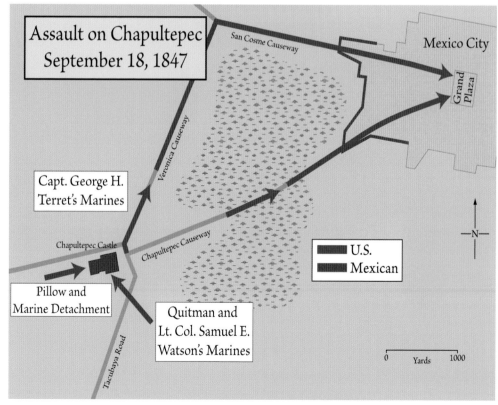

Assault on Chapultepec
September 18, 1847

Capt. George H. Terret's Marines

Pillow and Marine Detachment

Quitman and Lt. Col. Samuel E. Watson's Marines

San Cosme Causeway

Mexico City

Grand Plaza

Veronica Causeway

Chapultepec Castle

Chapultepec Causeway

Tacubaya Road

U.S.
Mexican

Yards   0   1000

approaching American columns. Scott chose Quitman's division to assault the castle, and Quitman chose Twiggs's Marines to lead the assault.

Twiggs understood Marines. He formed the battalion around Captain John G. Reynolds, one of the most able commanders in the Corps, to lead the first wave. He chose Watson to support the storming party and lead the division during the attack.

At daylight on September 13, army artillery bombarded Chapultepec for two hours. At 8:00 a.m. the guns fell silent. Reynolds' men pressed forward with pickaxes, crowbars, and scaling ladders. Behind Reynolds came Watson and the rest of Quitman's division. While the Mexican defenders attempted to pin down Reynolds' pioneers, the Marines grew tired of waiting for the bugler to sound the general charge and swept over the castle walls, bayoneting the enemy as they advanced. At a cost of twenty-four casualties, including 2nd Lieutenant Charles A. Henderson, the commandant's son, the Marines collected 550 prisoners, including a general, ten colonels, seven guns, and a thousand muskets. Thirteen of twenty-three Marine officers at Chapultepec received brevets.

On another section of the battlefield, Marine Captain George H. Terrett of Company C initiated his own campaign. He outflanked the Mexican artillery defending the causeway, and instead of wheeling toward Chapultepec he pursued the enemy fleeing into Mexico City. Terrett's Marines broke up a counterattack by Mexican lancers, assimilated twenty-six men from Lieutenant Ulysses S. Grant's command, forced the gateway, and became the first Americans to enter the city. The following morning Reynolds came through the gate and formed his men under the shadow of the cathedral in the Grand Plaza. While Reynolds mopped up the city, 2nd Lieutenant Augustus S. Nicholson climbed to the top of the Montezumas, cut down the Mexican flag, and raised the Stars and Stripes.

The Marines now had another stanza for *The Marines' Hymn*. For forty years the Marine standard

The Marines' Hymn

From the halls of Montezuma
To the shores of Tripoli
We fight our country's battles
In the air, on land, and sea.
First to fight for right and freedom,
And to keep our honor clean,
We are proud to claim the title
Of United States Marines.

Our flag's unfurled to every breeze
From dawn to setting sun;
We have fought in every clime and place
Where we could take a gun.
In the snow of far-off northern lands
And in sunny tropic scenes,
You will find us always on the job —

The United States Marines.
Here's health to you and to our Corps
Which we are proud to serve;
In many a strife we've fought for life
And never lost our nerve.
If the Army and the Navy
Ever gaze on Heaven's scenes,
They will find the streets are guarded
By United States Marines.

had carried only the traditional motto, "To the Shores of Tripoli." When the Marines returned to Washington in 1848, the city presented General Henderson with a new blue and gold standard, emblazoned with the words: "From Tripoli to the Halls of Montezumas." From that, a lyricist reversed the sequence because no words rhymed with Montezumas, and after eliminating the "s," put Montezuma before Tripoli. No record exists of when the hymn was completed, but the melody dates back to Jacques Offenbach's 1859 opera, *Geneviève de Brabant*.

LEFT: General John A. Quitman became so impressed by the rugged battalion of fighting Marines assigned to his army division that he let the battle-grimed leathernecks and their drummer lead the division's victory parade to Mexico City's Placido Nacional.

A CENTURY OF DEVELOPMENT 1814–1898

RIGHT (TOP): *The Federal Armory at Harpers Ferry began producing muskets and bayonets in 1842. Because workmen fit every firing mechanism by hand, there were few inter-changeable parts. These were the muskets with which John Brown intended to free the slaves.*

RIGHT (BOTTOM): *The popular breech-loaded Sharps rifle went through many modifications and became one of the most accurate single-shot weapons prior to the Civil War. Soldiers preferred the pictured 1863 model, but most of them carried rifled muskets.*

After the Mexican War, Commandant Henderson reduced the Corps to its authorized peacetime strength of 1,224 officers and enlisted men. For the next twelve years the Corps would be stretched thin serving around the world. Privates still drew only six dollars a month, but during the 1850s Henderson ensured that wherever a Marine went, he would be noticed, and began enhancing the Marine uniform. Enlisted men wore white cross-belts, white trousers for summer, and light blue trousers for winter. Officers and NCOs wore similar trousers distinguished by dark blue stripes edged with scarlet. Then, as now, the Marine Band wore gold-trimmed scarlet coats.

To supplement a private's wretched pay, every enlisted man received an annual clothing allowance of thirty dollars. He could not waste it capriciously because the Uniform Regulations of 1859 prescribed his wardrobe as:

1 uniform cap	1 blanket
2 uniform coats	8 pairs of socks
2 sets of epaulettes	8 pairs of drawers
7 pairs linen trousers	4 fatigue caps
8 pairs woolen trousers	4 fatigue coats
12 shirts	8 blue flannel shirts
6 pairs of shoes	1 greatcoat
2 stocks, leather	
(The stock, worn around the neck, gave rise to the Marines' nickname—"Leathernecks.")	

A Marine private owned a greater wardrobe than the ordinary civilian of the 1850s or the typical GI of World War II. No one has explained how a Marine at sea squeezed all his clothing into a single ditty bag.

If clothing did not overburden an enlisted man, his next stop at the Marine Corps Depot of Supplies would have done, for there, depending upon his particular specialty, an inductee would receive from Major D. J. Sutherland's four-story quartermaster house at 226 South 4th Street in Philadelphia several pounds of accoutrements:

Musket	Bayonet
Bayonet belt	Drum
Scabbard	Fife
Knapsack	Haversack
Cartridge box	Canteen
Cartridge belt box	Slings, musket
Sword, NCO only	Sling, drum
Sword, musician only	Sword belt

An Expanding and Strife-torn Nation

With the signing of the Treaty of Guadeloupe Hidalgo on February 2, 1848, the United States acquired from Mexico an additional 500,000 square miles, which included today's California and parts of several other southwestern states. The ink had barely dried on the instrument when California's gold rush spawned a fleet of fast new clipper ships that rounded Cape Horn for San Francisco. During the next twelve years foreign trade doubled, and so did America's merchant fleet.

Marines found themselves serving on ships in busy ports from South America to China. When in September 1856 some 4,000 Cantonese armed with 176 cannon opened without warning on American merchantmen, Captain John D. Sims, USMC, took 287 Marines and bluejackets ashore and in three days of hard fighting captured four forts, killed 500 Chinese, and routed an army of thousands. During the assault, Sims lost seven men killed and twenty wounded.

In 1857, Commandant Henderson had barely enough men serving stateside to suppress a growing agitation between the North and the South over states' rights and slavery. On June 1 the self-styled "Plug-Uglies" of Baltimore attempted to disrupt elections in Washington, D.C., and Henderson formed a company of Captain Jacob Zeilin's Marines and confronted the troublemakers himself. He stood before the muzzle of their brass cannon and sternly warned, "Men, you had better think twice before you fire this piece at Marines." Somewhere in the crowd a drunken ruffian made the mistake of discharging his musket. Zeilin's Marines returned the fire, and the rioters fled.

On January 6, 1859, Henderson died in office. He had guided the Marine Corps through troubled times. He would always be remembered as "The Grand Old Man of the Corps," but his successor, 61-year-old Colonel John Harris, was a man of Southern sympathies who came close to dismantling Henderson's work during the calamitous years ahead.

While John Brown's Harpers Ferry raid is sometimes cited as the beginning of the Civil War, Israel Greene put the incident in perspective when he wrote: "[Colonel Lee] treated the affair as one of no great consequence, which would be speedily settled by Marines. It was."

Israel Greene: "The Capture of John Brown," North American Review, *December, 1885.*

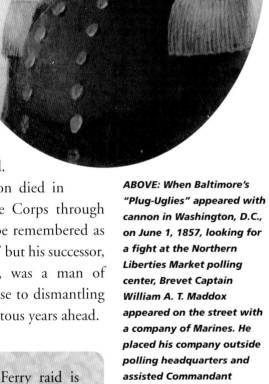

ABOVE: When Baltimore's "Plug-Uglies" appeared with cannon in Washington, D.C., on June 1, 1857, looking for a fight at the Northern Liberties Market polling center, Brevet Captain William A. T. Maddox appeared on the street with a company of Marines. He placed his company outside polling headquarters and assisted Commandant Henderson in driving the ruffians away.

Marines at Harpers Ferry

On October 16, 1859, abolitionist John Brown attempted to foment a national crisis by raiding the federal armory at Harpers Ferry, Virginia, and using the weapons to incite a slave uprising in the South. His plans began unraveling on the morning of October 17 when Virginia's governor Henry Wise wired President James Buchanan for help. The only forces available in Washington were Commandant Harris's Marines, and the only officer available to lead them was Brevet Colonel Robert E. Lee of the army. Harris entrained eighty-six Marines under Lieutenant Israel Greene and instructed them to wait until Lee arrived. In the meantime, Brown and his revolutionaries barricaded themselves in the armory's engine house and skirmished with local militia.

At daylight on October 18, Lee ordered Greene to assault the engine house. In an action lasting little more than one minute, Marines battered through the swinging doors of the building with a ladder and rushed inside. During the turmoil, one of the raiders killed Marine Private Luke Quinn. A hostage caught Greene's

eye, pointed to a silver-bearded man reloading a Sharps rifle, and said, "That's Brown!" Greene leaped through the doorway and cut down Brown with a sword-bending backhand slash. Days later, after Brown and several of his men recovered from wounds, Greene escorted the survivors to Charles Town, Virginia, for incarceration, trial, and execution.

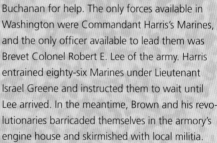

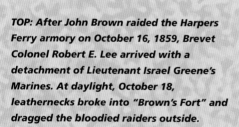

TOP: After John Brown raided the Harpers Ferry armory on October 16, 1859, Brevet Colonel Robert E. Lee arrived with a detachment of Lieutenant Israel Greene's Marines. At daylight, October 18, leathernecks broke into "Brown's Fort" and dragged the bloodied raiders outside.

ABOVE: Lieutenant Israel Greene's Marines took under two minutes to batter through the heavy doors of the armory's fire-engine house with a ladder, subdue John Brown and his raiders, and rescue the civilians being held as hostages.

Outbreak of Rebellion

The November 6, 1860, election of Abraham Lincoln triggered the December 20 secession of South Carolina. During the four months before Lincoln's inauguration, six more states seceded. Southern delegates formed the Confederate States of America and elected former U.S. Senator Jefferson Davis president. Lincoln had barely settled into the White House when on April 12, 1861, batteries in the harbor of Charleston, South Carolina, opened on Fort Sumter and initiated the Civil War.

The outbreak of war ripped apart the army, the navy, and the Marine Corps. The Corps suffered the greatest setback, losing half its men to the Confederacy, among them the best. Captain John D. Sims, who had led the charge at Canton, and Israel Greene, who had captured Brown's raiders at Harpers Ferry, joined the Confederacy. To make up the losses, Congress increased the Marine Corps to 93 officers and 3,074 enlisted men. Lincoln added a thousand more. During the war the Corps never exceeded 3,900 men, many of whom never received any military training. Commandant Harris relied on his 1812 experiences. He planted most of the Marines among the navy's blockading squadrons and failed to organize them into an effective amphibious fighting force to spearhead assaults. The Confederacy also formed a marine corps but never attracted more than 600 men. Most of them served in forts.

First Bull Run

After the first new recruits reported for instruction, Major John G. Reynolds created a 353-man battalion and attempted to whip them into fighters. Only seventeen officers and NCOs had previous experience, including company commander Major Jacob Zeilin. Secretary of War Simon Cameron wanted to augment Brigadier General Irvin McDowell's Union army of green recruits with veterans and asked Secretary of the Navy Welles for a battalion of Marines. Harris detailed Reynolds' battalion, which drew the assignment of

LEFT: Majors John G. Reynolds and Jacob Zeilin gathered together a 353-man battalion of Marines and on July 21, 1861, led them into the furious battle on Henry House Hill, First Bull Run's bloodiest engagement.

ABOVE: The Marine Barracks in Washington, D.C., contained the commandant's quarters and the parade ground. During the Civil War there were many parades because Marines were seldom sent anywhere to fight.

supporting army Captain Charles Griffin's six-gun "West Point Battery."

On the morning of July 21, 1861, as erratic combat between two untrained armies commenced. Reynolds and Griffin found themselves defending the crest of Henry House Hill, the epicenter of the battle of First Bull Run. Neither side had a battle plan. The Confederates made three desperate attempts to seize Griffin's guns. Three times the Marines fell back under a hail of minié balls, and three times their officers and NCOs herded them back to the crest. At 4:40 p.m. the Union Army broke and ran. Having lost ten killed and thirty-four wounded, the Marines soon followed, chased by Confederate cavalry under the command of Colonel James E. B. "Jeb" Stuart.

The clash of arms demonstrated a lack of tactical leadership on both sides. Commandant Harris had the unpleasant duty of informing Welles of "the first instance in [Marine Corps] history where any portion of its members turned their backs to the enemy"—an immensely bitter pill for men like Reynolds and Zeilin to swallow.

The Struggle for Redemption

Colonel Harris did not bother to witness the Battle of First Bull Run, nor was he inclined to elevate the Marine Corps' role in the Civil War. When on August 20, 1862, Secretary Welles grumbled, "Almost all the elder officers [of the Marine Corps] are at loggerheads and ought to be retired," he might have solved the problem immediately by retiring Harris. When Reynolds lobbied to have the commandant replaced, Harris responded by having Reynolds court-martialed. Reynolds was acquitted and preferred charges against Harris. Welles exhausted his patience with both men, but instead of solving the problem he sent them letters of reproof.

ABOVE: Colonel John Harris served as the Corps' sixth commandant until May 12, 1864, when he died in office. Exhausted by a half-century of service, Harris muffed marvelous opportunities to demonstrate the skills of his Marines during the Civil War.

LEFT: Alfred R. Waud captured a panoramic scene when 250 Marines and army regulars assaulted and captured two Confederate forts at Hatteras Inlet, North Carolina, in one of the few assaults involving ships' Marines.

Despite the quarreling and with no help from Harris, the Marines worked their way into the Civil War. From Chesapeake Bay to the Rio Grande, they served at sea, where Harris had put them. On August 28, 1861, six weeks after the disaster at Bull Run, a

ABOVE: Marines serving at the Washington Navy Yard were understandably among the best dressed in the service. The officer standing to the left was expected to ensure that rifles, clothing, brass buttons, and headgear always looked sharp.

250-man assault force of Marines and army regulars landed from surfboats and stormed Fort Clark at Hatteras Inlet, North Carolina. Following a softening-up bombardment by navy ships, Marines entered the works and raised the Stars and Stripes. Fort Hatteras surrendered the following morning after a shell touched off its magazine. The first joint amphibious operation of the war demonstrated the capabilities of Marines at a time when Harris was still engaged in his squabble with Reynolds.

In November 1861 Welles assembled seventy-seven ships—at the time the largest fleet ever under a U.S. flag—and ordered Flag Officer Samuel F. DuPont to seize an advance base for the Atlantic blockading squadrons at Port Royal Sound, South Carolina. The 16,000-man expeditionary force under Brigadier

General Thomas W. Sherman included a 300-man Marine battalion commanded by Major Reynolds. This time Marines encountered the worst possible luck. DuPont put them on an old, unseaworthy transport that foundered on the way to Port Royal. Reynolds found near-miraculous ways to save all but seven of his men and most of the equipment. Instead of investigating the root cause of the catastrophe, Harris disbanded the amphibious battalion and reassigned the men to ships.

Davy Farragut's Marines

Some of Reynolds' Marines were fortunate enough to join the West Gulf Blockading Squadron commanded by Flag Officer David G. Farragut. In April 1862 he took them into the Mississippi River and put them to work during the New Orleans campaign. On the night of April 24, Farragut pressed thirteen of his ocean-going warships through a cordon of fire laid down by Forts Jackson and St. Philip, and destroyed the Confederate river squadron. Next day he demanded the surrender of New Orleans from a group of obstinate politicians. Having no army nearby to force his demands, Farragut turned to his handful of Marines.

Second Lieutenant John C. Harris of the screw-sloop *Pensacola* led the first Marines ashore. Armed with rifled muskets and two boat howitzers, Marines rowed to the levee where a hostile crowd of civilians armed with pistols, knives, and clubs shouted threats. Harris set up the howitzers to bear on the mob, formed his men, marched them to the nearby U.S. Mint, hauled down the Confederate colors, raised the Stars and Stripes, and placed a guard.

After local politicians still refused to surrender the city, Captain James L. Broome, Farragut's senior Marine officer, formed a 300-man battalion from the remainder of the squadron and landed at the levee. Broome ignored the mob, led his battalion through

narrow streets, stopped at the customhouse to raise the Stars and Stripes, and proceeded to city hall. For three days Broome's Marines held New Orleans, the South's largest city, while waiting for Major General Benjamin Butler's 12,000-man army to arrive upriver.

The same Marines remained with Farragut until the end of the war. In 1863 Broome became personally involved in General Grant's Vicksburg campaign. With Farragut's support, he went ashore and personally reconnoitered the Vicksburg area. Broome suggested that Grant's army pack a week's rations and cross the Mississippi below Grand Gulf, then, by taking a circuitous route, assault Vicksburg from the rear. Grant put Broome's plan into operation and three months later (July 4, 1863) forced the unconditional surrender of Vicksburg.

Marines in the Atlantic

By mid-1863, most Confederate ports had been closed to munitions-carrying blockade-runners. Among those that weren't were Charleston, South Carolina, and Wilmington, North Carolina. Welles wanted to close both ports but agreed to assault Charleston first. On April 7, 1863, after Admiral DuPont muffed an attack on Charleston, Welles suggested an assault on Fort Sumter, which stood near the entrance to the harbor. At midnight, September 8, Rear Admiral John A. Dahlgren sent a force of 500 Marines and bluejackets in thirty-five converging whaleboats to storm the fort's bulwarks. Captain Charles McCawley, a future commandant, led the Marines. During the unrehearsed operation, the boats became separated in the ink-black darkness, and the squealing of their oarlocks alerted

ABOVE LEFT: Corporal John Mackie became the first Marine to be awarded the Medal of Honor. After the USS Galena was disabled during operations on the James River, Mackie put fires out on the gundeck, dragged casualties clear, and put three guns back in action.

ABOVE: Marines on the USS Kearsarge stand ready for inspection. In 1864, the men of the Kearsarge won honors for sinking the long-sought Confederate commerce raider Alabama in the English Channel.

LEFT: *When Marines and bluejackets went ashore to assault Fort Fisher on January 15, 1865, they were disorganized. Lieutenant Commander K. R. Breese, USN, muffed the assignment, but he blamed it on Marines instead of reporting his own blunders.*

RIGHT: *Admiral David D. Porter's squadron shelled Fort Fisher for more than two days before launching the ground assault. The combined Marine-bluejacket force reached the fort's palisades before being repulsed by heavy fire.*

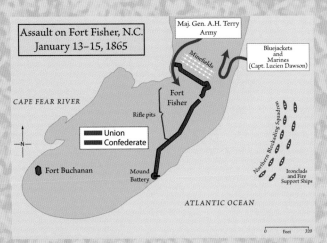

The Assault on Fort Fisher

On December 23–27, 1864, Marines attached to Admiral Porter's North Atlantic Blockading Squadron watched from the rail as General Benjamin Butler bungled another military expedition. Butler put half of his 6,500-man infantry force ashore near Fort Fisher. Because of high seas he sailed away and left them there. Porter rescued the men and swore he would never cooperate with Butler in another military operation.

General Grant agreed. He replaced Butler with Major General Alfred H. Terry and implored Porter to try again. Terry planned to make the assault with 8,500 infantry, but Porter had already decided that he wanted a larger share of the

action. So on January 15, 1865, after softening-up Fort Fisher with a naval bombardment, Porter formed a diversionary amphibious force of 400 Marines and 1,600 bluejackets. The flaw in Porter's scheme resulted from sending the entire force ashore from different ships with no instructions other than to form into companies after landing and assault the fort from the Atlantic side of the peninsula while Terry's infantry assaulted the fort from the opposite side. Porter expected the Marines to advance on the fort while under fire, dig rifle pits in the sand, and support the bluejackets' assault on the palisades. The plan, according to future Admiral George Dewey, was "sheer, murderous madness" because the naval officers entrusted with

the operation had no experience in assault tactics.

Nevertheless, the Marines wanted action. When every steam whistle in the fleet screeched the signal and every gun stopped firing, Marines tumbled into boats and landed on the neck of the peninsula, north of Fort Fisher. Without pausing to organize, Marines hit the beach yelling, and with bayonets fixed began running towards the fort. A barrage of Confederate fire met the attack and sent the survivors reeling back in disorder. Captain Lucien L. Dawson, commanding the Marines, attempted to reorganize the men and carry out his part of the assault, but Fleet Captain K. Randolph Breese, in overall charge of the operation, failed to issue a

comprehensible order. As the bluejackets fell back, Dawson's men followed, leaving behind 309 dead sailors and Marines.

To protect his own career, Breese blamed the failure of the assault on the Marines. Porter, who later became a Marine Corps advocate, accepted Breese's distorted account. General Terry praised the men who made the diversionary attack, because a few hours later he captured the fort. Breese's accusations, however, resonated for thirty years, causing many navy officers to question whether an independent force of Marines was really necessary. The fumbled Fort Fisher assault set back progress on amphibious operations until the Spanish-American War, and almost destroyed the Marine Corps.

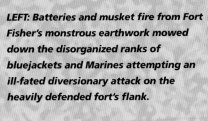

LEFT: *Batteries and musket fire from Fort Fisher's monstrous earthwork mowed down the disorganized ranks of bluejackets and Marines attempting an ill-fated diversionary attack on the heavily defended fort's flank.*

RIGHT: *As naval guns fall silent on January 15, 1865, boats filled with Marines and bluejackets from Admiral Porter's North Atlantic Blockading Squadron head for shore but with no organized plan for assaulting Fort Fisher.*

Resolved: That the Committee on Naval Affairs be directed to consider the expediency of abolishing the Marine Corps, and transferring it to the Army . . .

House Report No. 22, 39th Congress, 2nd session, February 21, 1867.

Confederate sentinels. Firepower from huge guns knocked several of the boats to pieces. Men who landed found the base of the fort littered with mounds of masonry. After losing a third of his Marines, McCawley re-embarked the survivors and rowed back to the fleet. Until February 1865, Charlestown remained under Confederate control.

On May 12, 1864, Commandant Harris died aged seventy-four after having wasted his Marine Corps during the Civil War. Lincoln ignored the tradition of seniority, retired four senior Marine officers, and named 57-year-old Major Jacob Zeilin commandant. Brevetted during the Mexican War and wounded at First Bull Run, Zeilin had earned a distinguished record as a Marine. During his twelve-year career as commandant, he would become the Marine Corps' first general.

As the war wound down, Zeilin looked for one final expedition to demonstrate the amphibious skills of his men. The opportunity came when Welles ordered Rear Admiral David D. Porter to cooperate with the army

I beg leave to say that I would consider it a great calamity if the Marine Corps should be abolished or turned over to the Army. In its organization it should be naval altogether. A ship without Marines is no ship of war at all.

Admiral Farragut's Testimony to the Naval Affairs Committee, February 22, 1867.

and capture Fort Fisher, thereby closing the Cape Fear River to blockade-runners attempting to reach Wilmington.

Major Zeilin to the Rescue

When Zeilin became the 7th commandant, he never anticipated spending the next twelve years fighting to preserve the Corps. Because of Harris's mismanagement, when the Civil War ended in April 1865 the Marine Corps had not established a meaningful purpose, and Breese's accusations only made the situation worse. Facts also counted. In a war that killed or wounded 600,000 men, the Marines lost only 148 men in battle and 312 from other causes.

Zeilin was not a politician, but when it came to defending the Corps he applied exceptional skill in using admirals like Farragut, Porter, and other supportive navy officers to espouse his cause. They all appeared before the Committee on Naval Affairs, which in February 1867 finally concluded: "No good reason appears either for abolishing . . . the Marine Corps, or transferring it to

TOP: A small team of Marines work with army volunteers under annoying Confederate fire as they lay pontoons across the Rappahannock River in preparation for the Army of the Potomac's mismanaged Battle of Fredericksburg in December 1863.

the Army; on the contrary, the Committee recommends that its organization as a separate Corps be preserved and strengthened . . . and its commanding officer shall hold the rank of brigadier general."

Welles promptly advanced Zeilin to brigadier general, and the Corps' existence remained unchallenged for another seven years. During those years Zeilin introduced an esprit that became the body and soul of the Corps. He restored the officers' Mameluke sword and equipped NCOs with a brawny saber. He then convinced the secretary of the navy to adopt a distinctive insignia containing a spread eagle atop a globe of the western hemisphere superimposed over a canted anchor, thereby tying the Corps' sea-going tradition to the navy. In another morale-bonding action, Zeilin introduced the Corps' motto—*Semper Fidelis* ("always faithful")—a Latin phrase that has carried through the decades with the same meaning it has today.

Marine Operations Between the Wars

Formosa (1867)
Japan (1867) and (1868)
Uruguay (1868)
Mexico (1870)
Korea (1871)
Colombia (1873)
Hawaiian Islands (1874)
Egypt (1882)
Isthmus of Panama (1885)
Korea (1888)
Egypt (1888)
Samoa (1888)
Hawaiian Islands (1889)
Argentina (1890)
Chile (1891)
Bering Sea (1891)
Navassa Island, Hawaii (1891)
Korea (1894)
Nicaragua (1894)
North China (1894 and 1895)
Isthmus of Panama (1895)
Nicaragua (1896)

McCawley's Marines

When Zeilin retired in 1876, he set the stage for 49-year-old Charles G. McCawley to carry on his work. McCawley had been brevetted during the Mexican War and again for leading the attack on Fort Sumter during the Civil War. For nearly thirty years, commandants continued to use the Corps in its traditional role at sea, and during those years Marines made their presence known around the world.

With a smaller budget to run the Corps, McCawley concentrated on improving the quality of his officers and men. He establish higher enlistment standards, improved the training of recruits, and beginning with the class of 1881 recruited all his officers, some fifty in number, from the U.S. Naval Academy. Five of his selections would become commandants; thirteen others would become generals.

On the eve of McCawley's retirement in 1891, a faction of young naval officers led by Lieutenant William F. Fullam made a determined effort to force

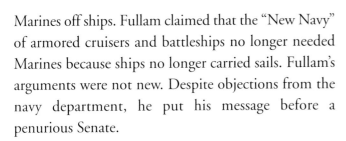

Marines off ships. Fullam claimed that the "New Navy" of armored cruisers and battleships no longer needed Marines because ships no longer carried sails. Fullam's arguments were not new. Despite objections from the navy department, he put his message before a penurious Senate.

TOP LEFT: After capturing the Citadel on the Salee River, Captain McLane Tilton's Marines relax under trees. When the Korean defenders fled, they left behind 481 guns, one of which the Marines carried off as a trophy.

ABOVE: During a presentation ceremony on board the screw-steamer USS Vandalia in 1886, Marines form on deck for inspection at Portsmouth Navy Yard, where the Vandalia serves as a receiving and guard ship.

LEFT: Congress authorized the first two U.S. Navy modern armored cruisers in 1886. Marines considered themselves fortunate on August 15, 1895, when they were detailed to participate in the commissioning ceremony for the USS Texas.

ABOVE LEFT: For their daring assault on the Korean Citadel, Medal of Honor recipients Corporal Charles Brown (left) and Private Hugh Purvis (center) stand with Captain McLane Tilton in front of the huge Korean flag they captured.

Preserving the Corps

As a new attack on the Marine Corps gathered steam, McCawley resigned and on June 30, 1891, passed the problem to 51-year-old Colonel Charles Heywood, the ninth commandant. Heywood avoided becoming involved in a political fight and let the battle be fought by his supporters in the navy department. An August 1894 Senate bill proposed that the Corps become a "Corps of Marine Artillery" and transferred to the army. Exasperated by the proposal, Secretary of the Navy Hilary A. Herbert convinced the Senate Naval Affairs Committee to pigeonhole the legislation, and by doing so he also pigeonholed Fullam and his followers.

Meanwhile, Heywood created a new School of Application in Washington for lieutenants and promising NCOs, which stressed naval gunnery, mine warfare, electricity, and high explosives. The program soon evolved into the Marine Basic Schools system and the construction of the Marine base at Parris Island in South Carolina. Heywood de-emphasized drill and put the emphasis on improving marksmanship. Marines became the best sharpshooters in uniform, and when the navy tried to induce Heywood to accept a few new bolt-action .236-caliber Lee magazine rifles, he held onto his old single-shot Springfields until Congress appropriated enough money for 3,000 Lees, better target ranges, and enough ammunition for Marines to continue their marksmanship program. That Heywood made all his demands—which also included better rations, better bedding, and better uniforms—during Secretary of the Navy Herbert's fight to preserve the Marine Corps demonstrated the commandant's stubborn determination to look after his men.

In 1895 Captain Robley D. Evans, USN, took command of the new battleship *Indiana* (BB-1). He still bore a grudge against the Marines because of Breese's account of the Fort Fisher operation. Evans had nearly lost his leg during the assault and informed the secretary that he wanted no Marines on the *Indiana*. Herbert took Evans aside and made it clear that "one captain, one subaltern, and 60 noncommissioned officers, privates, and musics" would be on board whether Evans liked it or not. Herbert's proclamation set matters straight, and though "Fighting Bob" Evans demonstrated occasional bursts of obstreperousness, Marines today still serve on ships of the navy.

Congress Goes to War

On February 15, 1898, the battleship USS *Maine* mysteriously exploded in the harbor of Havana, Cuba, and "Remember the Maine" became the hue and cry of the angry American public, who concluded that the Spaniards were to blame. Ten days later Assistant Secretary of the Navy Theodore Roosevelt secretly cabled Commodore George Dewey, commanding the Asiatic Fleet, to prepare for operations in the Philippines. On March 8, Congress upstaged President William McKinley by appropriating $50 million for national defense. Two weeks later the navy formed the Flying Squadron for the "defense" of the eastern seaboard, placing Acting Commodore Winfield Scott Schley in command. On March 26, after being repeatedly goaded by Congress to act, President McKinley sent an ultimatum to Spain demanding, among other matters, independence for Cuba. Spanish officials continued to stall, and their agreement for an armistice came too late. On April 19, Congress swiftly approved McKinley's request to declare war on Spain. When Secretary of the Navy John D. Long cabled the Asiatic Squadron, he was aghast to find Dewey all ready poised to strike Manila Bay.

Commandant Heywood now had a war of vast opportunities, a promotion to brigadier general, and authorization to bring the Corps' strength to 119 officers and 4,713 enlisted men. He also had the navy's new Lee high-velocity, bolt-action rifles that used smokeless powder, and the first opportunity to use them in battle.

John Philip Sousa and the President's Own

While Zeilin served as commandant, a floor fight in the House of Representatives barely succeeded in preserving the Marine Band. McCawley persisted for more than another decade to keep the band immune from congressional cost-cutters. In October 1, 1880, he solved the problem for $94 a month by appointing John Philip Sousa the band's new director.

In 1868 Antonio Sousa, a member of the band, forced his 13-year-old son John Philip to join the Marines as a "music boy" because the lad "needed discipline." Twelve years later Antonio was still playing trombone but under the direction of his son. During the years that followed, the younger Sousa became internationally known as "The March King." He led the Marine Band for twelve years, composed 136 marches, and elevated the "President's Own" to the finest military band in the nation. No national event, such as the dedication on July 4, 1886, of the Statue of Liberty, occurred without music provided by Sousa's Marine Band.

After his long service with the Marine Corps, Sousa retired and formed his own band. When the United States entered World War I, 62-year-old Sousa joined the Naval Reserve with the rank of lieutenant and became the first musician ever to become a naval officer. He loved life and he loved music. In 1932, during the celebration of George Washington's 200th birthday, Sousa took the stand and conducted the combined bands of the army, navy, and Marine Corps. Fourteen days later he died. The last composition played under the direction of his baton was the immortal *Stars and Stripes Forever*. Sousa would have wanted it that way.

TOP: Sousa would have been proud of the way that the "President's Own" developed to equal in professionalism any civvy street band. Here, the Marine Band peforms at one of the Inauguration Day functions for President George H. W. Bush, January 1989.

ABOVE: U.S. Marine Band leader John Philip Sousa.

RIGHT: After Commodore George Dewey defeated Spain's fleet in Manila Bay on May 1, 1898, Marine First Lieutenant Dion Williams took ashore the first Marines to occupy Spanish territory and secured the Cavite Navy Yard.

FAR RIGHT: Lieutenant Colonel Robert W. Huntington led Marines on the first amphibious assault of Cuba on June 11, 1898. A few hours later, leathernecks raised the Stars and Stripes near Fisherman's Point on Guantánamo Bay.

Marines in the Philippines

On the morning of May 1, 1898, nine days after the president's declaration of war, Commodore Dewey steamed into Manila Bay with seven ships, and before lunchtime defeated Admiral Patricio Montojo y Pasarón's Spanish squadron. Two days later Marines under the command of 1st Lieutenant Dion Williams headed ashore from the USS *Baltimore* (C-3), secured the Cavite navy yard, and hoisted the first American colors on Spanish territory. Then they waited. Two months passed before the army arrived, causing Dewey to grumble, "If there had been 5,000 Marines under my command at Manila Bay, the city would have surrendered to me on 1 May 1898." He believed the delay enabled an insurrection to be organized that could otherwise have been snuffed out before it began.

While Dewey waited for the army to arrive, Captain Henry Glass sailed the USS *Charleston* (C-2) to Guam and bombarded the island. First Lieutenant John Twiggs Myers took a Marine detachment ashore and raised the American flag. The local Spanish garrison had not heard of war being declared and thought the bombardment was meant as a salute.

Marines in Cuba

On April 17, 1898, four days after the president declared war on Spain, Heywood ordered Lieutenant Colonel Robert W. Huntington to prepare a Marine battalion for amphibious operations in Cuba. Huntington mixed veterans with new recruits and formed the men into five companies of infantry and one of artillery. On April 22 he marched them through the streets of Brooklyn, New York City, embarked them on an old merchantman re-christened *Panther,* and sent them off to Key West, Florida, with four 3-inch artillery pieces, medical stores, mosquito nets, tents, pick-axes, shovels, barbed-wire cutters, a three-months' supply of provisions, and other accoutrements.

The *Panther's* skipper, Commander G. C. Reiter, nursed an old grudge against Marines that dated back to the Civil War. Now with an opportunity to get even, he disembarked the battalion at night near a swamp swarming with bloodthirsty insects instead of on Key West's sandy beaches. As Reiter stood offshore smirking, Huntington put the Marines through battle-hardening tactical exercises while awaiting orders.

On May 28, Schley's Flying Squadron cornered the Spanish Fleet at Santiago and blockaded the harbor. Navy Secretary Long cabled Rear Admiral William T. Sampson, Atlantic Fleet commander, and asked, "Can you take possession of Guantánamo [and] occupy [it] as a coaling station?" Sampson replied, "Send Colonel Huntington's Marines." On June 7 Reiter re-embarked the colonel's battalion and steamed for Guantánamo Bay, forty miles east of Santiago.

On June 10, supported by the guns of the battleship *Oregon* (BB-3), Huntington's battalion went ashore and became the first American troops on Cuban soil. After they landed, Reiter tried to sail away. He refused to unload small arms ammunition, claiming he needed it for ballast. Commander Bowman H. McCalla of the USS *Marblehead* (C-11) curtly ordered Reiter to "break out or land" all the ammunition and supplies Huntington requested. In appreciation for the commander's intervention, Marines named their beachhead Camp McCalla.

For four days enemy snipers pestered the camp while Huntington's scouts probed the countryside for enemy outposts. During one skirmish, two rifle companies under 52-year-old Captain George F. Elliot (later to become the Corps' tenth commandant) defeated a 500-man Spanish detachment near the village of Cuzco. The booming voice of 1st Lieutenant Wendell C. Neville, another future commandant, could be heard above the chatter of rifle-fire as he led his men into the fight.

Marine Sergeant John C. Quick distinguished himself during the heat of battle by performing a new role that would increase in importance during future wars—spotting for artillery and naval batteries. When firing from the gunboat *Dolphin* (PG-24) came dangerously close to falling among Marines, Quick improvised a semaphore flag and stood calmly on a rise wigwagging it while bullets whined about his head. For heroism and courage at Guantánamo Bay, Quick earned the Congressional Medal of Honor.

A Glimpse of the Future

Spain's forces in Cuba had no chance of winning the Spanish-American War, which ended on August 14, 1898. In the settlement four months later, the United States paid $20 million for Guam, Puerto Rico, and the Philippines, and forced Spain to relinquish control over Cuba. During the short war, Commandant Heywood capitalized on every opportunity to put the Marine Corps back in business.

The operations of Huntington's battalion in Cuba inadvertently introduced a new chapter in Marine Corps doctrine. In 1898, nobody envisioned the term "Fleet Marine Force," but Huntington demonstrated what a strong assault force from an armed attack transport could accomplish, despite Commander Reiter's efforts to make the amphibious operation a failure. By landing on an enemy shore and securing an advanced base for the fleet while gathering intelligence for broader operations, Huntington created a model that became adopted in every war of the 20th century where Marines became involved.

On March 3, 1899, Congress finally recognized both the true and the potential value of the Marine Corps by defeating the Fullam clique and passing the Naval Personnel Bill, which provided for a permanent Corps of 201 officers and 6,062 enlisted men. Heywood and his successors could now begin work on a new Marine doctrine. For every leatherneck, the future had finally come.

ABOVE: At Marine headquarters tent on Guantánamo, (left to right) First Lieutenant Herbert L. Draper, Lieutenant Colonel Robert W. Huntington, and Captain Charles L. McCawley find a quiet moment for a photograph.

FAR LEFT: Returning to the Portsmouth Navy Yard in 1899 after six months at sea, sailors and Marines stand together on the deck of the cruiser Chicago before going ashore for a well-deserved respite from sea duty.

LEFT: After nightfall, July 4, 1898, the Spanish attempted to blockade the channel to Santiago by scuttling the cruiser Reina Mercedes across it. The U.S. Navy destroyed the ship before it could be scuttled, and Marines found no survivors.

THE CHALLENGING YEARS 1898–1940

The Spanish-American War catapulted the Marine Corps into an indispensable and flexible fighting force. With a new far-flung empire, the United States suddenly needed a strong navy with a responsive fleet Marine force. Alfred Thayer Mahan, former head of the Naval War College in Newport, Rhode Island, wrote in *The Influence of Sea Power upon History* that national power could only be achieved with naval power.

Trouble was already brewing in the Far East. On November 4, 1898, the Asiatic Squadron responded to threats in Peking, China, and landed a detachment of Marines to guard the U.S. legation. Late in 1898 intertribal warfare erupted in the Samoan Islands, and a detachment of Marines went ashore from the USS *Philadelphia* (C-4) to protect the American consulate. On April 1, 1899, Samoan tribesmen ambushed an Anglo-American patrol in the jungle near Apia. Private Henry L. Hulbert was awarded the Medal of Honor for covering the withdrawal. Bloody jungle engagements continued into mid-May, during which sergeants Bruno A. Forsterer and Michael McNally also earned Medals of Honor for heroism in action.

On February 4, 1899, Filipinos led by General Emiliano Aguinaldo expressed their anger over the annexation of the Philippines and revolted. Trouble first began at Cavite, Admiral Dewey's naval base. Dewey asked for a battalion of Marines, and Commandant Heywood sent him fifteen officers and 260 men under Colonel Percival C. Pope, who had been Colonel Huntington's executive at Guantánamo. Five months later Heywood sent a second battalion,

this one under another veteran, Major George Elliott. By the end of 1900, five battalions of Marines were dueling with Aguinaldo's insurrectionists. Pope formed the battalions into the First Marine Brigade, consisting of two rifle regiments and two artillery companies totaling fifty-eight officers and 1,547 enlisted men. From this brigade, three future commandants emerged: Elliott (1903–1910), William P. Biddle (1911–1914), and Ben H. Fuller (1930–1934).

Congress soon recognized that the expanding empire required more ships, which meant more Marines. In 1899 Heywood proposed that the Corps be doubled from an authorized strength of 3,073 in 1898 to 201 officers and 6,062 enlisted men. After Congress authorized the increase, Heywood rebelled

Come on, you sons-of-bitches. Do you want to live forever? *Sergeant Dan Daly at Belleau Wood.*

when the navy's general board wanted Marines to serve as colonial infantry in addition to developing advance base capabilities while performing its traditional role as shipboard troops for expeditionary operations.

Marine Lieutenant Smedley D. Butler became livid when he found his unit guarding the Cavite navy base while the army occupation force on the Philippines did the fighting. Butler chafed because the army fought defensively. Marines received their opportunity when Muslim Moros on Samar attacked and crushed an army company. On October 24, 1899, Major Littleton W. T. Waller's Marine battalion landed at Basay, Samar, absorbed the army unit, drove the Moros out of Samar's jungles, and restored peace to the island. Two Marine captains, David D. Porter and Hiram I. Bearss, received Medals of Honor for gallantry.

The Advanced Base Initiative

In 1900, Admiral George Dewey's navy board informed Secretary of the Navy Long that the Marine Corps was the "best adapted and most available for immediate and sudden call" than any other branch of the service. Long directed Commandant Heywood to select personnel and develop techniques that would expand the Corps' mission to include rapid deployment. In 1902, a year before George Elliott became commandant, Heywood organized and placed in training the first battalion of the new Advanced Base Force. Elliott took the next step and in 1910 established the first Advanced Base School in New London, Connecticut, which he later moved to Philadelphia. Although the school was intended for officers, the first class contained forty NCOs. Secretary of the Navy George L. Meyer upped the ante and authorized Elliott to acquire the weapons necessary to carry out the advanced base mission.

In conjunction with the advanced base concept, the Marine Corps stepped up recruiting at large naval stations and, for greater efficiency, consolidated training at two bases: Parris Island, South Carolina, on

The Boxer Rebellion

On May 18, 1900, American and European commercial penetration of China provoked a violent uprising of the Righteous Society of Heavenly Fists. Thousands of so-called Boxers went on a rampage. They burned railway facilities and threatened foreign legations. On May 31 the first of 112 Marines and bluejackets arrived from the cruiser *Newark* (C-1) and the battleship *Oregon* (BB-3). They fought their way to Tientsin, where Marine captains John T. Myers and Newt H. Hall attempted to load the men on trains to Peking. In early June, however, Boxers shut down all rail transportation and snipped telegraph lines, thereby isolating Peking's legations.

On June 10 an international relief force under British Vice Admiral Edward Seymour departed from Tientsin to repair the railway, but six miles from the city they met stubborn resistance and settled into a fort. Ten days later, Major Waller arrived from the Philippines with 140 Marines and found Tientsin in the hands of the Boxers. He joined forces with Seymour, and the unified force, now 2,000 strong, fought its way back to Tientsin. By mid-July, Seymour's international force consisted of 5,650 troops, including 1,021 men of the 1st Marines and the U.S. 9th Infantry, all under Marine Colonel Robert W. Meade. On July 13-14 the allied force attacked and crushed 20,000 howling Boxers and captured Tientsin. Operations then shifted to the relief of

Peking, where legations had been under a fighting siege against thousands of Boxers for eight weeks. By August 3 the small international garrison at Peking had become desperate, having nearly exhausted their supplies and ammunition. They did not know that an international relief force of 18,600 men under General Sir Alfred Gaselee was advancing from Tientsin. With the army came a fresh battalion of Marines under Major William P. Biddle. Gaselee's force, which included 482 Marines, reached the outskirts of Peking on August 13 and raised the siege. Biddle's Marines marched through the Imperial City the following day. For acts of individual heroism, thirty-three Marines received the Medal of Honor.

ABOVE LEFT: In 1900 the Boxer Rebellion threatened Americans residing in the international legation compound in Peking, Cina. Major William P. Biddle's Marine battalion arrived just in time to drive the insurgents away.

ABOVE: A detachment of 140 Marines under Major Littleton Waller arrived in China from the Philippines on June 19, 1900, and marched ninety-seven miles in five days against stubborn resistance in an effort to reach Tientsin.

Fifteen Years of Foreign Interventions

Boxer Rebellion	1900–1901
Philippine Insurrection	1900–1901
Panamanian Interventions	1901–1902
Honduran Expedition	1903
Dominican Republic Insurrections	1903–1904
Panamanian Intervention	1903–1904
Beirut Intervention	1903
Ethiopian Mission	1903
Korean Intervention	1904
Morocco Intervention	1904
Cuban Pacification	1906
Honduran Intervention	1907
Nicaraguan Intervention	1909–1910
Panamanian Intervention	1910
Guantánamo Intervention	1911
Peking/Shanghai Intervention	1911
Cuban Peacekeeping Intervention	1912
Nicaraguan Intervention	1912
Mexican Intervention	1914
Haitian Gold Intervention	1914

the East Coast, and Mare Island, California, on the West Coast, which in 1923 moved to San Diego. Like Heywood, Elliott promoted the importance of marksmanship. When on February 3, 1911, William Biddle became commandant, he continued Elliott's program of improving artillery, adopting automatic rifles, adding more reliable machine guns, and increasing the overall firepower of the Corps.

In January 1904, President Teddy Roosevelt sent a provisional Marine brigade (actually an embryonic advanced base force) to Panama to settle a territorial conflict with Colombia over the establishment of the ten-mile-wide Canal Zone. Commandant Elliott accompanied the three-battalion force, marking the last time a commandant took personal command of military operations in the field. Colombian soldiers were no match for Marines and the dispute swiftly ended. Congress was not certain what to do with Roosevelt's ditch, to which the president replied, "I took the Canal Zone… let Congress debate."

The Advanced Base Force

On December 13, 1913, Commandant Biddle formed the first Advanced Base Force from two Marine regiments and placed it under Colonel George Barnett, who two months later became the Marine Corps' 12th commandant. After completing a series of amphibious exercises, the unit began functioning as a combat-ready, brigade-sized, combined-arms unit trained for assault or defense in either environment. Fifteen years of unrest and interventions in foreign lands necessitated the creation of a highly mobile force of rapid responders.

When in early 1914 tensions in Mexico threatened American interests, Colonel Barnett embarked Colonel John A. Lejeune's Advanced Base Force and sent it to Veracruz, Mexico. The Marines arrived on four ships: Lieutenant Colonel Charles G. Long's 1st Regiment on the *Hancock* (AP-3): Lieutenant Colonel Wendell C. Neville's 2nd Regiment on the transport *Prairie*; Major Smedley Butler's Panama battalion on the cruiser *Chester* (CS-1); and Major Albertus W. Catlin's 3rd Provisional Regiment on the battleship *New Hampshire* (BB-25). Every Marine intended to demonstrate the effectiveness of his training as a member of the Advanced Base Force.

On April 21, President Woodrow Wilson ordered the navy to seize the customs house at Veracruz. Lejeune sent Neville's and Catlin's regiments ashore and landed the other two units below the city the following morning. Some 6,429 officers and men took part in the operation, including 2,469 Marines.

Lejeune intended to prove the merits of the Advanced Base Force, and did. Neville's regiment stormed Veracruz on April 22 and engaged in house-to-house fighting. When temporarily stopped by fire from the Mexican Naval Academy, Neville called for and directed fire support from the *Chester*. Unlike bluejackets fighting from the ground, Neville sent sharpshooters to the city's rooftops to pick off snipers.

ABOVE: During the Mexican crisis in 1914, more than 700 Marines went ashore on the morning of April 21 and circulated through Veracruz to protect American interests and prevent rebel groups from toppling the government.

awarded the Medal of Honor, among them Neville and Butler. The Corps' first amphibious operation under the Advanced Base Force doctrine worked with precision. From this doctrine the Marine Corps would build and grow. Three months later, on July 28, 1914, World War I erupted in Europe.

The Fourth Marine Brigade

On June 14, 1917, Colonel Charles A. Doyen's newly organized 5th Marine Regiment sailed to France with the U.S. Army's 1st Infantry Division to become the first ground units of the American Expeditionary Force (AEF). On October 23, after the arrival of the Colonel Catlin's 6th Marine Regiment and the 6th Machine Gun Battalion, Brigadier General Doyen organized the units into the Fourth Marine Brigade. The 3,600-man units were different from any regiment in the past. Each contained three 1,100-man infantry battalions

ABOVE: Sergeant Major John H. Quick, USMC, aids another Marine in raising the Stars and Stripes at Veracruz, Mexico, on April 21, 1914.

LEFT: Marines disembark from the battleship Florida and the transport Prairie at Veracruz on April 21, 1914, and wait while navy officers advise Mexican authorities that troops have landed and to discourage resistance.

Butler's Panama battalion, which was thoroughly acquainted with street fighting, cleared the city block by block. By nightfall, Marines reached the edge of the city but had to pull back to rescue a trapped bluejacket battalion. With the exception of occasional sniper fire, the fight sputtered out at dusk.

Marines lost four killed and thirteen wounded in two days of erratic fighting. Nine Marines were armed with M1903 Springfield rifles, a regimental machine gun company armed with Hotchkiss guns, and a headquarters and supply company. Transportation consisted of one automobile for the regimental colonel, three motorcycles, fifty-nine mounts for officers, and an assortment of wagons, water carts, and rolling kitchens drawn by 332 fractious mules. The Fourth Marine Brigade became the centerpiece of Marine Corps' operations in World War I, but the men saw no action until the spring campaign of 1918.

On March 17, 1918, Marine units entered the trenches on the front line for the first time at Toulon, France. The sector lay on the heights above the Meuse River southeast of Verdun. On that day, the Fourth Marine Brigade consisted of 258 officers and 8,211

The Beginning of Marine Aviation

Marines performing duties around the world missed one of the developments at home that would one day become a hallmark of the Corps—aviation.

On May 22, 1912, 30-year-old Marine 2nd Lieutenant Alfred A. Cunningham reported to the navy aviation center at Annapolis, Maryland, for flight training. On August 1, after a modest amount of instruction, Cunningham went to the Burgess Company plant at Marblehead, Massachusetts, and after two hours and forty minutes of additional instruction made his first solo flight in a Curtiss seaplane. Designated as Naval Aviator Number 5, he joined six navy officers and became a member of Washington I. Chambers' board, a committee formed to draft "a comprehensive plan for the organization of a naval aeronautical service." Cunningham's influence led to the formation of the Aviation Detachment, Advanced Base Force. His career as a pilot took a temporary setback after he catapulted from a moving battleship: the successful exploit shocked his new bride, who forbade him to fly, so Cunningham turned in his wings.

First lieutenants Bernard L. Smith and Francis T. Evans took over Cunningham's work and equipped two seaplanes for aeronautical experiments. Smith succeeded in dropping small bombs from a seaplane while Evans worked on air maneuvers and looping tactics.

Unable to console himself with ground operations, Cunningham repudiated the agreement with his wife and retrieved his wings. By the outbreak of World War I, he had become a major in charge of a seven-pilot squadron that included Smith, Evans, and forty-three enlisted men. The group became the cadre for the Aeronautical Company, Advanced Base Force, which formed the first exclusively Marine Flying Field outside Miami, Florida.

On April 15, 1918, Commandant Barnett split the 1st Marine Aviation Force into four squadrons and a head-quarters company and sent them to Europe under the command of Major Cunningham. Major Roy S. Geiger, the fifth Marine aviator, served as second-in-command.

Marine pilots flew one of the most poorly designed,

single-engine bombers of the war, the British De Havilland DH-4, nicknamed "The Flaming Coffin" because of its exposed fuel tank. On October 14, 1918, while returning from a bombing raid over Belgium, 2nd Lieutenant Ralph Talbot and his observer, Gunnery Sergeant Robert Robinson, became separated from a Marine squadron of eight DH-4s and had to fight off a swarm of German fighters. Robinson downed a Fokker D-VII, and then suffered wounds fighting off more attacks. Talbot turned the DH-4 around and shot down another Fokker with his fixed gun. Coming under heavy attack, Talbot swooped toward the ground and, flying fifty feet above German lines, landed safely on a Belgium airfield. Both Marines received the Medal of Honor.

By the end of the war, the Marine Aviation Force in Europe had grown to 1,095 officers and men. The unit was credited with inflicting 330 German casualties, shooting down twelve enemy planes, and dropping 52,000 pounds of bombs during fifty-seven raids.

ABOVE: Major Ross E. "Rusty" Rowell, commander of Marine Observation 1, stands beside his DeHavilland DH.4 bomber on a field in Nicaragua after performing the first actual dive-bombing attack in history.

ABOVE: A Curtis pusher-type observation plane is prepared for launch from a catapult on the USS North Carolina. Pilots of early observation planes preferred having props in the rear for clearer view.

ABOVE: Marine pilots considered the two-seat DH.4 the best bomber of World War I, but other flyers dubbed the aircraft "Flying Coffins" because the exposed fuel tank, if struck by bullets, engulfed the plane in flames.

When [World War I] was declared, I tendered, ready and equipped, two regiments of Marines to be incorporated into the Army. Some Army officers were not keen to accept them.

Secretary of the Navy Josephus Daniels in The Wilson Era.

TOP: Marines were among first to arrive in France and went immediately into combat training, which included the wearing of gas masks during drill and field exercises.

ABOVE: A detachment from the 6th Marines snakes through a field outside the German troop-infested town of Bouresches and occupies a deserted trench, from which they pummel the enemy with grenades and rifle fire.

enlisted men who all described fighting from trenches as repugnant and demeaning. In the eight battles that followed, the brigade would suffer 11,968 casualties, including 2,461 killed.

Doyen's Fourth Marine Brigade, along with the army's Third Infantry Brigade and an artillery brigade, became part of the 28,000-man 2nd Infantry Division. Doyen became the first Marine to command an army division, but in December 1917 was inevitably superseded by Major General Omar Bundy of the U.S. Army.

On March 21, 1918, when Germany launched the Somme offensive, General Erich F. W. Ludendorf planned to drive a wedge between the British and French armies, capture Paris, and defeat the two allied armies separately. The German offensive penetrated to within sixty-five miles of Paris and paused to regroup. Two offensives followed, the Lys offensive on April 9 and the Aisne offensive on May 27, where fourteen German divisions broke across the Aisne, advancing ten miles a

ABOVE: Of the many campaign posters nailed to billboards and telephone poles across America, none was more proudly displayed than the Marine Corps' claim of being "First in France."

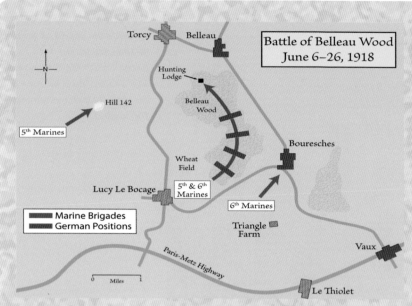

Battle of Belleau Wood
June 6–26, 1918

- Torcy
- Belleau
- Hunting Lodge
- Hill 142
- 5th Marines
- Belleau Wood
- Bouresches
- Wheat Field
- Lucy Le Bocage
- 5th & 6th Marines
- 6th Marines
- Triangle Farm
- Vaux
- Paris-Metz Highway
- Le Thiolet

Marine Brigades
German Positions

0 — Miles — 1

LEFT: *The Battle of Belleau Wood began on June 6 and seesawed back and forth for another twenty days. Although the veteran German IV Corps struck back with mustard gas and artillery, the Marines would not be stopped.*

RIGHT: *After decades of struggling for survival as a service, the advance of Marines into Belleau Wood opened the eyes of the world to the toughness and determination of a special breed of fighters who would not retreat.*

Belleau Wood

On the night of June 5, 1918, the Fourth Marines marched east along the Paris-Metz highway, passing through columns of retreating French infantry. A French officer stopped Marine Captain Lloyd W. Williams and suggested he join the withdrawal. "Retreat, hell!" Williams replied. "We just got here!"

The brigade turned off the highway, fanned out around the village of Lucy-le-Bocage, and spent an uneasy night holding the road to Torcy. Off to the east they could see an ominously silent square-mile of woods and rocks—the Bois de Belleau. Marines did not know they were about to encounter a body of the most combat-seasoned troops in the German army.

At daybreak Major Julius S. Turrill led the 1st Battalion, 5th Marines, through a wheat field and struck Hill 142 west of Belleau Wood. After a bloody fight, the battalion captured the hill, suffering 410 combat casualties.

The next phase of the fight began when the 3rd Battalion, 5th Marines, and the 2nd and 3rd Battalions, 6th Marines, entered the southwestern fringe of Belleau Wood. At a cost of 1,087 casualties, Marines held the southern portion of the woods and the nearby village of Bouresches. The penetration might have collapsed but for the individual heroism of Lieutenants Charles B. Cates and James F. Robertson, who fought off two counterattacks, and of Sergeant John H. Quick, already a Medal of Honor recipient, who drove an old Model-T Ford truck loaded with ammunition through a gauntlet of machine gun fire to Major Thomas Holcomb's pinned-down battalion. War correspondent Floyd Gibbons went into the battle with Gunnery Sergeant Dan Daly's platoon. He remembered Daly raising his rifle and with a forward sweep of his arm shouting to his men, "Come on, you sons-of-bitches. Do you want to live forever?"

For five days the Fourth Marine Brigade obstinately hammered their way—tree by tree—through Belleau Wood, taking enormous casualties, among them Colonel Catlin, shot through the lungs. At nightfall, June 12, Colonel Frederic W. Wise's 2nd Battalion, 5th Marines, broke through the last German defensive position and cleared the northernmost sector of the woods. At daybreak the German IV Corps counterattacked with artillery and mustard gas, and streamed toward the woods. Marines, using their old, reliable 1903 Springfield rifles, began dropping the enemy at 800 yards. Still the Germans came.

General Harbord watched from a distance, expecting to see Major John A. Hughes's 1st Battalion, 6th Marines, withdraw from Bouresches, but despite 450 gas casualties, the Marines stuck fast, fighting at close quarters and smashing attacks while shielding themselves behind stony outcroppings and shattered tree-stumps. When asked for a report, Harbord informed division skeptics: "There is nothing but U.S. Marines in the town of Bouresches."

A final attack by the 3rd Battalion, 5th Marines, now commanded by Major Maurice Shearer, drove the last Germans from the woods. Shearer, a man of few words, reported, "Woods now U.S. Marine Corps entirely."

The fight for Belleau Wood lasted twelve days. The Germans lost 9,500 men and more than 1,600 prisoners. In the opinion of French Prime Minister George Clemenceau, the Fourth Marine Brigade "saved Paris."

day. Within thirty-six hours, the German spearhead reached Château-Thierry, forty miles from Paris.

To meet the crisis, French Field Marshal Ferdinand Foch pulled reserves from quiet sectors, one such outfit being the Fourth Marine Brigade. With some hesitation, Foch moved the untested 2nd U.S. Infantry Division into the nose of the German attack. When the Fourth Marines reached the front lines, army commander Major General John J. Pershing placed the brigade under Brigadier General James G. Harbord, USA, and said, "Young man, I am giving you the best brigade in France—if anything goes wrong, I'll know whom to blame." Harbord knew very little about Marines, but he knew the two regimental commanders,

> The [Marines] looked fine, coming in there, tall fellows, healthy and fit—they looked hard and competent. We watched you going in, through those little tired Frenchmen, and we all felt better. We knew something was going to happen.
> *John W. Thompson, in* Fix Bayonets!

Neville and Catlin, were both Medal of Honor recipients. Harbord deployed the Fourth Marines near a scattered stand of trees known as Belleau Wood, where Ludendorf's spearhead had inadvertently set the stage for the future of the Marine Corps.

A Moment of Reflection

For most of their 142-year history, Marines had seldom faced a professionally trained, well-equipped enemy. At Belleau Wood they met and defeated veteran troops employing modern tools of war. The German IV Corps had been specifically instructed to inflict the severest punishment on Americans fighting their first big battle to destroy their morale. Instead, the Germans were shocked by the ferocity of Marines, who by courage, discipline, and the Corps' own doctrine of *esprit de corps* won the field. During the battle at Belleau Wood (June 5–17, 1918), thousands of Marine officers and men learned a great deal about war.

On July 14, General Harbord received his second star and command of the 2nd Army Division. Colonel Neville received his first star and took command of the Fourth Marine Brigade. Nobody any longer questioned whether Marines could fight. Though the brigade had lost half its men at Belleau Wood, rugged veterans still nursing wounds began stumbling back to their units.

Spearheading the Allies

On July 15, Germany mounted its last offensive of the war, a thrust by thirteen divisions under General Oscar von Hutier to capture Rheims and then Paris. To meet the attack, Field Marshal Foch put Harbord's 2nd Army Division beside the French XX Corps. Harbord now understood Marines and chose the Fourth Brigade as the spearhead. At dawn, massed French XX Corps artillery opened on German positions, and the 5th Marines jumped off behind the barrage, the 1st Battalion on the right and the 2nd Battalion on the left, and struck the rail center at Soissons. On July 19, the 6th Marines pushed through rapidly intensifying resistance and ran head-on into a counterattack by a full German Corps. The Marines had learned a trick at Belleau Wood. They scratched out a shallow rifle pit and, relying on their marksmanship training, began decimating the advancing enemy. A correspondent heard someone call the shallow pits "foxholes." He added it to his column, and the era of the foxhole began.

GOOD PAY :: FOREIGN TRAVEL
CONGENIAL EMPLOYMENT

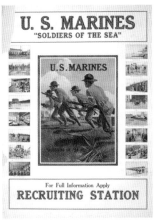

ABOVE: An earlier recruiting poster referring to Marines as "Soldiers of the Sea" lost some significance during World War I because most of the fighting occurred in northern France, 150 miles from the English Channel.

LEFT: Another earlier World War I poster promising "Good pay, foreign travel, congenial employment," and showing Marines coming ashore from ships, did not quite sit comfortably with the horrendous casualties piling up in France.

> Surrendering wasn't popular at the time, and the only way to capture a Marine was to knock him senseless first.
> *Colonel Albertus W. Catlin,* With the Help of God and a Few Marines

ABOVE: *During a post-Armistice visit to the 5th Marine Brigade at Pontanezen, France, Brigadier General Smedley Butler (center) leads Major General John A. Lejeune (right) and Major General Charles A. Summerall into the compound.*

RIGHT: *In "The Greatest Single Achievement" of the war, the 5th and 6th Marines astounded the French army by rolling up the German line holding Blanc Mont Ridge, which during four years of fighting France had failed to do.*

Marines, he had waited too long. Fifty thousand Germans slipped through the closing ring. The 6th Marines charged into the fray and in sharp fighting overran positions held by a heavy force of Germans, repelled four counterattacks, and demolished the fortifications screening the strategic Hindenburg Line.

Field Marshal Foch now realized that the best troops in the American army were not doughboys but leathernecks, and he moved General Lejeune's division into General Henri Gouraud's French Fourth Army. In late September, during the first few days of the Meuse-Argonne offensive, Gouraud retained Lejeune's 2nd Army Division in reserve. Four days later the French offensive ground to a halt, stopped by Blanc Mont Ridge, a precipitous massif occupied by the enemy since the beginning of the war.

The German mincing machine went to work on the Fourth Marine Brigade, but the men held. At one point Lieutenant Cates reported being in an old trench with only two men from his company and twenty from other companies, and with a German Corps confronting him. Cates closed, adding, "I will hold!"

The Fourth Brigade lost 1,972 men to reach and hold the main road leading to General von Hutier's salient. After nightfall, a fresh division relieved the 2nd Army Division. By then, German intelligence had captured a few Marines and realized they were up against a new breed of fighters who knew how to kill with long-range rifles.

After Soissons, the Fourth Brigade lost General Harbord to another round of promotions but gained Brigadier General Lejeune, who became the first Marine general to lead a World War I army division in combat. During the fierce engagement for the Saint Mihiel salient (September 12–16, 1918), Lejeune held back the decimated Fourth Brigade because of its shattered ranks. The American attack caught the Germans in the middle of a tactical withdrawal. When I Corps commander Lieutenant General Hunter Liggett finally called for

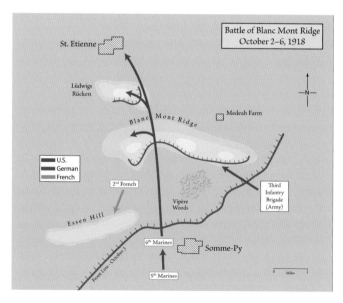

"I Will Take Blanc Mont"

For four years the terrain around Blanc Mont had been gutted by shell and soaked with the blood of both armies. When the Allied offensive stalled, French officers asked Gouraud to split up the 2nd U.S. Infantry Division and spread its components among French divisions. Lejeune strenuously protested, and said, "I will take Blanc Mont." Gouraud did not believe him, but he smirked and replied, "Done!"

Lejeune put the Fourth Marine Brigade on the left to spearhead the attack and the Third Infantry Brigade on the right to disconcert German defenders. With both flanks of the enemy engaged, he intended to pierce the trenches in the center with the rest of the division. He left the demoralized French Fourth Army in the rear with instructions to capture the already decimated Essen Trench and then follow the Marines. Instead of laying down the usual prolonged bombardment, which would have signaled the attack, Lejeune asked Gouraud for just a five-minute barrage from 200 guns.

At dawn, October 3, 1918, the 6th Marines, followed by the 5th Marines and French tanks, assaulted the left side of Blanc Mont Ridge, and three hours later signaled Lejeune, "Objective taken." Captain Leroy P. Hunt's 17th Company, 5th Marines, assaulted the machine-gun-studded Essen line after the French failed to take it, and after driving the Germans out of the trenches, presented the position to the French. A German counterattack drove out the French, and the 5th Marines had to take it back.

The French could not keep pace with the Marines, who found themselves two miles deep in enemy territory with their flanks unprotected all the way back to the Essen Trench. Instead of withdrawing, they pushed forward and on October 8 captured St. Etienne. The French continued to lag behind. Gouraud could not believe that a single brigade of U.S. Marines could accomplish in five days what the French army had been unable to do during four years of fighting.

On October 10, fresh army troops relieved Lejeune's 2nd Division, and for the Fourth Marine Brigade the second phase of the Meuse-Argonne offensive ended. The toll came high. Blanc Mont cost the Marines 2,538 casualties. The Fourth Marine Brigade won its third citation in the French Army, entitling the regiment to carry the streamer of the *Croix de Guerre* on

ABOVE: Men from Major George Hamilton's 3rd Battalion, 5th Marines, set up a .30-caliber machine gun nest in the woods during the war-ending Meuse-Argonne offensive on November 10–11, 1918.

its colors. Individual members received the *fourragère*, irreverently known by Marines as "the pogey rope."

Perhaps the greatest honor came from Marshal Foch, who said, "The taking of Blanc Mont Ridge is the greatest single achievement in the 1918 campaign."

Expansion of the Marine Corps

Unlike Commandant Harris during the Civil War, General Barnett used every opportunity to deploy and expand the Marine Corps during World War I. In addition to creating Marine aviation, Barnett used the "reserve clause" in the Navy Appropriations Act of 1916 to created the Marine Corps Reserve, which by war's end included 496 officers and 6,760 enlisted personnel. When on August 12, 1918, Secretary of the Navy Josephus Daniels authorized Barnett to enroll women as "Marinettes," Opha M. Johnson immediately volunteered and became the first woman Marine. Some 277 women served as enlisted Marines, and some became sergeants.

During World War I, 78,839 Marines served in the Corps. Fewer than half (31,871) went to Europe, and

Meuse-Argonne: The Last Campaign

ABOVE: During "The Last Night of the War" on November 10–11, 1918, with only one hundred men still standing, the 1st Battalion, 5th Marines, surge against a German counterattack and push the enemy back to St. Etienne.

On October 10, the Fourth Marine Brigade went to the rear of the French Fourth Army to mend. During the final phase of the Meuse-Argonne offensive (November 1-11, 1918), General Lejeune, commanding the 2nd Infantry Division, received a call from General Pershing to knock out two strongholds on the Hindenberg Line, called Brünhilde and Freya Stellung. Lejeune turned to Brigadier General Neville, asking that the Fourth Brigade capture Barricourt and push the Germans across the Meuse.

On November 1, the Marines took position on the 2nd Division's left flank. At 5:20 a.m., after 300 guns pounded the trenches at Barricourt, the 1st Battalion, 5th Marines, bounded across "No Man's Land" and pushed forward behind a rolling barrage. The rest of the brigade—battalions from the 5th Marines on the right and the 6th Marines on the left—leapfrogged through Kreimhilde Stellung and Freya Stellung and gained five miles in one day. After capturing Barricourt Heights, the Marines experienced a few anxious hours waiting for the infantry to catch up. The Marine attack on November 1 set one of the speed and distance records of World War I. When relieved by the Third Infantry Brigade, the Marines marched back to division headquarters with 1,700 German prisoners.

On November 9, the 2nd Army Division reached the Meuse River and regrouped for the crossing. Lejeune called for Neville's Fourth Marine Brigade to spearhead the attack. He sent the 6th Marines to seize a bridgehead near Mouzon and the 5th Marines to cross the Meuse at Villemontry.

After nightfall on November 10, assault battalions from the 5th Marines ran into vicious enemy shelling as they attacked across fire-swept footbridges but succeeded in gaining a foothold on the opposite shore. At Mouzon, enemy fire pinned down engineers constructing bridges, so the 6th Marines spent the night hunkered in foxholes until the firing slackened.

At dawn, November 11, both Marine regiments moved rapidly against weak enemy resistance. At precisely 11:00 a.m. they noticed an enormous burst of artillery fire from both sides, followed by sudden silence. An hour later they learned that Germany had surrendered. The Marines collapsed on the ground, built fires, and silently rejoiced. Weeks later, while the doughboys went home, the tattered Fourth Marine Brigade marched into Germany to serve as part of the army of occupation.

RIGHT: With the war in Europe expected to last another year, hundreds of young men volunteer for the Marine Corps in 1918 and are sworn in at the recruiting station in New York City.

FAR RIGHT: As part of the USMC publicity effort to attract recruits under the banner of the "First to Fight," some of the men posing for the photograph looked more like disgruntled draftees than enthusiastic volunteers.

those that did paid a heavy price. Between March and November 1918, Marines in France suffered 12,179 casualties, including 3,284 deaths or missing in action. From the time they entered into combat in March 1918 until war's end, Marines sustained more casualties than they had suffered during the preceding 142 years.

Twelve Medals of Honor went to Marines. Another six went to navy doctors and corpsmen serving with the Fourth Marine Brigade. Other members of the brigade received 744 Navy Crosses or Distinguished Service Medals, together with another 1,720 American and foreign decorations.

By July 1920, the Marine Corps had been sliced from its wartime strength of 78,000 to 17,165 officers and men. Every Marine went home a hero, whether he served with the Fourth Marine Brigade or never left the

John Archer Lejeune (1867–1942)

LEFT: Colonel John Archer Lejune (center) confers with Commandant Colonel George Barnett (left) and staff officer Lieutenant Colonel Powers (right) in Washington regarding the construction during June 1917 of the new Marine training base at Quantico, Virginia.

In August 1919, Major General John A. Lejeune came home from Germany and during the victory parade in New York City marched at the head of the 2nd Infantry Division, which included veterans from the Fourth Marine Brigade. Secretary of the Navy Josephus Daniels admired the 53-year-old general and in 1920 named him the Marine Corps' 13th commandant.

Lejeune made his own way in life. Born January 10, 1867, during the reconstruction years in Louisiana, he grew up in poverty but managed to obtain a tuition-free education at Louisiana State University. He worked to obtain an appointment to the Naval Academy, graduated in 1888 at the age of twenty-one, and went to sea for the compulsory two years as a navy midshipman. He wanted to be a Marine and took his commission as second lieutenant in the Corps.

Lejeune fought in the Spanish-American War, took a battalion into Panama in 1903, commanded in the Philippines in 1907, served in Cuba during 1912–1913, and led the Second Advanced Base Brigade at Veracruz, Mexico, in 1914. Prior to World War I, Commandant Barnett made Lejeune an assistant and soon discovered his understudy could deal with Congress better than anyone else in the Corps. In 1918, Lejeune demonstrated the fighting qualities of Marines in France, and became the Corps' most distinguished general. He improved the training of officers and enlisted men and organized company-grade and field-grade schools at Quantico, Virginia, which became the home and headquarters of the 1st Advance Base Force. He also understood the value of public relations and fielded varsity-quality football and baseball teams and organized the Marine Corps League. Most importantly, for nine years he prepared the Marines for war with Japan by putting a tactical team together to develop the science of amphibious warfare. The team included Lieutenant Colonel Earl H. "Pete" Ellis, whose "Orange Plan" (Operation Plan 712) laid the foundation for victory in the Pacific during World War II.

When Lejeune retired in 1929, he carried on the work to improve the Corps by becoming superintendent of the Virginia Military Institute. In February 1942 the Marine Corps advanced Lejeune to the rank of lieutenant general. Eight months later he died and was buried with full military honors in Arlington Cemetery.

TOP: Marine Corps women reservists prowl the streets of New York City with paste buckets to adorn brick buildings with recruiting posters in support of their male counterparts during World War I.

ABOVE: To promote recruitment in 1917–1918, the Marine Corps fitted Broadway diva Lillian Russell with the uniform of a woman reservist and surrounded her with three bogus privates named O'Keefe, Kelly, and Spike.

states. Thousands returning to civilian life wanted to retain their connection with the Corps and joined the reserves. Nine Marinettes stayed with the Corps and worked for the chief clerk, some for thirty years, and eventually became indispensable supervisors. Deceived politicians hailed the conflict as "the war to end all wars." Another generation would pay the price for reckless bluster and shoddy statesmanship.

Two Decades of Brush Fires

Haitian intervention	1920–34
Guatemala City intervention	1920
Guarding the U.S. mails	1921
Nicaraguan intervention	1922–25
Taku, China, intervention	1922
Matsu Island, China, intervention	1923
Tungsham, China, intervention	1923
Moros revolt, the Philippines	1924
Honduran revolution intervention	1924
Chinese civil war intervention	1924–29
Nicaraguan intervention	1926–33
Guarding the U.S. mails	1926–27
Shanghai, China, intervention	1932
Foochow, China, intervention	1934
Spanish Civil War intervention	1936
Japanese invasion of China	1937
Beginning of World War II	1939

TOP: World War I did not end skirmishes for the Marine Corps. Duty took them around the world, where "Horse Marines" on occasion functioned as cavalry and rode on the backs of bucking "ships of the desert."

ABOVE: The Caco rebellion in Haiti spanned a decade, but in February 1926 the 2nd Marine Regiment deployed enough heavier firepower to the skirmishes to suppress the insurgents permanently.

TOP RIGHT: Marines served off and on for more than two decades, supporting the Nicaraguan government. During the 1932 presidential election, trucks mounting Browning machine guns prevented riots at polling centers.

LOWER RIGHT: When a Sino-Japanese incident in Shanghai put the 4th Marines on alert at the United States' Peking embassy in 1932, the 24th Company set up defensive positions in anticipation of a possible attack.

Marines at Home and Abroad (1920–1939)

During the two decades following World War I, four more commandants served the Marine Corps: Wendell C. Neville (1929–1930), Ben H. Fuller (1930–1934), John H. Russell (1934–1936), and Thomas Holcomb (1936–1943). Together they advanced Marine amphibious doctrine while simultaneously inserting forces of rapid responders wherever Americans or U.S. legations were threatened.

The Fleet Marine Force (FMF)

While Marines served wherever called, in 1922 Lejeune's staff began conducting amphibious maneuvers at Guantánamo, Cuba, and Culebra Island, Puerto Rico. Lejeune wanted mistakes made so that he could correct them, and plenty of mistakes occurred.

In 1923, Lejeune replaced the Advance Base Force by creating the Marine Corps Expeditionary Forces, which in 1924 consisted of 3,300 officers and men working on amphibious doctrine using both offensive and defensive tactical exercises. Lejeune soon discovered that Marines were not loading their transports to be unloaded efficiently. Nor did they have suitable landing craft for getting themselves and their equipment ashore. In 1925, when army-navy war games moved to Oahu, Hawaii, the only beneficiaries of the highly theoretical exercise were the 1,500 men who successfully simulated a 42,000-man Marine landing force. Lejeune's staff went back to the drawing board to add more improvements. Meanwhile, problems in Nicaragua and China enabled the Marines to make mini-landings, though rarely under fire.

When in 1930 Major General Ben H. Fuller became the 15th commandant, he faced the problem of nursing the Marines through the Great Depression, during which Congress reduced the Corps from 18,000 to 15,350. In 1934 he passed the baton to Major General John Russell, his understudy, who had never liked Lejeune's term "expeditionary." While still serving under Fuller in 1933, Russell succeeded in renaming the two units on the East and West Coast the Fleet Marine Force. After taking office, Russell immediately launched a program to resume amphibious assault exercises and improve tactics with better landing craft. Russell's Marine Corps Equipment Board went to work testing and developing what became the LCVP (landing craft, vehicle and personnel), the LCM (landing craft, mechanized), and the LVT (landing vehicle, tracked).

One might wonder how the Marines would have gotten ashore on dozens of islands in the Pacific without such vehicles.

Between the Wars in the Air

Without fully capitalizing on the potential of air power during the 1920s, the Marines continued to work on the development of air-ground cooperation and close air support. In July 1927 Marine aviators were still flying World War I DH.4s. During operations against Nicaraguan guerrilla leader Augusto Sandino, Major Ross E. "Rusty" Rowell became involved in a rescue operation over jungle terrain. Captain Gilbert D. Hatfield's 110-man battalion had been surrounded and pinned down by Sandino's rebels. Rowell overflew the area, strafed the guerrillas, returned to base, and

ABOVE: The Marine Corps were often recipients of aircraft neither the navy nor the army wanted, but for Advanced Base concept exercises, old Curtiss pushers launched from cruiser catapults were used for observation. This biplane was already obsolete and discarded before World War I.

TOP LEFT: *Chance-Vought SU-2s scout planes from Marine squadron VO-8M fly over San Diego, California, during routine observation exercise in 1933.*

ABOVE: *Grumman F3F-2 fighters, powered by 750-horsepower Pratt & Whitney engines, were among the last of biplane-class of pursuit aircraft. Both F3F-2s and F3F-3s gave way to Grumman F4F-3s in 1937.*

TOP RIGHT: *The Chance-Vought OS2U-3 Kingfisher performed observation-scout duties from 1936 until the outbreak of World War II. The aircraft also operated as a dive-bomber for the navy but was too slow.*

ABOVE: *The Grumman F4F-3, delivered in 1937, became the Marine Corps' first monoplane fighter. At 298 miles per hour the F4F-3 was no match for Japanese Zeros and paid a heavy price when in combat.*

loaded four 25-pound fragmentation bombs on each of his five DH.4s. With all the machine gun ammunition the planes could carry, he flew back to Hatfield's position. Having been a postwar pioneer of dive-bombing, Rowell had taught his squadron the technique and now prepared to put the training into practice.

At 1,500 feet, Rowell approached Sandino's base, keeping one eye on the ground and the other on an approaching storm. Sandino watched with curiosity as Rowell's squadron tipped over, leveled off at 300 feet, glided over the base, and plastered the position. The guerrillas scattered in different directions, and Hatfield's Marines mopped them up.

Young Marine flyers took notice of Rowell's escapades and soon began improving air tactics with better aircraft. Many years passed in the transition of DH.4s to F6C Curtiss "Hawks," SU-2 Scout planes, F-4B3 Boeing fighters, and finally in 1938, Grumman F3F-2 fighters, all of which were biplanes and unfit for World War II. Even early monoplanes like the Vought SB2U-3, which introduced folding wings, became instantly obsolete on the world air stage.

The Blending of Assets

In 1936, when Major General Thomas Holcomb became the 17th commandant, the approaching war defined his efforts. A well-decorated Marine, Holcomb had served at Belleau Wood and Soissons during World War I and later in China, where he learned the language. President Franklin D. Roosevelt pulled him out of the Marine schools at Quantico and gave him the task of increasing the Corps from 17,000 to 300,000 men. Holcomb's massive task included building up the Fleet Marine Force while integrating the Marine Air Wing with ground forces and the navy for the fighting anticipated in the Pacific.

On September 1, 1939, war erupted in Europe. Holcomb sent the 1st Marine Division to Camp

Lejeune for training on 111,710 acres of water, coastal swamp, scrub pines, and sand flats in North Carolina's wastelands near Morehead City. One officer grumbled, "This division won't be fit for anything but jungle warfare." As the Marines gathered strength, the supreme test approached with breathless speed.

ABOVE: Marines recruited in 1940 were still being trained on Quantico's World War I trench warfare assault course, which had no resemblance to the jungle fighting that would distinguish the Corps during World War II.

CRISIS IN THE PACIFIC 1941–1943

Having invaded China in 1937, Japan waited until France surrendered to Germany on June 14, 1940, before sending troops into Indochina. On July 19, President Franklin D. Roosevelt responded by signing the Naval Expansion Act creating a two-ocean navy, more than doubling the existing combat fleet, and providing for a corresponding increase in the Marine Corps. Commandant Holcomb found mobilizing the Corps during peacetime a slow and tedious recruiting and training process.

On September 26, 1940, three days after Japanese troops moved into northern Indochina, Roosevelt reduced oil shipments to Japan. One day later Japan intensified operations in Tonkin (North Vietnam) and on September 27 signed a Tripartite Pact with Germany and Italy.

On July 26, 1941, Roosevelt froze Japanese assets in the United States. Japan reacted by invading Cochin China (South Vietnam) and on August 11, 1941, called for a general mobilization. Occupation of

RIGHT: The Marine Statue at Parris Island, South Carolina, harkens back to October 28, 1915, when Commandant General George Barnett recovered the post from the navy and made it a fourteen-week basic training base for recruits.

. . . the basic amphibious doctrines which carried Allied troops over every beachhead of World War II had been largely shaped—often in the face of disinterested and doubting military orthodoxy—by U.S. Marines . . .

General Alexander Vandegrift in Jeter A. Isley and Philip A. Crowl, The U.S. Marines and Amphibious Warfare, 4.

Indochina provided Japan with a springboard for launching assaults on Malaya and the oil-rich islands of the Dutch East Indies.

The war in Europe, which officially began on September 1, 1939, when Germany attacked Poland, provided Japan with the impetus to dominate the Far East. Easy victories in China and Indochina merely encouraged War Minister General Hideki Tojo, who in October 1941 became prime minister, to expand operations in the Pacific, including U.S. possessions and the Philippines. Admiral Isoroku Yamamoto questioned the advisability of drawing Americans into the war, but Tojo prevailed, theorizing that by destroying the U.S. Pacific Fleet at Pearl Harbor, America would be unable to respond to Japan's offensive.

In December 1941, Commandant Holcomb's Marine Corps consisted of 65,000 officers and enlisted men. Twenty thousand were still in training, 4,000 were serving on navy ships or at naval stations, and others were scattered all over the world. Of the total,

4,500 Marines were stationed at Pearl Harbor on Oahu in the Hawaiian Islands.

The Day of Infamy

At dawn on December 7, 1941, a Japanese task force commanded by Vice Admiral Chuichi Nagumo and composed of six carriers (*Akagi, Hiryu, Kaga, Shokaku, Soryu,* and *Zuikaku*), two battleships, three cruisers, and nine destroyers, turned into the wind 230 miles north of Honolulu. Minutes later forty-three Mitsubishi "Zero" fighters, eighty-nine Nakajima "Kate" torpedo-bombers, and eighty-one Aichi "Val" dive-bombers began assembling in the sky for a surprise attack on the U.S. Pacific Fleet anchored in Pearl Harbor. As the first wave disappeared from sight, a second wave of fighters and bombers began forming on the decks of the carriers.

Admiral Husband E. Kimmel, commanding the navy's Pacific Fleet, had been warned of a possible Japanese attack, but the naval base at Pearl Harbor had

ABOVE: Vice Admiral Chuichi Nagumo, commanding Japan's Pearl Harbor strike force, believed that his carrier planes had dismantled the U.S. Pacific Fleet at Pearl Harbor, unaware that he had planted the seeds for his nation's defeat.

ABOVE: As a second wave of torpedo-bombers begin their strike on Pearl Harbor, a Japanese pilot looks through the glazing of his cockpit to view the damage his comrades had earlier inflicted on the U.S. Pacific Fleet.

RIGHT: During the Japanese strike on Pearl Harbor, the magazine explodes on the battleship USS Shaw. All efforts to keep her afloat fail. That day, Marines in ships' detachments lost 108 killed and 49 wounded. In all, 2,280 Americans were killed and 1,109 wounded.

not been mentioned in the message. A lone U.S. radar station searching the skies reported dozens of aircraft heading for Oahu, but the sleepy communications center in Honolulu ascribed the blips to a squadron of bombers expected from the mainland, and did nothing. On the eight American battleships anchored off Ford Island and the eight cruisers lying nearby, sailors chatted at breakfast. At the three airfields around Honolulu, flyers lounged in their bunks or in mess halls.

After a casual Sunday morning breakfast, Marine Captain Leonard Ashwell, officer of the day at Ewa airfield, sauntered outside and spotted two formations of Japanese torpedo-bombers, followed by twenty-one Zeroes, heading east toward Pearl Harbor. Before he could react, Zeroes swooped low over Ewa and strafed the forty-seven planes, parked wingtip to wingtip, of Marine Air Group 21 (MAG-21). Two minutes later, Japanese torpedo-bombers struck Pearl Harbor.

The firing, explosions, and the sound of many aircraft alerted the men of MAG-21 that something horrific was occurring on the airfield. Sirens blared. Marines piled out of barracks and mess halls to get to their stations. Pilots tried unsuccessfully to get planes in the air. Three separate strafing attacks followed by dive-bombers destroyed every plane but one.

There were no antiaircraft guns on Ewa. Marines tried frantically to set up a makeshift defense. They broke out machine guns and pulled others from wrecked planes. Some fought back with rifles and pistols. Master Technical Sergeant Emil S. Peters pulled Private William C. Turner into the rear cockpit of a parked dive-bomber and used its machine gun to shoot down a Val. At 9:45 a.m. Japanese planes headed back to sea. The aircraft at Ewa resembled a junkyard, but the Marines kept the field open to receive army and navy planes from other smashed airfields. Four Marines died on Ewa, including Private Turner, and thirteen suffered wounds.

Six minutes after the Japanese struck Ewa, Colonel Harry K. Pickett sent for the Marines stationed at the navy yard. After the men reached the airfield they pulled together thirty-eight machine guns and shot down three Vals. When Pickett sent for more guns from storage, he discovered that all the ammunition had been secured in hills twenty-seven miles away.

The destruction was devastating. Five of eight battleships sank to their superstructures or capsized. Three more were severely damaged but eventually limped to the West Coast for repairs. Of 877 Marines stationed on ships, 108 were killed and 49 wounded. In

all, the United States lost 2,403 servicemen killed and 1,178 wounded on a Sunday morning President Roosevelt called "the day of infamy."

Owing to good luck, the Pacific Fleet's three aircraft carriers—*Enterprise* (CV-6), *Lexington* (CV-2), and *Saratoga* (CV-3)—were not at Pearl Harbor where they might have been. Had they been destroyed, the Japanese might not have been stopped.

Admiral Kimmel paid the price for poor vigilance at Pearl Harbor, and on December 31, 1941, Admiral Chester W. Nimitz took command of the Pacific Fleet.

The Philippines (1941–1942)

For the United States, the military situation in the Pacific looked bleak indeed. On December 8 Marines surrendered on Guam. Although army Major General Lewis H. Brereton, commanding General Douglas MacArthur's Far East Air Force on the Philippines, had been alerted on November 27 to the possibility of a Japanese attack, all but one of his planes were parked on Clark Field when at 12:15 p.m., December 8, some 108 twin-engine Japanese bombers and thirty-four Zeroes struck the airfield and destroyed the air wing. Two days later, after Japanese bombers wrecked the naval base at Cavite and disabled the ships in Manila Bay, Lieutenant General Masaharu Homma's Fourteenth Army landed unopposed on the Philippines.

In late November, Colonel Samuel L. Howard's 4th Marine Regiment of forty-four officers and 728 enlisted men had reached the Philippines from China.

In the first six to twelve months of a war with the United States and Britain, I will run wild and win victory after victory. After that, I have no expectation of success.

Admiral Isoroku Yamamoto's prewar admonishment to Imperial General Headquarters.

Wake Island

On December 8, 1941, thirty Japanese bombers dropped bombs on the small airstrip on Wake Island and destroyed seven of the twelve Grumman F4F Wildcats that had been delivered four days earlier by the carrier *Enterprise*. The attack also destroyed the airfield's 25,000-gallon fuel tank, leaving VMF-211, Major Paul A. Putnam's Marine fighter squadron, in desperate shape. Putnam had no radar—it was still in a box at Pearl Harbor—and for reconnaissance relied on lookouts atop two fifty-foot water towers. On December 9 enemy bombers returned, and Putnam's four patrolling Wildcats shot one down. When the bombers reappeared on December 10, Captain Henry Elrod shot down two.

On December 11, after three days of air strikes, the Japanese launched a seaborne assault supported by three light cruisers and six destroyers. Major James P. Devereaux's 388 officers and men of the 1st Defense Battalion, aided by VMF-211, inflicted 700 casualties in repulsing the assault force. Devereaux's seacoast guns sank one destroyer and Elrod's aerial bombs sank another. The cruiser Yubari limped away spewing smoke. Wildcats damaged two destroyers, and shore batteries crippled two transports. In Japan, the setback against a handful of Marines produced an unexpected shock.

Devereaux had six good 5-inch seacoast guns, twelve 3-inch antiaircraft guns, dozens of machine guns, but too few Marines. Admiral Kimmel, Pacific Fleet commander, had been remiss in not adequately reinforcing Wake Island, which lay 2,000 miles west of Hawaii. Then in mid-December he recalled a relief expedition containing more planes and another

battalion of Marines. Japan wanted Wake because it lay inside their defensive perimeter. The Americans needed Wake as a strategic outpost. Kimmel's decision made Devereaux's force expendable.

Daily strikes by Japanese bombers eventually disabled Putnam's five Wildcats, and after midnight on December 23, a thousand Japanese troops waded ashore on four beaches. In ferocious hand-to-hand combat, Marines resisted the attack at the water's edge, but after several hours of hopeless fighting, navy Commander Winfield Scott Hamilton, the island commander, told Devereaux to surrender.

After sinking four Japanese ships and inflicting more than 1,000 casualties, the Marines laid down their arms. The defense of Wake Island became a rallying point in America. In 1942 William Bendix and Robert Preston starred in the movie "Wake Island," luring thousands of young men into the Marine Corps.

ABOVE LEFT: Under constant air attack, and with only a handful of Grumman F4F-3 Wildcats on Wake Island, pilots from VMF-211 watched grimly as damaged fighters began piling up on the pock-marked airfield.

ABOVE RIGHT: Major James P. Devereux reached Wake Island with the 1st Defense Battalion and VMF-211 on October 15, 1941, but his F4F-3 Wildcats did not arrive until November 27. After a valiant defense, Devereux spent the next four years in a Japanese prison camp.

RIGHT: During the Battle of the Philippines in March 1942, endless columns of Japanese troops jam the few narrow roads leading to the Bataan Peninsula.

FAR RIGHT: Japanese soldiers stand proudly after forcing the surrender of Corregidor on May 6, 1942. Marine Colonel Donald Curtis, somewhere in the pack, expressed shame for becoming the first Marine officer "ever to surrender a regiment."

ABOVE: The Japanese celebrate the capture of Orion on the Bataan peninsula. On April 9, 1942, some 75,000 Americans and Filipinos surrender. Only 105 Marines were trapped in the net, others having escaped to Corregidor.

Had they remained in China longer, they would have shared the fate of 500 Marines taken prisoner at Peking and Tientsin. Howard had only two battalions, each short one company and each company short one rifle platoon. MacArthur sent the 1st Battalion to Bataan and the 2nd Battalion to Cavite. On December 20 he rounded up all the Marine units scattered among the navy, put them into Howard's regiment, and sent most of them to Corregidor, a rocky lizard-shaped island at the entrance to Manila Bay. A few Marine Rifle platoons remained on Bataan to slow the enemy.

On January 9, 1942, Japanese forces attacked the Bataan peninsula, inflicting and taking heavy casualties. MacArthur fell back to a reserve line formed across the neck of the peninsula, where his dwindling army held out for two months. On March 12, under orders from President Roosevelt, MacArthur departed for Australia and turned his command over to army Lieutenant General Jonathan M. Wainwright. Before leaving, he awarded Distinguished Service Crosses to all units except the Marines. Wainwright corrected the oversight the day he took command.

Four weeks later, 80,000 U.S. and Filipino troops, including 1,500 Marines, surrendered on Bataan. Before the infamous Bataan "Death March" began, a few Marines escaped and joined their comrades on Corregidor. Of 11,000 men isolated on the tiny island, 1,430 were Marines.

In late March, after enemy artillery pounded Corregidor, 2,000 Japanese landed in assault boats. They came ashore near the 1st Marine Battalion and were cut to pieces in the moonlight. More enemy soldiers followed and established a beachhead. They captured Battery Denver and forced Colonel Howard to commit his last reserves—Marines attached to headquarters and service units. By daylight, more than 150 Marines lay dead or wounded.

Marines took over most of Corregidor's batteries and turned them on Japanese tanks crawling across the island, but at noon, May 6, with water and food supplies knocked out and ammunition nearly exhausted, General Wainwright notified Homma that he intended to surrender. When Colonel Howard learned of the order, he turned to his adjutant, and with tears in his eyes, ordered the regiment's colors and standard burned. Then reality struck. "My God," he gasped, "I [am] to be the first Marine officer ever to surrender a regiment." Howard no longer had a regiment to surrender. Of 1,430 Marines, 687 lay dead or wounded. Another 239 men from the 4th Marines later died in Japanese prison camps.

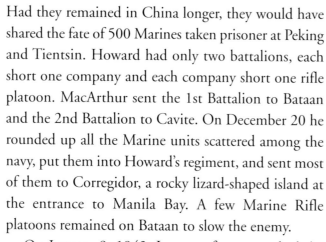

The battle of the Philippines took much longer than Imperial General Headquarters anticipated. The delay only slightly slowed the enemy's overall campaign. By early May, Japanese forces had isolated China from its allies, overrun the Dutch East Indies, Singapore, Malaya, and Burma, and began driving south through the Solomon Islands to New Guinea. Two American carriers—*Lexington* (CV-2) and *Yorktown* (CV-5)—stood in the way, and, during the battle of the Coral Sea on May 7–8, 1942, turned back a Japanese invasion force headed for Port Moresby, New Guinea. Exactly six months had passed since the attack on Pearl Harbor. The U.S. Navy was back in the fight, and so were the Marines.

Marines at Midway

After the fall of Wake Island, Midway had become America's most advanced base in the central Pacific. The small island group lay 1,150 miles west of Honolulu. Admiral Nimitz's cryptanalysts had broken the Japanese code, warning that Admiral Yamamoto planned a massive attack on Midway for the purpose of drawing out the Pacific Fleet and destroying it. Nimitz prepared his own surprise. He mustered the carriers *Enterprise* (CV-6) and *Hornet* (CV-8) under Rear Admiral Raymond A. Spruance, and the carrier *Yorktown* (CV-5) under Rear Admiral Frank Jack Fletcher, and sent them with their task forces to meet Admiral Nagumo's Carrier Strike Force, consisting of the carriers *Akagi, Hiryu, Kaga,* and *Soryu,* the Main Body battle force under Yamamoto, and the Midway Occupation Force under Vice Admiral Nobutake Kondo.

Nimitz also instructed Colonel Harold D. Shannon, commanding Marines on Midway, to keep scout planes in the air. Shannon passed the order to Lieutenant Colonel Ira E. Kimes, whose Marine Air Group 22 (MAG-22) flew some of the Corps' more antiquated aircraft. Marine Scout-Bomber Squadron 231 (VMSB-231) operated seventeen Vought SB2U Vindicator dive-bombers. Marine Fighter Squadron 221

(VMF-221) flew fourteen equally vulnerable Brewster F2A-3 Buffaloes and a handful of older vintage Grumman F4F-3 Wildcats. In March, a squadron of sixteen Douglas SBD-2 Dauntless dive-bombers joined the group, giving MAG-22 a slightly more potent punch.

At daybreak, June 4, Midway's radar detected blips from Admiral Nagumo's first wave of thirty-six Val dive-bombers, thirty-six Kate torpedo-bombers, and thirty-six Zeroes. Fifteen minutes later, Colonel Kimes sent every available plane from MAG-22 into the air. Major Floyd B. Parks headed the Buffaloes from VMF-221 directly at the approaching Japanese strike force. Major Lofton R. Henderson led his sixteen SBD-2 Vindicator dive-bombers from VMSB-241 to a rendezvous area forty miles east to wait for word on the location of Nagumo's carriers. Major Benjamin Norris followed behind Henderson with the slower SB2U Vindicators.

Fifteen minutes after takeoff, Parks sighted Vals with Zero escorts about thirty miles from Midway. From 17,000 feet, the old Buffaloes tipped in a dive designed to pass through the Zeroes and attack the bombers. During the first run, seven of the twelve Buffaloes burst into flames. During the second attack, six more Buffaloes spiraled into the ocean, followed by two Wildcats. After a twenty-minute one-sided dogfight,

TOP: Marines began flying Douglas SBD-1 Dauntlesses in 1939. Many variations followed. The aircraft was armed with three 12.7mm machine guns and could carry a 1,000-pound bomb under the fuselage and two 100-pound bombs under each wing.

ABOVE: Grumman F4F Wildcats traced back to the early 1930s. When World War II began, most models flown by Marines were F4F-3s. Compared with Zereos, they were slow and eventually replaced by F4F-4s and F6F Hellcats.

ABOVE: Survivors from the Japanese carrier Hiryu, the last of Admiral Nagumo's four carriers sunk at Midway, are herded ashore at Pearl Harbor under Marine guard. The Battle of Midway on June 5–6, 1942, proved to be the beginning of the end for the Imperial Japanese Navy in the Pacific.

not much remained of VMF-221, but thirty-two Japanese Vals never made it to Midway.

Meanwhile, Major Henderson received coordinates on the location of Nagumo's carriers. He led his sixteen Vindicators to 9,000 feet and peeled off to plant 500-pound bombs on the flight decks of the enemy flattops. Zeroes flying cover above the carriers cut through the diving SBDs and shot down half the planes, including Henderson's. Eight pilots returned to Midway, reporting no hits.

A second group from VMSB-241, seventeen old Vindicators led by Norris, closed on the battleships *Haruna* and *Kirishima* instead of the carriers. Zeroes shot down three Vindicators before they came in striking range of the ships. During the dive, flak struck Captain Richard E. Fleming's plane and set it on fire. Fleming nosed the aircraft towards the closest Japanese ship and crippled the cruiser *Mikuma,* an act for which he was posthumously awarded the Medal of Honor.

Having scored no hits, Norris took the squadron back to Midway, which was covered by a pall of smoke from oil fires. At nightfall, he and other flyers got back into the air with six flyable Vindicators. Failing to find an enemy carrier, the pilots returned them to Midway, all, that is, except for Norris's, which never returned.

The reason for the disappearance of the enemy carriers soon became evident. During the day, dive-bombers from the *Enterprise, Hornet*, and *Yorktown* had destroyed them. The victory of the American carriers at Midway—which signaled the first major turning point of the war—completely overshadowed the contribution of the Marine Air Group. MAG-22 lost forty-eight killed, thirty-nine wounded, and most of its aircraft, but Marine flyers knocked down forty-three enemy planes, and AA guns of the defense battalion on the ground downed ten more.

The Organization in the Pacific

Admiral Chester W. Nimitz, who on December 31 assumed command of the Pacific Fleet, became a party to a somewhat confusing arrangement worked out by the Joint Chiefs of Staff (JCS) when he became commander-in-chief of operations in the Pacific and the eastern Solomons. General MacArthur obtained command of the Southwest Pacific area, which included the western Solomons, New Guinea, and Australia. Although the arrangement would eventually be modified, it temporarily defined the areas of responsibility for the army, navy, and Marines.

When on May 27, 1941, the United States and Great Britain signed the ABC-1 Staff Agreement, President Roosevelt committed American ground forces to defeating Germany. The agreement also committed British and American chiefs of staff to work together as combined chiefs of staff. After Pearl Harbor, the combined chiefs modified the agreement to include operations against Japan. This led to the understanding that the Royal Navy would be mainly responsible for the Atlantic and the U.S. Navy for the Pacific. Conversely, the U.S. Army would be mainly responsible for the war in North Africa and Europe, and Commandant Holcomb's Fleet Marine Force would be responsible for amphibious operations in the Pacific. Admiral Nimitz wanted his own ground force, and Holcomb provided it. General MacArthur would command U.S. Army and Allied forces in the Southwest

Pacific sector, but he was told to not expect much help.

Under this agreement, Admiral Ernest J. King, commander-in-chief, U.S. Fleet, authorized Nimitz to plan Operation Watchtower, an offensive against the southern Solomon Islands. King believed the incapacity of MacArthur's Southwest Pacific forces to take action against the Solomons required that the navy and the Marines fill the void. After asking the army for troops he had no expectation of receiving, King did not wait for a response and unilaterally set the wheels in motion for an assault on Guadalcanal by Marines.

King's argument for using Marines in the Pacific dated back to the 1921 Orange Plan for "Advanced Base Operations in Micronesia," authored by Marine Colonel "Pete" Ellis. For two decades the Marine Corps had worked on a series of Rainbow "what if" plans in the event of war. Rainbow-2 anticipated a war against Japan waged mainly by the navy during which the Marine Corps would play an important role. Plans for Rainbow-2 suffered a setback when Germany invaded Denmark and Norway, but revived when Congress authorized funds for a "two-ocean" navy. Commandant Holcomb made the decision to put the Marines on a war footing by increasing and modernizing the Fleet Marine Force. Amphibious warfare was not the navy's highest priority, but it was Holcomb's. This required an amphibious force of thirty large transports, eleven amphibious supply ships, 1,400 new landing craft, 500 amphibian tractors, ships for naval gunfire support, and an enormous increase in Marine aviation. It also meant the Corps would have to supply thousands of pilots and aviation support personnel. The legislation, signed by Roosevelt after his re-election in 1940, resulted in the formation of the 1st and 2nd Marine Divisions, the 1st and 2nd Marine Aircraft Wings, and several defense battalions for the Fleet Marine Force.

Although Admiral Harold R. Stark, former Chief of Naval Operations (CNO) before King assumed the post, had opposed the formation of a third Marine division, Holcomb eventually created six divisions and five aircraft wings, and he thrust them one by one into the battle for the Pacific.

As a result of the modified ABC-1 Staff agreement, Marines never became a factor in the European theater. Marines in that theater served almost exclusively on ships of the Atlantic Fleet, but on occasion served with the Office of Strategic Service (OSS) for covert

operations in North Africa and Europe. They worked with partisan groups in France, Germany, Italy, and Yugoslavia, and one Marine, Colonel Peter J. Ortiz, won two Navy Crosses for heroism with the French Resistance. Otherwise, Marines remained committed to the war in the Pacific.

ABOVE: Commandant Holcomb's vision of the Fleet Marine Force during the 1930s paid immense dividends during operations in 1942. The deck of the USS Enterprise is crammed with Douglas SBD Dauntlesses and Grumman F4F Wildcats, which were flown by both the navy and the Marine Corps.

Guadalcanal (Operation Watchtower)

Victory at Midway accelerated Operation Watchtower. In late June 1942, Major General Alexander A. Vandegrift had the 1st Marine Division spread about in New Zealand and Samoa for six months of training. The first elements of the 2nd Marine Division were on

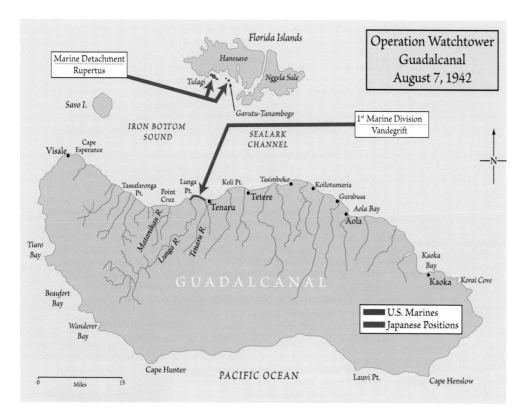

Operation Watchtower
Guadalcanal
August 7, 1942

U.S. Marines
Japanese Positions

TOP: The amphibious assault of Guadalcanal on August 7, 1942, occurred with more trepidation than opposition, but Marines assaulting the tiny islands across the sound ran into stiff resistance from well-concealed Japanese naval infantry.

ABOVE: Parris Island turned out pilots along with infantrymen. The pictured cadet, probably having recently completed flight training, could expect to be soon on his way to the Pacific.

the way, which he planned to place in reserve. Vice Admiral Robert L. Ghormley, commanding the South Pacific Fleet, objected to the operation, arguing that resources were inadequate. Guadalcanal had never been mapped and little was known about tides or reefs. Nor had any Marine division performed a large-scale exercise involving amphibious maneuvers. Vandegrift did not expect to go into battle until February 1943, but on July 2 the JCS approved Operation Watchtower and advanced the assault on Guadalcanal to August 7.

The acceleration of the campaign resulted after air reconnaissance reported a Japanese airfield under construction near Guadalcanal's Lunga Point. Because the enemy had already installed seaplane bases on Florida Island, opposite Guadalcanal, the JCS added Tulagi, Gavutu, and Tanambogo to the assault.

During July, Vandegrift assembled the 1st Marine Division in the Fijis. He worried that the division would not be ready for operations by D-Day, nor had naval support forces been properly prepared. A dress rehearsal

conducted off the Fijis resulted in a fiasco. Assault craft lodged on reefs, naval gunfire went wild, and supporting aircraft missed their targets. Admiral Fletcher balked at leaving his carriers off Guadalcanal for four days to protect Rear Admiral Richmond Kelly Turner's amphibious assault force and promised only two days of air coverage. Turner wanted one regiment of Marines retained on ships "for further operations," though no additional operations ever materialized. While Fletcher and Turner continued to bicker, Vandegrift's Marines merely wanted to get on with the war and fight.

At nightfall, July 31, the 1st Marine Division sailed for the Solomons to lead the first American ground assault in World War II. The designation "First to Fight" gave new meaning to their long history as Marines, for they had been given the point position on the long road to final victory.

At dawn August 7, after a week at sea, thousands of nervous and sleepless Marines scrambled down cargo nets draped over the sides of transports and tumbled into landing craft. They listened nervously as hundreds of naval guns pounded an area designated as Red Beach. Stomachs felt queasy as boats moved into assault formation and sprinted toward the white, sandy beaches of Guadalcanal, a shimmering jungle-covered island ninety miles long and twenty-five miles wide in the southern Solomons.

At 9:10 a.m., boats transporting the first wave of the 5th Marine Regiment scraped against the shallows and stopped. Wide-eyed Marines splashed through green-colored water and raced for cover in a coconut grove. Not a sound could be heard but the steady whoosh of naval shells landing farther inland. The assault took 2,230 Japanese soldiers and Korean construction workers by surprise. They fled into the jungle. Not a shot was fired. General Vandegrift came ashore to direct the assault. None occurred. A detachment went forward to reconnoiter the near-complete airfield and found it deserted. Vast supplies of fuel and food lay undisturbed, along with construction equipment in good working order.

As units spread out on Guadalcanal to establish a perimeter, the 2nd Marine Regiment and the 1st Parachute Battalion went ashore on Tulagi, Gavutu, and Tanambogo. There they found Japanese in a fighting mood, a portent of things to come. The enemy hid in caves and dense foliage and came out at night to infiltrate Marine lines. One captain, anxious to demonstrate the technique for disposing of Japanese concealed in caves, overestimated the amount of TNT required and blew off his trousers. To clear out enemy positions, Marines called for the first naval gunfire support from a U.S. ship in World War II. Air support strikes proved as dangerous to the Marines as to the enemy. For three small islands across the sound from Guadalcanal, the Marines paid with 108 dead and 140 missing.

Isolation of Marines on Guadalcanal

Marines on Guadalcanal experienced their next shock on the night of August 8–9 when Admiral Fletcher informed Admiral Turner and General Vandegrift that he was removing his carrier task force from the area without waiting for permission to do so. Left with no air power and only a few cruisers and destroyers, ships of the amphibious task force lost their protection. After a Japanese squadron came down "the Slot" the night of August 9 and sank four heavy U.S. cruisers (Battle of Savo Island), Turner hastily withdrew before unloading all the supplies. Vandegrift made a quick inventory in the morning and concluded that his Marines had thirty-seven days of ammunition and supplies instead of the ninety-day arrangement provided for the operation. Turner had also carried off all the headquarters and regimental weapons for the 2nd Marines, along with the 3rd Battalion, 10th Marines.

Left with 11,000 Marines, Vandegrift established a broad perimeter around the airfield and put the 1st Engineer Battalion to work firing up Japanese earth-

moving equipment to finish the airstrip. If the navy would not help, perhaps flying leathernecks would if they had a place to land.

ABOVE: Survivors from Lieutenant Colonel Evans F. Carlson's 2nd Raider Battalion's Makin Island assault on August 17, 1942, wait on the deck of the USS Argonaut as the submarine eases into the dock at Pearl Harbor.

LEFT: After "Carlson's Raiders" won a tactically muddled action on Makin Island, which General Holland Smith later called "a piece of folly," the Marines returned to the USS Argonaut convinced they had fulfilled their mission.

> The thing that impresses me more than anything else in connection with the Solomons action is that we are not prepared to follow-up. We have seized a strategic position. Can the Marines hold it? There is considerable room for doubt.
>
> *Major General Millard F. Harmon, U.S.A., to General George C. Marshall, August 11, 1941.*

The Cactus Air Force

Imperial General Headquarters quickly understood the danger of allowing the United States to operate an airbase on Guadalcanal. Daily bombing raids and nightly naval shelling began to routinely pockmark Henderson Field, named for Lofton R. Henderson, who had lost his life during the Battle of Midway. Despite being sniped at by Japanese reinforcements deposited on the beaches at night, the 1st Engineer Battalion worked around the clock, finished the main landing strip, and carved two auxiliary strips out of the jungle.

On the night of August 18–19, Japanese destroyers disembarked 815 men twenty miles east of Lunga Point. Company A, 1st Marines, caught a Japanese patrol creeping along the beach and decimated it. Hours later, the 1st Special Weapons Battalion repulsed a heavy attack along the Tenaru River.

On August 20, two squadrons from the 1st Marine Aircraft Wing (MAG-1) landed on Henderson Field: F4F Grumman Wildcats from Major John L. Smith's VMF-223, and SBD Dauntless dive-bombers from Colonel Richard C. Mangrum's VMSB-232. The two squadrons became the first elements of the "Cactus Air Force," Cactus being the codename for Guadalcanal. Smith and Mangrum had the distinction of being the first pilots to land a squadron on an airfield captured by Americans in World War II. Henderson Field reminded them of "a bowl of black dust that fouled airplane engines...[or when it rained] a quagmire of

black mud which made the takeoff resemble...a fly trying to rise from a runway of molasses."

Vandegrift put the planes to work harassing Japanese efforts to land reinforcements. During its first ten days on Guadalcanal, the Cactus Air Force shot down fifty-six enemy planes but lost eleven.

When Japanese transports, screened by Rear Admiral Raizo Tanaka's cruisers and destroyers, arrived off Guadalcanal with a second and larger invasion force, Cactus flyers pounced on the squadron, set a transport and the cruiser *Jintsu* on fire, and forced Tanaka's "Tokyo Express" reinforcement system to retire. Tanaka soon changed his tactics and began landing reinforcements and supplies on Guadalcanal at night using destroyers. Marines on the ground called the nocturnal deliveries "Rat Runs" and celebrated when the Cactus flyboys sank the Japanese destroyer *Asagiri*.

TOP: Marines pull a Grumman F4F-4 Wildcat from a Henderson Field hangar struck by a Japanese bomb, and use dirt and chemicals to extinguish the flames. After a little scrubbing, the aircraft resumed combat operations.

ABOVE: Major John L. Smith of Marine Fighting Squadron 223 received the Medal of Honor on February 24, 1943, for heroism in the Solomons, where he downed sixteen enemy planes.

Battle of Bloody Ridge

In early September, Vandegrift needed every half-starved, malaria-infected, walking wounded Marine on Guadalcanal to hold the airfield against a steady build-up of Japanese forces on the island. He brought Colonel Merritt A. "Red Mike" Edson's 1st Raider Battalion and the Parachute Battalion from Tulagi to reconnoiter Japanese activity in the jungle east of the airfield. Edson made an amphibious landing near Tasimboko, collided with 1,000 Japanese equipped with artillery, struck the enemy flank, drove them into the jungle, and captured a pouch filled with top-secret documents, including the first accurate maps of Guadalcanal. After deciphering the papers, Vandegrift correctly surmised that Major General Kiyotake Kawaguchi, the Japanese commander, had taken forces on a circuitous maneuver through the jungle for the purpose of capturing a 1,000-yard ridge overlooking Henderson Field. Vandegrift sent Edson's command to the forward sector of the ridge with the 11th Marines' 105mm howitzers and two disease-weakened infantry battalions.

Kawaguchi believed his three-pronged assault, coordinated with naval and air support, would not be discovered until it was too late for Vandegrift to save Henderson Field. He overlooked that his troops would be severely fatigued before reaching the ridge, and he did not expect to find Edson's Marines dug-in and waiting.

After nightfall on September 12 an enemy plane, mirthfully known as "Washing Machine Charlie," flew over Henderson Field and dropped a green flare, signaling Kawaguchi to begin moving 3,450 Japanese troops over the ridge and onto the airfield. Edson's two battalions stopped two assaults before being pressed into the spurs of "Bloody Ridge." At dawn Edson counterattacked but found the enemy too strong. He pulled back, dug in again, and formed one line facing front and another facing rear. Throughout the day, Zeroes screamed overhead, strafing the ridge and dropping fragmentary bombs.

LEFT: Men from a Marine raider battalion had already become skilled jungle fighters when they landed on Cape Totkina, Bougainville, in January 1944. After capturing a Japanese dugout, they take a break for a photograph.

ABOVE, TOP: The gas-operated, magazine-fed Garand .30-caliber M1 rifle was adopted by the army on January 9, 1936, and eventually replaced the Springfields used by Marines.

ABOVE: Marines adopted the Thompson M1928A1 submachine gun during the 1930s. Unlike most submachine guns that had skeleton stocks, the .45-caliber Thompson had a wood stock and a clip carrying thirty-two cartridges.

After dark, September 13, Kawaguchi struck Edson's center. The Parachute Battalion buckled, fell back on the main line, and held. Edson called for support from the 105mm howitzers of the 5th Battalion, 11th Marines, and used the barrage to fall back to his rear line of defense. "Okay, Raiders, this is it," Edson shouted above the firing. "We stand here. If those little bastards get to the airfield, the whole 1st Division is in big trouble." To curb the Japanese assault, the 5th Battalion fired 1,992 105mm shells. Private Irving Reynolds, suffering from a fungus infection, crouched in a hole with his BAR and later recalled, "There were Japs mingling with us all night. Christ, you could smell them."

Throughout the night, Kawaguchi's men clawed at the ridge, only to be thrown back by grenades and BAR fire. Marine mortars, sited in defilade, arced shells into the enemy advance as fast as the next round could be fed down the tube. By daylight, September 14, some 600 Japanese corpses littered the ridge. Nine hundred wounded died during Kawaguchi's retreat through the jungle.

After two nights of hell, "Red Mike" Edson came to understand the discipline and fighting tactics of the Japanese soldier. "I hope the Japs will have learned something about the American fighting man. I certainly have earned respect for the Japs . . . They're good, all right. But I think we're better." Edson earned the Medal of Honor for holding Bloody Ridge and for serving as the rallying point for his Marines.

Guadalcanal Secured

On September 18, the first reinforcements arrived at Guadalcanal—4,262 men of the 7th Marine Regiment, which had been left behind at Samoa at MacArthur's insistence. Along with the regiment came Lieutenant Colonel Lewis B. "Chesty" Puller, a remarkable and experienced combat officer known by others as "everything from a warrior, born two hundred years too late, to a madman."

Vandegrift now had 23,000 troops, though one-third were already partially disabled by malaria, malnutrition, dysentery, jungle fungus, and battle fatigue. He would need them all because Japan refused to accept defeat and continued pouring thousands of suicidal fanatics into Guadalcanal. The Cactus Air Force, commanded by Brigadier General Roy S. Geiger, kept enough aircraft patched together to sink half the

ABOVE: Colonel Merritt A. "Red Mike" Edson, commanding the 1st Raider Battalion and the Parachute Battalion, took 850 Marines onto "Bloody Ridge" and repulsed 3,450 veteran Japanese assault troops bent on capturing Henderson Field.

General Alexander Archer Vandegrift (1887–1973)

Born in Charlottesville, Virginia, on March 13, 1887, "Archie" Vandegrift attended the University of Virginia and in 1908 enlisted in the Marine Corps. He received a 2nd lieutenant's commission in 1909 and spent the next fifteen years serving in the Caribbean and later in China as a field officer. In 1937 Commandant Holcomb brought Colonel Vandegrift home as his military secretary and assistant and kept him in the position for four years. Vandegrift requested field duty, so Holcomb promoted him to brigadier general and put him in charge of the 1st Marine Division.

On March 1942 Vandegrift took command of the division at Camp Lejeune, North Carolina. He had barely begun to organize the unit when in June he received orders to take the division to the South Pacific. On August 7, 1942, he led the Marines ashore on Guadalcanal. The fight for the island dragged on for months. Despite heavy odds, intense Japanese resistance, and unreliable naval support and logistics, Vandegrift's 1st Marine Division determinedly held Henderson Field. Relieved on December 9 by the 2nd Marine Division and the 25th U.S. Infantry Division,

Vandegrift took the Marines to Brisbane, Australia, for rest and recovery and to prepare for the invasion of Bougainville.

Ordered home to become the Marine Corps' 18th commandant on January 1, 1944, General Vandegrift expanded the Corps to a wartime strength of 485,000 and six divisions. His greatest moment came not at Guadalcanal, however, but in 1946 when Congress debated whether to package U.S. forces into three components—land, sea, and air—and eliminate the

Marine Corps. On May 6 he went before the Senate Naval Affairs Committee to testify, and said:

"Sentiment is not a valid consideration in determining questions of national security. We have pride in ourselves and in our past, but we do not rest our case on any presumed ground of gratitude owing us from the nation. If a Marine as a fighting man has not made a case for himself after 170 years of service, he must go. But I think you will agree with me that he has earned the right to depart with dignity and honor, not by subjugation to the status of uselessness and servility planned for him by the War Department."

The debate resulted in the National Security Act of 1947, which redefined the status of the Marine Corps as part of the U.S. Navy and gave the Fleet Marine Force, ground and air, permanent statutory standing.

ABOVE LEFT: Major General Alexander A. Vandegrift, commanding the 1st Marine Division on Guadalcanal, leads a group of officers including Commandant Holcomb and Colonel Edson on a November 1942 inspection of the base.

ABOVE: Brigadier General Roy S. Geiger commanded the 1st Marine Air Wing and in 1942 took over air operations on Guadalcanal. He later became a major general and commanded amphibious operations in the Pacific.

transports delivering Japanese reinforcements to Guadalcanal. Admiral William F. "Bull" Halsey, who in October replaced Admiral Ghormley as South Pacific commander, prevented another huge Japanese reinforcing effort from reaching Guadalcanal during the Battle of Santa Cruz Islands (October 26–27, 1942). Half the total of 36,000 Japanese troops who reached the island died on it. In mid-November the Imperial Japanese Army (IJA) decided to pull out and remove the survivors of the once powerful 23rd Imperial Army Division. The campaign cost the 23rd some 14,000 killed or missing, in addition to those who had been killed before. Marine and relieving army reinforcements lost 1,600 officers and enlisted men killed and 4,200 wounded.

With Guadalcanal secured on February 9, 1943, Marines took a breather before moving up the Solomon chain toward New Britain and the massive Japanese base at Rabaul.

The Solomons Campaign

To effectively threaten the Japanese air and naval base at Rabaul, the Marines faced the problem of first establishing intermediate airfields on islands in the central Solomons. After Guadalcanal, the Japanese had shifted to a defensive posture, making the task more difficult. As the year 1943 came into focus, MacArthur planned to use the army to flank Rabaul on New Britain by launching an offensive in New Guinea. Halsey planned to use his ships and Marines to isolate Rabaul by driving up the Solomons chain. As aircraft carriers and men became available, Nimitz began organizing a third amphibious force for operations in the Pacific.

On February 23, 1943, twelve days after securing Guadalcanal, Admiral Turner landed the 3rd Marine Raider Battalion and a battalion of Seabees on Russell Island, 150 miles northwest of Henderson Field. Unopposed, the Seabees went to work building an airstrip so that planes from MAG-21 could support the invasion of New Georgia.

On June 30, the same day that MacArthur commenced operations on New Guinea, Turner launched "Operation Toenail" and assaulted New Georgia. Turner landed the 9th Marine Defense Battalion on Rendova, across the lagoon from the enemy air base on Munda Point. Lieutenant Colonel Samuel B. Griffith's 1st Battalion of the 1st Marine Raider Regiment landed as a blocking force behind Munda Point. A landing on June 21 preceded the attack when Lieutenant Colonel Michael S. Curran's 4th Raider Battalion landed at Segi Point, east of Munda, to rescue coastwatcher Donald G. Kennedy, who the enemy had been relentlessly pursuing. Japanese defenders fought tenaciously. The New Georgia operation eventually required 30,000 men, including detachments from the army, five amphibious landings, and more than a month of treacherous jungle fighting to secure the Munda airstrip. Although the

Japanese lost 358 planes trying to hold Munda, the operation had been poorly planned and mismanaged. "We certainly took it the hard way," naval historian Samuel Eliot Morison later admitted.

By August 10, VMF-123 and VMF–124 began flying sorties out of Munda. This time Halsey capitalized from lessons learned on New Georgia— "Bypass enemy strongholds and hit them where they ain't." This time the Marines leapfrogged heavily defended Kolombangara, assaulted lightly defended Vella Lavella, and built another airbase fifty miles closer to Rabaul. During the operation, 31-year-old Major Gregory "Pappy" Boyington shot down five planes on his first mission. His Black Sheep Squadron, VMF-214, downed fifty-seven enemy planes in its first month of combat out of Vella Lavella. Boyington earned the Medal of Honor and became the Marine Corps' top ace with twenty-eight kills.

On November 9, 1943, Major General Geiger relieved Vandegrift, who had been called to

ABOVE: "Pappy" Boyington, when a "Flying Tiger," called the Brewster F2A fighters "a perfect dud in combat." When provided with nimble Vought F4U Corsairs, he shot down twenty-eight enemy planes in air combat, became the Marine Corps' top ace, and earned the Medal of Honor.

ABOVE: Major Gregory "Pappy" Boyington, one of the most flamboyant and belligerent pilots in the history of the Marine Corps, gives instructions to his rowdy fellow flyers of VMF-124, the so-called "Black Sheep Squadron."

Women Marines

During World War II, Marines had successfully kept women out of the Corps until February 13, 1943, when Secretary of the Navy Frank Knox announced, much to the chagrin of Commandant Holcomb, the Women's Reserve Program. Thousands of women swelled the ranks. Instead of calling their ladies WACS, as did the army, or WAVES, like the navy, the Marine Corps initially referred to their unwelcome reservists as "WRs," although many of the women joined the Corps with more enthusiasm than their male counterparts. By December 1943, "WRs" serving the Corps numbered 13,201.

In the midst of a war, Holcomb faced new problems as women filled the ranks. Activist groups urged him to make the Corps a sexless organization. Eleanor Roosevelt wanted him to put the women through basic training, including field and weapons training. Holcomb ignored the pressure and assigned his women reservists to administrative and clerical duties. The women never

moved into ground or air combat, but they met Marine Corps standards in appearance and discipline, and released men from rear-area jobs for duty in the Pacific.

After Colonel Ruth Cheney Streeter took over the reserves, she trained women to become motor mechanics, truck drivers, cryptologists, and parachute riggers, and prepared them for dozens of other jobs. By June 1944, she had built the reserve organization to its full complement of 1,000 officers and 18,000 enlisted women. By the end of the war, 23,000 women had joined the Marine Corps Reserve. Even Commandant Holcomb remarked, "There's hardly any work at our Marine stations that women can't do as well as men. They do some work far better than men . . . What is more, they are real Marines." Unlike WACS and WAVES, the reservists never became an acronym. As Holcomb belatedly but stoutly admitted, "They are Marines."

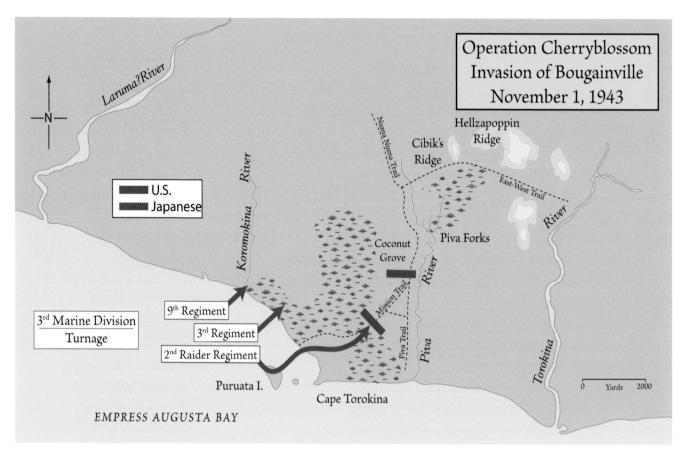

RIGHT: The 3rd Marine Division bypassed Japanese positions to the east and landed in Empress Augusta Bay, where the 2nd Raider Regiment pressed up the trail beside the Piva River and isolated thousands of enemy troops in the Bougainville jungle.

CENTER RIGHT: Pushed deep into the jungle surrounding Cape Gloucester, New Britain, Japanese troops reformed on December 30, 1943, and launched a counterattack. The 2nd Battalion, 1st Marines, responded with machine guns and repulsed the assault.

Operation Cherryblossom
Invasion of Bougainville
November 1, 1943

ABOVE: During operations in the jungles of Bougainville, Marines from the 2nd Raider Regiment relied on dogs for routing out the enemy, but always kept a few canines handy to trot messages back to the command post.

Washington as commandant, and took over the I Marine Amphibious Corps (I MAC). By then, three Marine divisions were in the Pacific. The 1st was preparing for an assault on New Britain's Cape Gloucester; the 2nd for Tarawa in the Gilbert Islands; and the 3rd for Bougainville, a large island with five airstrips, the closest being 200 miles from Rabaul.

Bougainville (Operation Cherryblossom)

On October 28, 1943, Lieutenant Colonel Victor H. Krulak's 2nd Parachute Battalion made a diversionary attack on the island of Choiseul to deceive the Japanese. The "Paramarines" killed only seven of a ten-man Japanese patrol so that the others could escape to misinform their superiors.

On November 1, while Japanese prepared for battle on Choiseul, Major General Allen H. Turnage landed the 3rd Marine Division at Empress Augusta Bay on

the west coast of Bougainville. Lessons learned from the mistakes made on New Georgia, especially in combat loading and logistics, added immensely to the success of the assault, despite some elements having landed near a virtually impassable marsh. The Marines also learned that on the large island of Bougainville it was easier to build an airfield than to waste casualties by slogging through jungles to capture one. The new strategy also coincided with an axiom of amphibious warfare: never hit a strongly defended beach when the objective can be reached over an undefended one.

Admiral Mineichi Koga mustered all his ships at Rabaul to crush the Marines on the Bougainville beachhead. Two U.S. Navy task forces met the attack in Empress Augusta Bay, sank a light cruiser and a destroyer, and repulsed the enemy without loss.

For three weeks, fighting side-by-side with the army, Marines plunged through some of the worst battle

LEFT: Marine pilots became experts at providing close air support. During operations on Eniwetok Atoll in February 1944, radiomen on the ground lay prone in the sand while flyers strafe enemy positions concealed in coral trenches a hundred yards away.

Perfecting Close Air Support

From airstrips laid down by Seabees on Bougainville, Lieutenant Colonel John Gabbert, air officer for the 3rd Marine Division, worked with pilots flying TBF Avengers from VMTB-143 and VMTB-144. He trained them to drop 100-pound bombs 120 yards in front of the 2nd Battalion, 9th Marines. Close air support was not new. There had been many prearranged air strikes in support of troops ever since Guadalcanal, but never one joined by radio communication controlled directly from the front lines. Marine close air support, born a decade earlier in the jungles of Nicaragua, sprang anew in the jungles of Bougainville when TBFs dropped bombs a few dozen yards in front of Marines and wiped out Japanese fortifications in the village of Piva.

conditions of the war. They had been involved in bloody battles before, but none so nightmarish as Bougainville. Swamps gave way to dense jungles, out of which emerged sharp ridges, only to become swamps and jungles again. Every few hundred yards the terrain repeated itself. Every step of the way, Marines encountered more concealed coconut-log fortifications and pillboxes.

Every afternoon it rained, making it impossible for clothes and shoes to dry. The sun never penetrated the jungle, locking humidity in with the terrible heat. When night came, Marines hunkered into a wet hole and covered themselves with a poncho. One Marine wrote that at night it "got so goddamn cold you thought you were going to die."

During the first days on Bougainville, nobody slept. Every noise sounded like Japanese creeping through the lines. Insects, unlike anything known, choked the nostrils

and feasted on fresh Marine blood. "Compared with Bougainville," one Marine lieutenant recalled, "everything I ever heard about Hell sounded like a picnic."

The Marines never intended to capture the entire island, just enough space for airstrips. Seabees followed closely behind, leaving thousands of Japanese to die of disease in the jungle.

By the end of 1943 it became clear to Halsey that a ground assault on Rabaul would never be necessary. Admiral Nimitz had already partially isolated Rabaul by launching his campaign in the Pacific. On December 26 the 1st Marine Division landed on the western side of New Britain and secured enough ground to build airstrips. Marines flying from the new fields destroyed the usefulness of Rabaul, and the Solomons campaign, except for mopping up operations, came to an end.

ABOVE: On December 26, 1943, Marines disembark from LCIs and wade ashore in Borgen Bay to establish a beachhead within striking distance of the important Japanese airfield east of Cape Gloucester, New Britain.

ISLAND-HOPPING IN THE PACIFIC 1943–1945

In mid-January 1943, during a joint meeting in Casablanca between Prime Minister Churchill and President Roosevelt, Admiral King obtained approval for opening in the central Pacific a second line of advance against Japan. After revisiting the 1921 Orange Plan, the JCS prepared the first operating initiative for Nimitz to leapfrog across the Pacific and acquire island airfields large enough to bring B-29 Superfortress bombers within range of Japan's homeland. The plan also called for establishing fighter-bomber bases for aggressive offensive operations against Japanese ground and naval forces each step of the way. To further the plan, Nimitz asked for more carriers, more aircraft, and more Marines.

A thousand miles northeast of the Solomons lay Tarawa and Makin atolls, equatorial outposts of Japanese strength in the Gilbert Islands. Though mere specks on a map, they provided stepping stones to the Marshalls and the Marianas. Atolls created new landing problems because they were not typical islands with

sandy beaches, but tips of submerged mountains ringed by razor-sharp reefs and underwater shoals, both crowned with coral. Natural landing sites were few, and the low contour of atolls offered little or no cover for amphibious assault vehicles bringing troops ashore.

Tarawa resembled a triangular necklace of flat coral islets with a thirty-one-mile hypotenuse and an eighteen-mile base that contained Betio, a 300-acre island on the atoll's western extremity. Betio contained the only airfield. Japanese defenders, burrowed deep into fortified bunkers, could withstand the heaviest air and naval bombardment with little loss, and these conditions remained unknown to American forces when planning Operation Galvanic, the assault on Tarawa, Makin, and Apamama.

> Even though you Navy officers do come into about a thousand yards [to support an assault], I remind you that you have a little armor. I want you to know that Marines are crossing the beach with bayonets, and the only armor they'll have is a khaki shirt.
>
> *Major General Julian Smith to Rear Admiral H. F. Kingman at Betio.*

Tarawa—Operation Galvanic

Nimitz put Admiral Spruance in charge of the Fifth Fleet, Admiral Turner in charge of the assault force, and Marine Major General Holland M. "Howling Mad" Smith in charge of the newly created V Amphibious Corps. The idea for the V Amphibious Corps grew from Marine doctrine developed during the Solomons campaign. For operations in the Pacific, Nimitz kept

amphibious assault responsibility with the Marines. Holland Smith formed the V Amphibious Corps around Major General Julian C. Smith's 2nd Marine Division and the army's 165th Infantry Regiment, the latter of which he assigned to assault Makin. Smith retained the Marine division for the Betio assault. Marines had trained for seven months in New Zealand and were in good fighting trim.

Admiral Spruance assembled the mightiest task force ever formed in the Pacific, and he expected his fleet to reduce Betio to a pile of rubble. He did not know that Admiral Meichi Shibasaki, commanding the 4,836-man Japanese garrison, had sited mines and erected anti-boat obstacles that would canalize assault vehicles into fire-lanes for shore batteries. A coconut-log seawall five feet high encapsulated Betio, and situated along its length were 106 steel-reinforced concrete pillboxes equipped with 13mm machine guns, augmented by fourteen coastal guns, twenty-five field guns, and fourteen tanks.

Marines had a better idea of what they would face going ashore than Spruance, who was usually thorough

RIGHT: Although the beaches on Tarawa Atoll had been distinctly delineated for the assault, the shallow reef lying inside the lagoon had not been reconnoitered. Landing craft operators became disoriented, some struck the reef, and others spent time under heavy fire looking for an opening into the shallows. As a result, many men were improperly disembarked. Some drowned in deep water; others struggled ashore on the wrong beach.

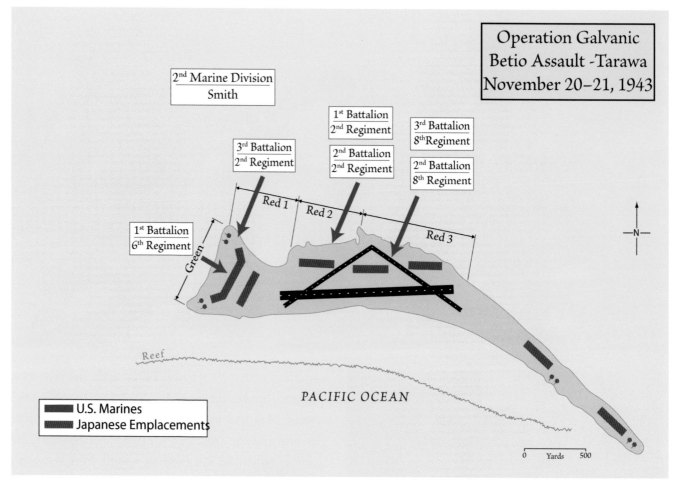

Operation Galvanic
Betio Assault -Tarawa
November 20–21, 1943

2nd Marine Division
Smith

1st Battalion
2nd Regiment

3rd Battalion
8th Regiment

3rd Battalion
2nd Regiment

2nd Battalion
2nd Regiment

2nd Battalion
8th Regiment

Red 1

Red 2

Red 3

1st Battalion
6th Regiment

Green

—N—

Reef

PACIFIC OCEAN

U.S. Marines
Japanese Emplacements

0   Yards   500

RIGHT: Although heavy navy fire had torn up the surface of Betio, the huge enemy bombproof between Red Beach 1 and Red Beach 2 remained untouched and held out for four days before Marines captured it by frontal attack.

and cautious. At 5:00 a.m., November 20, 1943, the campaign opened with battleships and cruisers delivering a sixty-minute bombardment. Carrier planes followed and bombed the remains of what appeared to be a desolate island. Marines began dropping into boats and formed for the assault. A few destroyers worked carefully into the lagoon to provide support. Clouds of smoke and dust reddened by fires hung like a pall over Betio. As the first wave of amphibious tractors approached shore, Marines doubted that anyone could still be alive there, but they were wrong. As soon as the shelling stopped, Japanese troops emerged from underground bunkers and began delivering a murderous fire against the assault force approaching Red Beaches 1, 2, and 3.

Some Marines walked through 700 yards of water to reach the beach. Each step they took made them bigger

LEFT: In the aftermath of the Betio assault on November 20–21, 1943, wounded Marines are towed on rubber boats to the reef, from where larger vessels will take them to base hospitals for proper care. More than 1,500 Marines were killed or wounded on Betio.

targets. Those off Red Beach 2 took temporary cover under a long pier jutting into the lagoon. Half of the LTVs were destroyed in the water, and those that made it ashore often landed on the wrong beach. None of the vehicles could mount the seawall, so there they sat. Unanticipated low tides stranded LCVPs on reefs hundreds of yards from shore. Marines dropped into the water, and some of smaller stature, weighted down by equipment, drowned. Marines coming ashore on the wrong beach could not find their units. Somehow they reorganized. Two battalions mounted an attack supported by medium tanks. They crossed the airstrip taxiway and established a 300-yard perimeter. Battalion commanders expected a night attack and called for reinforcements. None came, but neither did the expected night attack because the enemy's

LEFT: Taking refuge behind the remains of damaged coconut trees, Marine snipers pick off Japanese naval infantry in pillboxes by firing into the small slots used by the enemy for aiming and firing their weapons.

RIGHT: The Japanese had several small bases scattered along the necklace of Kwajalein Atoll. The most important targets were located near the top of the atoll at the twin islands of Roi and Namur, where the Japanese had built an airfield. Without much difficulty, the 23rd and 24th Marines landed on Roi-Namur on February 1, 1944, and captured the islands.

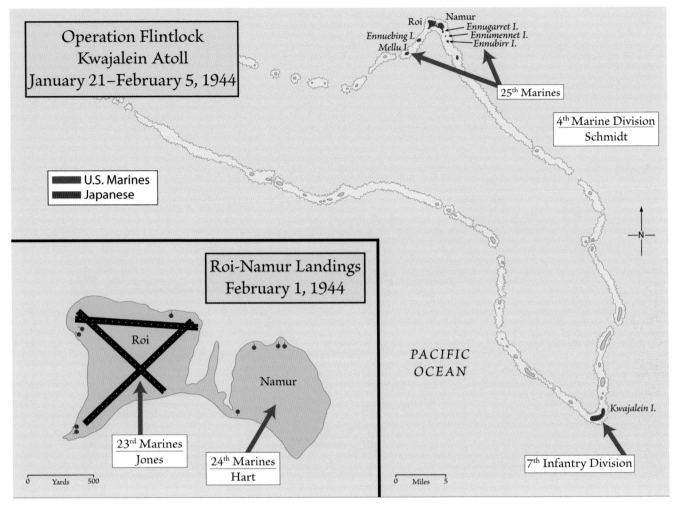

Operation Flintlock
Kwajalein Atoll
January 21–February 5, 1944

U.S. Marines
Japanese

Roi-Namur Landings
February 1, 1944

Roi

Namur

23rd Marines
Jones

24th Marines
Hart

Roi   Namur
Ennuebing I.   Ennugarret I.
Mellu I.   Ennumennet I.
         Ennubirr I.

25th Marines

4th Marine Division
Schmidt

PACIFIC
OCEAN

Kwajalein I.

7th Infantry Division

0   Yards   500

0   Miles   5

communications had been destroyed by the bombardment.

Throughout the night and early morning American units linked up as reinforcements arrived. The division inched forward with tanks and flamethrowers. By nightfall the second day, Colonel David Shoup's 2nd Marines pushed across the airfield to the southern shore, cutting Betio in two. On November 23 only 146 Japanese survivors surrendered: the others died fighting. To annihilate an enemy force of 4,836 naval infantry, the Marines lost 985 killed and 2,193 wounded. The butcher's bill raised eyebrows. On Tarawa, Marines had lost in four days half as many men as they had lost in six months on Guadalcanal. Clearly, something different had to be done.

Kwajalein Atoll—Operation Flintlock

With the Gilberts secured, Nimitz began final preparations for Operation Flintlock—the invasion of the Marshalls—but he gave the Marines time to make tactical amphibious adjustments. Because Spruance's pre-invasion bombardment had inflicted too little damage on Tarawa, the navy added armor-piercing shells for penetrating steel-reinforced bunkers and strongly barricaded defenses. Underwater Demolition Teams (UDTs) joined the assault to blast openings in reefs for landing vehicles. Marines obtained new amphibian tanks and tracked vehicles armed with bunker-busting weapons. Leathernecks had become the guinea pigs of the Allied powers, and Marine tactical planners predicted that with small improvements the

LEFT: Following the capture of Roi-Namur on Kwajalein Atoll, Pfc. N. E. Carling stands beside a medium tank "killer" on which is mounted a dead Japanese light tank.

ABOVE: With their equipment on Higgins boats stranded on reefs, 4th Regiment Marines wade ashore at Emirau Island in the St. Matthias group between New Ireland and the Admiralties, and on March 20, 1944, complete the encirclement of Rabaul.

Corps could get ashore despite obstacles.

Holland Smith beefed up the V Amphibious Corps for Operation Flintlock. Kwajalein Atoll, the next giant step toward Japan, lay 750 miles northwest of Tarawa. The Japanese naval base on Eniwetok, a second atoll, lay another 360 miles to the northwest. The twin islands of Roi-Namur, located 50 miles to the north of Kwajalein and at the apex of the atoll, came first because a major Japanese airfield covered the entire island of Roi. Smith assigned Major General Harry Schmidt's newly organized 4th Marine Division to assault Roi-Namur, and gave Major General Charles H. Corlett's 7th Infantry Division the task of assaulting Kwajalein.

On January 29, 1944, a three-day naval and aerial pre-invasion bombardment saturated the atoll, with devastatingly improved results compared with Tarawa. Vice Admiral Marc A. Mitscher's carrier aircraft virtually wiped out Roi's once-vaunted 24th Air Flotilla. UDTs cleared the lagoon of obstructions, and on the morning of February 1, some 240 LVTs and seventy-five armored tracked amphibians carried the 23rd Marines ashore on Roi and the 24th Marines ashore on Namur. The only misstep occurred when the navy failed to get the 24th Marines ashore on schedule. Japanese troops put up a savage fight but, capitalizing on lessons learned on Tarawa, Marines overran the defenders. Of 3,600 Japanese garrisoning Roi-Namur, only ninety-one were taken alive. The others fought to the death or committed suicide. The 4th Marine Division lost 195 killed and 545 wounded.

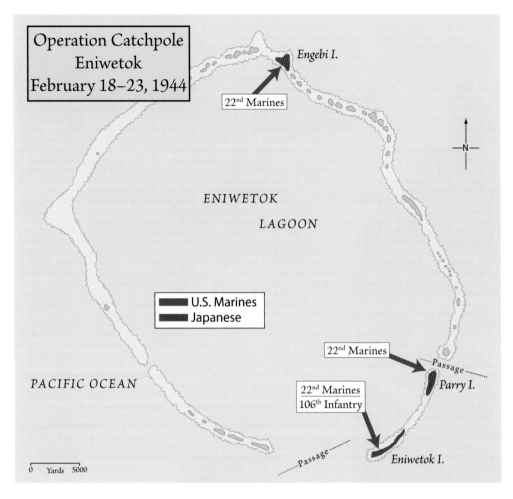

Operation Catchpole
Eniwetok
February 18–23, 1944

Engebi I.

22nd Marines

—N—

ENIWETOK

LAGOON

■ U.S. Marines
▨ Japanese

22nd Marines

Passage

Parry I.

22nd Marines
106th Infantry

PACIFIC OCEAN

Passage

Eniwetok I.

0 Yards 5000

ABOVE: Eniwetok Atoll provided another important stepping-stone in the Pacific. Only 2,586 Japanese troops held the three principal islands of the atoll. The 22nd Marine Regiment, aided by the 106th Infantry Regiment, began the assault on February 18, 1944, and quickly secured the islands.

RIGHT: After two days and two nights of fighting for control of the airfield on Eniwetok, three weary and begrimed Marines take a break; nineteen-year-old Pfc. Farris M. Touhy, is holding a coffee cup.

Eniwetok—Operation Catchpole

On February 18, 1944, because the V Amphibious Force's reserves had not been needed on Kwajalein, Holland Smith moved them up to Eniwetok lagoon. After Rear Admiral Henry W. Hill's fire-support squadron pummeled the three principal islands, Brigadier General Thomas E. Watson put the 22nd Marines ashore on Engebi Island, the strongest of the island bases and the only one with an airfield. At dark, the V Amphibious Corps Reconnaissance Company with light artillery battalions moved ashore on the two unoccupied islets next to Engebi and hammered the enemy throughout the night. In the morning the 22nd Marines landed from the lagoon in medium tanks, attacked straight across the island, wiped out half of the enemy's veteran 2,200-man 1st Amphibious Brigade, and secured Engebi during the afternoon.

Next came the assault of Eniwetok by the 106th Infantry Regiment, which encountered resistance and stalled. Watson sent in the 3rd Battalion, 22nd Marines, and later learned that the battalion had to do most of the fighting. On February 21, disenchanted by the performance of the 106th Army Regiment, Watson pulled it from the attack on Parry Island and sent in the 22nd Marines. The leathernecks pushed the last defenders into the tip of the island and declared Parry secured. At a cost of 339 killed, Watson's force annihilated the Japanese garrisons on all three islands.

During the Eniwetok campaign, Admiral Mitscher took his carrier task force southeast to the Caroline Islands, struck the Japanese naval base at Truk, sank 200,000 tons of shipping, and destroyed 275 Japanese planes.

The Tactical Learning Curve

Every campaign led to adjustments in Marine amphibious assault doctrine. Naval gunfire support drastically improved after Marines put specialized communication teams into key observation points to control targeting. New armored LCI-Gs (landing craft, infantry, gunboats) made their appearance, and when employed in mass, laid down a covering fire with rockets and 44mm guns. By early 1944, amphibian tractors were running off stateside assembly lines at the rate of 500 a month. With them came amphibian trucks (DUKWs) to provide logistics support. For the first time, naval star shells turned darkness into a panorama of light and illuminated enemy counterattacks. New rocket-carrying aircraft were able to pinpoint and demolish targets near the beach. The 4th Marine Division, which had taken casualties on Roi-Namur, developed the first highly effective system of tactical air observation, targeting on enemy ground positions not readily seen from the air. Specially designed command ships became available to provide mobile headquarters and communications centers for control and coordination of landing and beach-head operations.

With every battle, beginning with Guadalcanal, a persistent argument ensued over who would be responsible for amphibious operations: Admiral Turner of the navy or the Marine officer in charge of the expedition. In 1942 Admiral King ruled that the commander of the landing force should be co-equal with the naval commander. Nimitz defined the directive to mean that when time for the assault came the landing force commander would take full control of the fighting.

Turner still tried to muscle Holland Smith aside. King believed he could stop the bickering by giving Turner and Spruance another star, but not Holland Smith. Secretary of the Navy Frank Knox scuttled the scheme, overruled King, and made Smith a lieutenant general. Smith's advancement did not change his attitude toward Turner, and bickering continued over the issue of leadership.

Evolution of Tactical Air

Marine air wings made a significant tactical change during 1943 by switching from Grumman Wildcats to the gull-winged Vought F4U-1 Corsairs, which at 417 miles per hour could fly faster than any Japanese plane. The switch to Corsairs came when General Geiger commanded the 1st MAW, which he left in mid-1943 to become director of aviation for a second time. The aircraft arguably became the best-recognized Marine plane of all time. Marine aces flying Corsairs included Major Gregory "Pappy" Boyington with twenty-eight kills, 1st Lieutenant Robert M. Hanson with twenty-five kills, and 1st Lieutenant Kenneth A. Walsh with twenty-one kills.

During World War II, Marine aviation grew to five wings consisting of 31 groups, 145 squadrons, and 112,626 Marines, including 10,457 pilots. Admiral King thought the whole program too large, but the Marine Corps had to compensate for the lack of aircraft carriers by utilizing airstrips. Commandant Vandegrift agreed to drop one wing provided that King would use the pilots on escort carriers. Soon, composite squadrons built around Corsair fighters and Avenger torpedo-bombers began flying off carriers. In 1944 Marines also began flying new tactical aircraft, including the Grumman F6FN Hellcat night-fighters and naval versions of the North American B-25 Mitchell (PBJ) medium bomber.

TOP: A pilot flying close air support in a Vought F4U launches a load of rocket projectiles on the Japanese stronghold at Shuri during June 1945 operations on Okinawa.

ABOVE: During operations on Okinawa, ordnance men from Marine Air Group 33 hang five-inch rockets under the wing of an F4U Corsair. Safety pins will not be removed and or the rockets charged until takeoff.

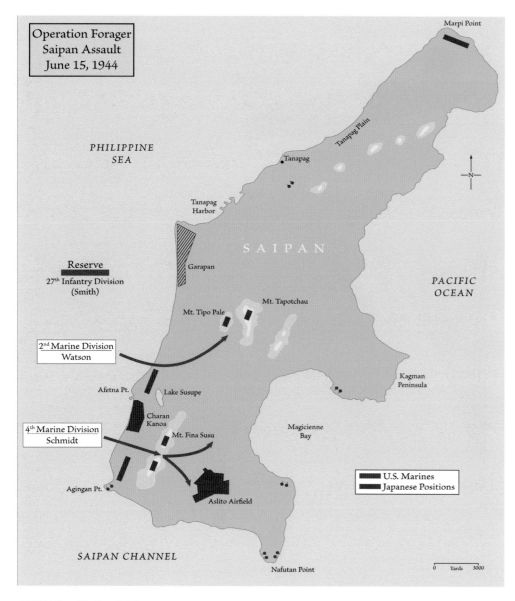

ABOVE: Two Marine divisions assaulted Saipan on June 15, 1944, in the first major amphibious operation in the Pacific. The entire effort centered around the capture of Aslito airfield, from which B-52 bombers could directly strike Tokyo. There were 29,662 Japanese defenders on Saipan, 10,000 more than intelligence at Pearl Harbor had predicted. As Brigadier General Merritt "Red Mike" Edson predicted, "This one isn't going to be easy."

We are through with flat atolls now. We learned how to pulverize atolls, but now we are up against mountains and caves where Japs can dig in. A week from today, there will be a lot of dead Marines.

General Holland Smith, quoted in On to Westward, *by Robert Sherrod.*

On to the Marianas

From the outset of the war, Admiral King maintained an unwavering conviction that the Mariana Islands held the key to the Central Pacific. Located a thousand miles west of Eniwetok, the airfields on Saipan, Tinian, and Guam offered strategic bases for attacking the enemy's sea-air communications. From Saipan, General Henry H. "Hap" Arnold's AAF B-29 Superfortresses could strike the Palaus, the Philippines, Formosa, China, and the Japanese mainland. King had been looking for a way to draw out the Japanese fleet, and he believed invading the Marianas would do it.

On March 12, 1944, Holland Smith and Admiral Turner began planning Operation Forager. Having mastered the problem of assaulting small islands on coral atolls, planners now shifted their efforts to invading large islands crowned with rugged mountainous, carpeted with deep forests, and defended by 60,000 enemy troops, half of which were on Saipan. Unlike atolls, Saipan consisted of seventy-two square miles enclosed by reefs and containing a large civilian population.

On February 23, 1944, as Operation Forager entered the final planning stage, Admiral Mitscher's carrier task force paid the Marianas a visit and plastered enemy airfields, and frequently returned to maintain air superiority. Admiral Spruance, commanding Operation Forager, used the time to pull together 800 ships to land and support three Marine divisions, two army divisions, and a reinforced Marine brigade—a total of 127,000 men. Turner headed the Joint Expeditionary Force while Holland Smith, commanding the V Amphibious Corps, led the assault. General Geiger, former director of aviation, commanded the III Amphibious Corps and drew the task of capturing Guam.

Operation Forager

On the morning of June 15, after a prolonged naval bombardment augmented by carrier air attacks, the 2nd and 4th Marine Divisions of the V Amphibious Corps fought their way ashore on Saipan's southwest coast to flank the principal city of Charan Kanoa. Four battleships, eight cruisers, and seven destroyers arced a rolling bombardment over the first wave of leathernecks while twenty-four LCI-gunboats with 44mm guns sprayed the beach. As Marines sprinted for cover, 700 amphibian tractors, sixty-eight with special armor and a new 77mm gun, pressed inland and cleared a path. Overhead, Corsairs from escort carriers flew close air support. Marines landed 8,000 men over a six-mile front. Smith trusted the beachhead to his Marines, retaining the 27th and 77th Army Infantry Divisions in reserve.

Major General Thomas E. Watson, commanding the 2nd Marine Division, swung north to attack Mount Tapotchau, a 1,554-foot ridge in the island's center. Major General Harry Schmidt, commanding the 4th Marine Division, moved on Mount Fina Susu, a long, narrow ridge blocking the way to Aslito Airfield. Japanese Lieutenant General Yoshitsugu Saito waited on the ridges with massed field artillery, partially buried tanks, and reserve infantry. Saito's plan to crush the Americans on the beach failed, and by nightfall Marines landed 20,000 troops, seven pack-howitzer battalions, and two armored units.

Progress inland became stoutly resisted. Only the battle-hardened 25th Marines, 4th Division, secured the first day's objective on the far right flank. Enemy troops sheltered on the ridges overlooking the beaches pinned down the 2nd Marine Division. Around

ABOVE LEFT: During early July men from the 2nd Marine Division capture an enemy howitzer while swinging north through the hills and turn the weapon against Japanese defending Garapan, the island's administrative center.

ABOVE: Men from the 4th Marine Division coming ashore south of Charan Kanoa crawl across the beach to their assigned positions as Japanese machine gun and sniper fire whines overhead.

LEFT: Men of the 2nd Marine Division move cautiously through the debris-littered outskirts of Garapan as they prepare to assault the island's main communication and control center, June 23, 1944.

TOP: *The first wave of the 4th Marine Division disembark from amphibious vehicles on beaches south of Charan Kanoa and take defensive positions as three more waves approach from the sea.*

ABOVE: *Short of vehicles for transportation on Saipan, Marines attempt to induce an uncooperative ox to move a cartload of supplies and ammunition to a battalion screaming for replenishments on the front line.*

midnight the enemy came out of their holes and launched a counterattack using a reinforced armored battalion against the 6th Marines. By failing to contest the landing, Saito hastened his own defeat. With the aid of naval gunfire, the 6th Marines threw the enemy back with heavy losses, but took significant casualties themselves. When General Smith learned that his Marines had lost more than 2,000 men and half of their armored amphibians, he pointed an accusing finger at the navy, and said, "We did not soften up the enemy sufficiently before we landed."

While Marines expanded the beachheads and repulsed counterattacks, another important development occurred at sea. As Admiral King predicted, the Imperial Japanese Navy dispatched Vice Admiral Jisaburo Ozawa to the aid of General Saito with five battleships, thirteen cruisers, twenty-eight destroyers, and nine aircraft carriers stacked with 473 planes. Not wanting to risk his ships, Ozawa sent planes against Mitscher's carriers. He intended that the pilots land on Mariana airfields after striking Mitscher's ships, refuel and rearm, and strike the American carriers again while returning to the Japanese fleet. Ozawa miscalculated. Mitscher's carrier aircraft had destroyed all the airfields and wiped out the land-based planes. Instead, Ozawa lost three carriers during operations in the Philippine Sea, and Mitscher's pilots shot down all but thirty-five of Ozawa's carrier planes and hundreds of others in what became known as the Marianas Turkey Shoot.

Meanwhile, on June 17, Holland Smith came ashore on Saipan, established a command post at Charan Kanoa, and landed the 27th Infantry Division in support of the 4th Marine Division. Five days later the Marines announced the southern section of Saipan secure, including Aslito Airfield.

As the Marines pressed north from Aslito, the pace noticeably slowed. Army and Marine commanders quibbled over doctrinal differences. Major General

The Holland Smith Controversy

ABOVE: Much inter-service controversy ensued when the irascible Lieutenant General Holland "Howling Mad" Smith, USMC, relieved the army's Major General Ralph C. Smith from command of the 27th Infantry Division on June 24, 1944. Here, Holland Smith (right) is shown at the V Amphibious Corps command post with (left) Vice Admiral Richmond Kelly Turner, USN, and Major General Harry Schmidt, USMC, following the Iwo Jima assault on February 19, 1945.

Sixty-two-year-old Holland "Howling Mad" Smith earned his nickname in 1916 while serving as a scowling, caustic lieutenant in the Dominican Republic. In June 1917 he went to France as a captain with the famous 5th Regiment, Fourth Brigade, and returned to take up the work of personally horse-powering the development of amphibious warfare.

Always combative, and among the most competent commanders in the Marine Corps, Smith was a superb tactician, a consummate strategist, also a harsh taskmaster,. Marines serving under Smith described him as a vigorous and demanding commander, irascible and quarrelsome, and, like General George Patton, one of America's colorful field commanders. When on June 24, 1944, he relieved Major General Ralph C. Smith, USA, from command of the 27th Infantry Division, the incident underscored the differences between the aggressive operational doctrine of the Marine Corps and the army's more conservative approach to warfare. The removal of Ralph Smith sparked a heated controversy with the army for Admirals Turner and Spruance, who approved it, and for Nimitz, who attempted to ignore it.

During the war in the Pacific, five army generals were relieved, but only one by a Marine officer. Whether Ralph Smith lacked "aggressive spirit," as Holland Smith claimed, can be debated, but for reasons that remain unclear today, the 27th Infantry Division's attack moved much slower than those of the Marine division's on each flank. During the advance on Garapan, Saipan's other principal city, the 2nd Marine Division on the left pushed to the outskirts of the city, and the 4th Marine Division stormed through stiff opposition on the right and pushed across Saipan to the Kagman Peninsula. Both wings overlapped the 27th Infantry Division, which had bogged down in the center. After Holland Smith relieved Ralph Smith, news correspondents fueled the controversy into a bitter interservice rivalry.

On July 12, before fighting stopped on Saipan, Lieutenant General Robert C. Richardson, USA, arrived without consulting Nimitz, for whom he worked, to vindicate Ralph Smith, a personal friend. Richardson convened a board to clear Smith's name, and by doing so thrust himself into the position of passing judgment on Marine and navy officers neither under his command nor answerable to him. Richardson then went directly to the 27th Infantry Division and improperly passed out decorations without approval from Holland Smith. Spruance pleaded with Holland Smith not to explode when he met with Richardson, which was no easy task for "Howling Mad." Despite one of the greatest victories in the Pacific, due mainly to Marines, Richardson cornered Major General Harry Schmidt of the 4th Marine Division, and said, "You and your commanders aren't as well qualified to lead large bodies of troops as general officers in the Army. We've had more experience in handling troops than you've had, and yet you dare to remove one of my generals! You Marines are nothing but a bunch of beach runners anyway. What do you know about land warfare?"

Holland Smith controlled his temper, but Turner and Spruance kept the controversy going until 1948. The debate lost steam until January 12, 1967, when Holland Smith died, giving veterans and historians an opportunity to rekindle an almost forgotten episode of interservice rivalry.

Ralph Smith of the 27th Infantry Division advocated a cautious advance. Holland Smith, aware of the vulnerability of the fleet offshore and anxious to assault Tinian, urged utmost speed. On June 24, when Ralph Smith balked, Holland Smith relieved him and put in motion another skirmish between the army and the Marine Corps that had nothing to do with the Japanese.

On July 6, Marines pinned down the last Japanese force in the northern reaches of Saipan. General Saito gathered together his staff and feasted on sake and canned crabmeat. With his stomach full, he cleaned off a rock, faced east, shouted "Banzai!" and carved out his bowels with a ceremonial sword. A day later in a cave nearby, Admiral Chuichi Nagumo, the man who had launched the attack on Pearl Harbor, put a pistol to his head and blew out his brains.

Marines pressed ahead and on July 9 secured Saipan after an episode of mass suicide performed by thousands of Japanese soldiers and islanders. Soldiers stood in line atop a cliff to be ceremonially beheaded by their comrades. Entire families stepped to the edge of 1,000-foot Marpi Point and threw themselves into the

ABOVE: Japanese trapped by the 2nd Marine Division north of Garapan attempt to escape to the few ships not already burning in Tanapag harbor. Time had already run out on a dead Japanese soldier lying on the beach.

sea because Japanese officers had told them that, should they be captured by the Americans, they would be prostituted and sold into slave labor. Marines set up loudspeakers in an effort to stop the slaughter, but Japanese officers persisted until the waters below Marpi Point became so cluttered with the dead and dying that the propeller blades of rescue boats clogged when attempting to recover those still alive.

When the fighting ended on July 12, only a handful of prisoners remained from the 30,000-man Japanese garrison on Saipan. American forces suffered 16,525 casualties, including 3,426 deaths. Of those, 12,934 were Marines.

The battle of Saipan, the Marianas Turkey Shoot, and the repulse of the Japanese navy in the Philippine Sea permanently changed the character of the war. Japanese strategists, aware that B-29s would now reach the homeland, admitted that the "war was lost with the loss of Saipan." A ripple effect ensued. On July 18, 1944, Japanese Emperor Hirohito forced General Tojo and his military cabinet to resign, and in November Franklin Roosevelt won an unprecedented fourth term as president.

Tinian—"The Perfect Amphibious Operation"

On July 12, 1944, and despite his altercation with the army, Holland Smith assumed command of the new Fleet Marine Force Pacific and turned the V Amphibious force over to General Schmidt. In turn, Schmidt yielded command of the 4th Marine Division to Major General Clifton B. Cates, who four years later became the Corps' 19th commandant.

On July 24, Schmidt focused his attention on Tinian, a smaller island three miles south of Saipan. Surrounded by reefs and heavily defended by coastal guns, Tinian created another difficult task for Marines. Schmidt posted the XXIV Army Corps artillery on the south side of Saipan to shell powerful enemy batteries lodged in the hills of northern Tinian. Because the dismissal of Ralph Smith still reverberated at headquarters, Schmidt kept the 27th Army Division on Saipan and used his two battered Marine divisions to spearhead the assault. He planned to have General Watson's 2nd Division feint against Tinian Town to the south while Cates's 4th Division landed on the northwest coast.

Admiral Kakuji Kakuta and Colonel Kiyochi Ogata, together commanding 9,162 Japanese troops, expected the attack to come near Tinian Town because the island had no other suitable beach for landing. Kakuta stopped work on fortifications on the north side of the island because the shelling from Saipan had driven the workers away, and he brought them south to strengthen Tinian Town.

Schmidt's strategy worked perfectly. On July 24, Watson's 2nd Division executed a masterful feint off Tinian Town while Cates's 4th Division landed three companies of Marine riflemen in twenty-four amphibian tractors on the northwest shore. By dusk, Cates had three regiments and four pack howitzer battalions ashore—15,614 Marines in all. On August 1, at a cost of 328 killed and 1,571 wounded, the 4th Division secured the island in what Holland Smith praised as "the perfect amphibious operation of the Pacific War."

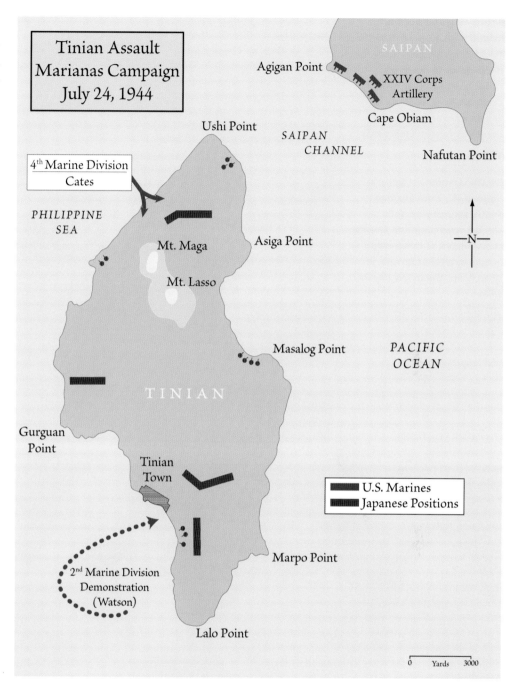

ABOVE: Twelve days after the fighting ended on Saipan, the 4th Marine Division, already battle-scarred and weary, makes a surprise attack on the northern coast of Tinian, while the 2nd Marine Division makes a demonstration against the island's principal city of Tinian Town.

RIGHT: A "water buffalo" loaded with a squad from the 4th Marine Division heads for the beaches in northern Tinian, while U.S. Army XIV Corps artillery located on Saipan hammers Japanese coastal defenses 3,000 yards away.

BELOW: Lieutenant General Holland M. "Howling Mad" Smith, second from left, confers with navy and Marine commanders at temporary headquarters set up near Asan Point, Guam, on July 22, 1944.

Guam—Operation Stevedore

The assault on Guam required a different plan. The island resembled Saipan's topography but was much larger, with more jungles, mountains, and ridges. Unlike Saipan, Guam's Chamorro inhabitants wanted to be liberated, so the recapture of the island became both symbolic and strategic.

On Guam, Lieutenant General Takeshi Takashima commanded the 19,000-man 29th Army Division, which included a large naval defense force armed with fifty-five guns in coastal batteries. However, Takashima did not have large supplies of ammunition, but he did have large quantities of whiskey, sake, and Asahi beer, which he distributed to inspire his men to fight to the death.

General Geiger drew the task of capturing Guam. He planned to spearhead the attack with the 3rd Marine Division, commanded by Major General

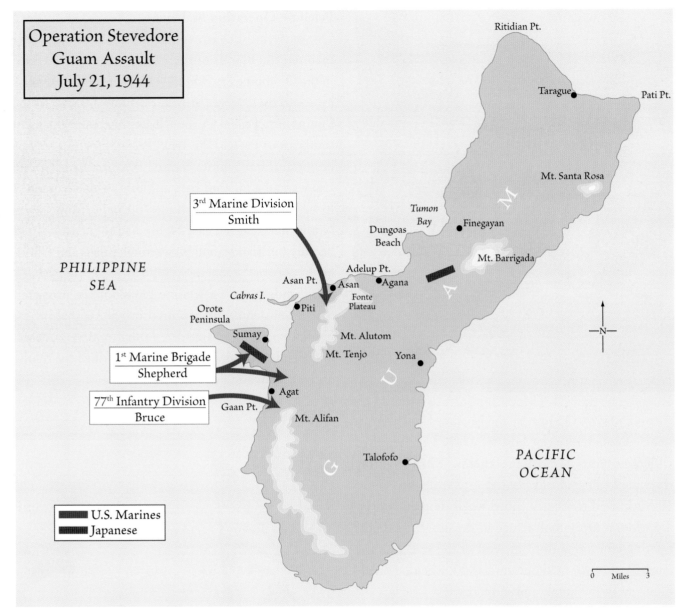

Operation Stevedore
Guam Assault
July 21, 1944

PHILIPPINE
SEA

Ritidian Pt.

Tarague   Pati Pt.

Mt. Santa Rosa

Tumon
Bay   Finegayan

Dungoas
Beach   Mt. Barrigada

3rd Marine Division
Smith

Adelup Pt.

Asan Pt.   Asan   Agana

Cabras I.   Fonte
Piti   Plateau

Orote
Peninsula   Mt. Alutom

Sumay   Mt. Tenjo   Yona

1st Marine Brigade
Shepherd

Agat

77th Infantry Division
Bruce   Gaan Pt.   Mt. Alifan

Talofofo

PACIFIC
OCEAN

—N—

U.S. Marines
Japanese

0   Miles   3

Andrew H. Turnage, and deploy Brigadier General Lemuel C. Shepherd's First Provisional Marine Brigade and Major General Andrew G. Bruce's 77th Infantry Division on another beach. For the assault, Geiger teamed with Rear Admiral Richard L. Connolly, another no-nonsense veteran, who looked Geiger straight in the eye, and said, "My aim is to get the troops ashore standing up. You tell me what you want done to accomplish this, and we'll do it." Connolly made good on his promise. For thirteen days prior to the assault, battleships, cruisers, and carrier-based aircraft pounded the enemy's coastal and inland defenses.

On July 2, the 3rd Marine Division landed on Guam's west coast near the capital of Agana. Signs on the beach read: "Welcome Marines." The First Marine Provisional Brigade and the 77th Infantry Division came ashore near Agat, south of the Orote Peninsula. In a brilliantly executed pincers movement, Geiger trapped the Japanese on the peninsula and surround the

Peleliu—Operation Stalemate

One of the most controversial operations in the Pacific involved the islands of the Palaus, Ngulu, and Ulithi in the Philippine Sea. On July 31, General MacArthur's forces secured New Guinea, opening the way to the Philippines. Peleliu in the Palaus lay about 500 miles southeast of Leyte. Like Truk, Peleliu now seemed less important, but Nimitz wanted it neutralized. Nimitz also wanted a forward base at Ulithi, which happened to be undefended and about 700 miles from Leyte. Nimitz also decided that Ngulu had to be neutralized because the island stood between the Palaus and Ulithi. Had Major General William H. Rupertus, commanding the 1st Marine Division, not predicted that Peleliu could be captured in two or three days, Nimitz might have considered other options because, in the end, "Stalemate" accurately described the results of the Peleliu assault.

ABOVE: A leatherneck from the 3rd Marine Division ascends a stairway to a second story balcony where one or more Japanese snipers are operating from a cottage on the shore near Asan, Guam.

RIGHT: Eight minutes after army and Marine assault troops landed on Guam, two U.S. officers planted the Stars and Stripes on a strip of beach after borrowing a boat hook to use as a staff.

enemy's airstrip. On July 25, the Japanese launched two frenzied counterattacks, both of which were repulsed with enormous loss to the enemy. Bitter fighting continued, but gradually petered out. Finally, on August 10, organized resistance ended when thousands from Takashima's army took refuge in the jungle. Sporadic fighting continued until the end of the war. The last Japanese survivor held out until 1960, when he finally came out of the jungle and surrendered.

The tactics developed between Geiger and Connolly at Guam set new standards for amphibious operations. Working with navy and Marine pilots, Connolly perfected a system that allowed naval gunfire and air support to be delivered against the same target at the same time. Navy vessels were able to deliver flat trajectory fire while aircraft delivered plunging fire. The tactic was largely responsible for putting Marine aircraft on escort carriers and implementing the Marine air-ground team for the specific purpose of supporting infantry units on the ground.

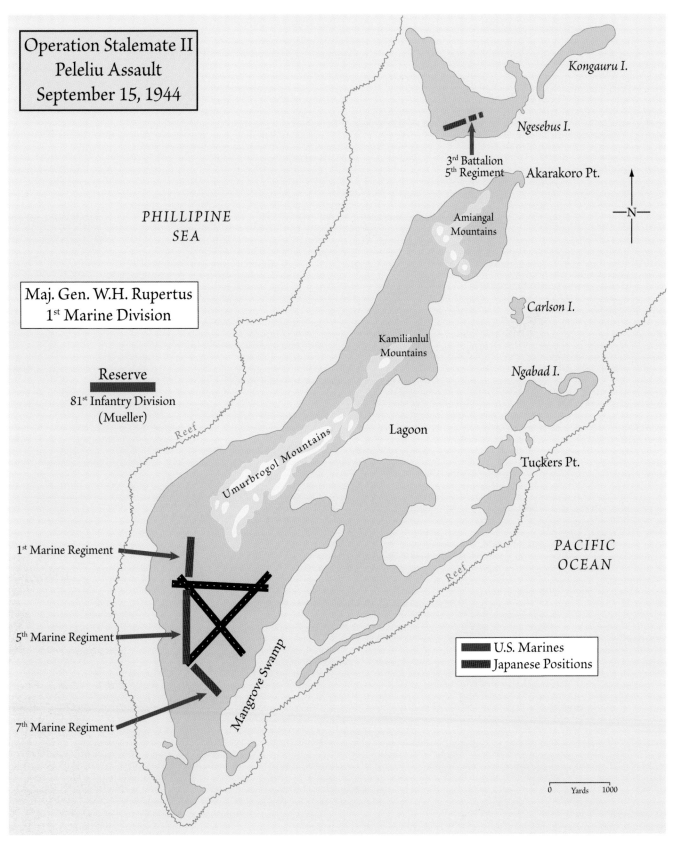

Operation Stalemate II
Peleliu Assault
September 15, 1944

Maj. Gen. W.H. Rupertus
1st Marine Division

Reserve
81st Infantry Division
(Mueller)

PHILLIPINE
SEA

Kongauru I.

Ngesebus I.

3rd Battalion
5th Regiment

Akarakoro Pt.

—N—

Amiangal
Mountains

Carlson I.

Kamilianlul
Mountains

Ngabad I.

Lagoon

Tuckers Pt.

Umurbrogol Mountains

1st Marine Regiment

5th Marine Regiment

PACIFIC
OCEAN

Reef

U.S. Marines
Japanese Positions

7th Marine Regiment

Mangrove Swamp

Reef

0   Yards   1000

LEFT: Before assaulting
Peleliu on September 15,
1944, Major General William
H. Rupertus, commanding the
1st Marine Division,
predicted: "We're going to
have some casualties, but let
me assure you that this is
going to be a short one, a
quickie. Rough but fast. We'll
be through in three days. It
may take only two." Nothing
went according to plan. The
Marines captured the airfield
only after a stubborn fight
and then spent the next two
months rooting the enemy
out of Umurbrogol Ridge.

LEFT: Along a tenuous perimeter established at the far end of Peleliu's airfield, Marine Pfc. Douglas Lightstreet (right) cradles his .30-caliber machine gun and takes time out for a smoke with his buddy, Pfc. Gerald Churchby.

For Operation Stalemate, General Geiger offered Rupertus part of the 81st Infantry Division. Because of ripples from the Ralph Smith affair, Rupertus decided to assault the island without the army's help. Though Geiger warned that Colonel Kunio Nakagawa's 10,700 defenders came from one of Japan's best infantry divisions, Rupertus remained unimpressed. Aerial reconnaissance showed hundreds of honeycombed caves imbedded in the Umurbrogal Ridge, which ran through the center of the island and stopped short of an airfield near the island's southwestern tip. Rupertus expected to capture the airfield quickly and mop up the island using 1st Marine Division veterans.

On September 15, 1944, Rupertus landed three regiments 500 yards from the Japanese airfield and spent the next five days engaged in fierce fighting before capturing the airfield. The 1st Marine Regiment, commanded by Colonel Lewis B. "Chesty" Puller, ran into stiff resistance at Umurbrogal Ridge and called for reinforcements. Puller concluded that 1,406 tons of navy projectiles hurled at the island had not touched the enemy burrowed in the ridge.

FAR LEFT: Unexplored coral ridges and mangrove swamps slowed the assault on Peleliu, forcing one scattered squadron of Marines to take shelter under a "duck" while two amphibious tractors burned on the beach.

ABOVE: Operations on Peleliu ground to a standstill in late September 1944 when Marines moved toward Umurbrogol Ridge. With a walkie-talkie flimsily strapped to his back, and clutching a radio in his right hand, a Marine reconnoiters the ridge looking for signs of the hidden enemy.

Now far behind schedule, Rupertus decided to encircle the ridge instead of attacking it, thereby leaving thousands of Japanese hidden in caves to harass the airfield. Geiger became impatient and ordered in the 321st Army Infantry Regiment. Rupertus then discovered that Umurbrogal was not one ridge but a series of five ridges all interlocked with tunnels that had to be blown one by one. What Rupertus envisioned as a three-day "quickie" took one day more than a month and delayed operations elsewhere. On October 16, after the 18th Infantry Division relieved the Marines, six weeks elapsed before the army declared the island secure. The Marine Corps lost 1,252 killed and 6,526 wounded on Peleliu, and the army lost 208 killed and 1,185 wounded, the highest ratio to date of American to Japanese casualties in any campaign. Only 302 Japanese surrendered. Rupertus spent the rest of his career wondering what went wrong.

> If military leaders were gifted with the same accuracy of foresight that they are with hindsight, undoubtedly the assault and capture of the Palaus would never have been attempted.
> *Rear Admiral Jesse B. Oldendorf, March 25, 1950.*

Marines on the Philippines

On October 20, 1944, MacArthur launched his promised return to the Philippines and assaulted Leyte. The expedition would be mainly an army-navy event with the Marine Corps playing a secondary role. The four embattled Marine divisions needed a rest, and the 5th and 6th Marine Divisions were still in training.

Holland Smith lent the V Amphibious Corps artillery, about 1,500 Marines under Brigadier General Thomas E. Bourke, to the XXIV Army Corps. During the Leyte assault, Bourke demonstrated the special skills born of Marine doctrine for amphibious operations by coordinating all artillery, naval gunfire, and supporting aircraft during and after the landing.

ABOVE: Operations soon shifted to the Philippines where on October 20, 1944, landing barges loaded with troops are shown churning toward the beaches of Leyte Island, while American and Japanese planes duel to the death overhead.

LEFT: General Douglas MacArthur, positioned directly beneath the flag, and members of his staff attend a ceremony on March 2, 1945, to re-raise the Stars and Stripes on the liberated island of Corregidor.

ABOVE: The hard-worked 4th Marine Division, recently reinforced after operations on Tinian, begin moving onto the beaches near Iwo Jima's Airfield No. 1 on D-Day, February 19, 1945. The assault will be the fourth in thirteen months for the 4th Marine Division. An LSM (landing ship, medium) is offloading equipment further up the beach.

On October 25, Major Ralph J. Mitchell, commanding the 1st Marine Air Wing, touched down on Tacloban Field, Leyte, looking for work for his flyers. A few days later he brought in MAG-12, commanded by Colonel William A. Willis, whose group included night-fighter squadron VMFN-541. When the Leyte operation ended in late December, five Marine squadrons had destroyed sixty-three enemy aircraft, seven destroyers, seventeen transports, and damaged another twelve vessels. MacArthur awarded MAG-12 an army citation, saying, "Your night-fighter squadron has performed magnificently repeat magnificently."

During December, before MacArthur invaded Luzon, Mitchell observed that neither the army nor the navy understood close air support the Marine way. He brought Lieutenant Colonel Keith B. McCutcheon's MAG-24 up from the Solomons to teach close air support to army pilots. When MacArthur ordered the 1st Cavalry Division to capture Manila, he sent MAG-24 along to cover the division's left flank. During the assault Brigadier General William C. Chase, USA, whose First Brigade led the division, insisted that the Marine air liaison jeep stay beside him. In reporting progress, he informed division headquarters, "I have never seen such able . . . and accurate close support as Marine flyers are giving us." When the 1st Cavalry entered the outskirts of Manila, Marines jury-rigged an airstrip on Quezon Boulevard and flew dive-bombing sorties from the street. By February, every army unit in the Philippines wanted Marine squadrons to support their ground movements.

Iwo Jima—Operation Detachment

Iwo Jima, an eight-square-mile volcanic island, lay exactly in the middle of a near-straight line drawn across 1,800 miles of ocean between Saipan and Tokyo. The small Japanese-controlled island operated two airfields with a third underway. In the overall strategy to assault Japan, Iwo meant very little. As a mid-ocean airbase to rescue B-29 bombers damaged over Japan, it meant everything. AAF chief General Arnold convinced Nimitz to capture the island, thereby enabling fighters to fly top cover for bombers, offer a haven for cripples, and provide an intermediate fueling stop, thereby enabling B-29s to carry more ordnance. On October 3, 1944, the JCS authorized Operation Detachment and put Nimitz's planners to work organizing another mission for the Marine Corps.

During 1944, Imperial General Headquarters sent Lieutenant General Tadamichi Kuribayashi to the island to turn it into an invader's death trap. With the exception of Mount Suribachi, an extinct volcano situated on the southern tip of the island, Iwo Jima's terrain consisted of coarse black sand, fissures emitting

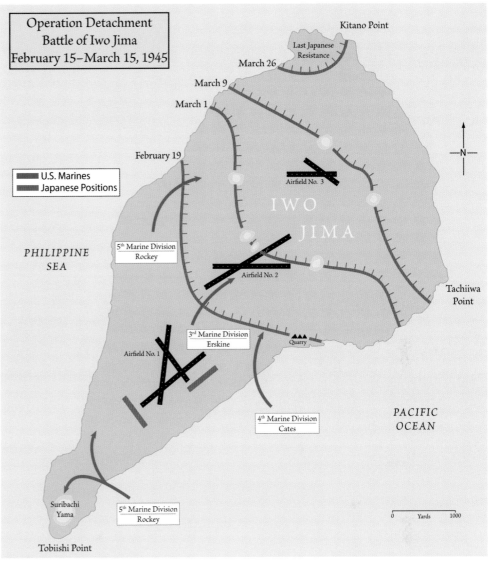

LEFT: During a pre-invasion briefing, Marine Lieutenant Wade gives his company specific landing and target acquisition instructions on the day before the scheduled assault of Iwo Jima.

ABOVE: Three Marine divisions participated in the assault of Iwo Jima, an eight-square-mile island defended by 21,000 veteran Japanese troops. General Holland Smith predicted: "We may expect casualties far beyond any heretofore suffered in the Central Pacific." Smith even underestimated the losses: the brutal five-week campaign that began on February 19, 1945, cost the V Amphibious Corps some 5,981 killed and 19,920 wounded.

ABOVE: When members of the 2nd Battalion, 27th Marines, went ashore near the southern tip of Iwo Jima, they crawled up a natural barrier of coarse black sand and came in view of Suribachi Yama, the ominous dead volcano they had been ordered to assault.

sulfurous fumes, and a few stunted shrubs. Kuribayashi garrisoned the island with 21,000 infantry and put them to work building pillboxes, blockhouses, masked batteries, and concrete-lined caves interconnected by 13,000 yards of tunnels. He fortified the island with hundreds of large coastal guns, masked artillery batteries, ninety mortars and rocket-launchers, sixty-nine anti-tank guns, two hundred machine guns, enormous quantities of ammunition, and twenty-four tanks dug hull-down into pockets.

In October 1944, Holland Smith and Turner began planning Operation Detachment. Smith chose General Schmidt to lead the assault, and Turner chose Admiral Hill to provide naval support—two veterans with impressive records for executing amphibious landings. Smith wanted the V Amphibious Corps assault to be exclusively a Marine operation and gave Schmidt two battle-hardened divisions, the 3rd and 4th, and added the rookie 5th Division, also led by seasoned veterans. Schmidt placed the 3rd Division, led by Major General

Graves B. Erskine, in floating reserve while General Cates's 4th Division stormed the beach adjacent to Airfield No. 1, and Major General Keller E. Rockey's 5th Division landed on the southern shore near Mount Suribachi. The plan called for the 4th and 5th Divisions to wheel north and assault the heavily fortified Motoyama Plateau, leaving the 28th Regiment with the daunting task of capturing Suribachi, a prominence providing the enemy with a full view of the battlefield.

From early December until mid-February 1945, B-24s and B-29s bombed the island for seventy-two days in a row. Smith wanted the assault set back to allow for another ten days of bombing but was given only three. He provided aerial reconnaissance photographs showing that during the bombardment the enemy had actually increased major land defensive positions from 450 to 730 and more than doubled its coastal gun emplacements. On February 16, Rear Admiral William H. P. Blandy's six battleships and five

ABOVE: After 5th Division Marines piled ashore on Iwo Jima, they began inching their way to the crest of Suribachi Yama and quickly came under fire from Japanese mortars, artillery, and machine guns concealed in a network of tunnels carved in the volcanic ash and rocks of the mountain.

cruisers, augmented by escort carrier Hellcats and Avengers, began hurling 14,000 16-inch, 14-inch, and 8-inch shells at Kuribayashi's coastal batteries and AA installations. Rain and misty conditions made targeting difficult, and when the weather cleared on D-minus-1 Day, Blandy discovered far more guns emplaced than anyone had anticipated. When Holland Smith predicted 15,000 casualties, nobody believed him.

On February 19, as dawn broke over a calm sea dotted by 450 ships of Spruance's Fifth Fleet, Smith watched as 482 LVT(A)s assembled under Blandy's rolling barrage. Sixty-eight LVT(A)s peeled off for the 4,000-yard dash to shore. Forty-five minutes later amtracs hit the black sand beaches with Rockey's 5th Division on the right and Cates's 4th Division on the left. Kuribayashi made a fatal mistake by allowing the Marines to push 300 yards inland before opening with raking fire on the flanks. Marines weathered the fire and fought back. By nightfall, more than 30,000 Marines supported by tanks and artillery commanded

LEFT: A few hours after Marines established a foothold on Iwo Jima, hundreds of landing craft began arriving with tons of ammunition and supplies.

ABOVE: By afternoon on D-Day, dozens of disabled trucks and amtracs litter the beach while first aid stations receive the wounded and prepare to have them transferred by boat to hospital ships.

ABOVE: Shortly after the first wave of Marines hit the beaches on Iwo Jima, an LST pulls alongside the USS Hartford and begins loading a medium tank.

ABOVE: A Marine observer on the front lines of Iwo Jima spots a Japanese machine gun nest, orients its location on a map, and transmits the coordinates to supporting artillery and mortar units in the rear.

RIGHT: Associated Press photographer Joe Rosenthal captures on film the historic moment when Marines reach the crest of Mount Suribachi and raise the Stars and Stripes. After more than sixty years, the photograph is still recognized by most Americans as a World War II icon.

the beachhead. At a cost of 2,400 casualties with 600 dead, Rockey's and Cates's divisions secured the southern neck of the island, isolated the enemy on Suribachi from the main Japanese force, and gained a foothold on Airfield No. 1.

With Marines firmly established on the island, it became a matter of time and casualties before exterminating the enemy. On the left flank the 28th Marines, commanded by Colonel Harry B. Liversedge, spent three horrific days using flamethrowers and satchel charges to blow the enemy out of their holes on Mount Suribachi, and on February 23 they planted the Stars and Stripes on the summit. The following day the 3rd Marine Division came ashore to break through General Kuribayashi's iron belt of cross-island defenses protecting Airfield No. 2. Now with 82,000 men ashore, the 4th Division on the right, the 5th Division on the left, and the 3rd Division in the center, the men snaked through stinking sulfur pits, lunar-like crags, and sunken pockets to flush out the enemy. Directly across from Airfield No. 2, all three divisions struck heavily fortified hills running through the center of the island. Smoke from high explosive shells shot into one hole puffed out another. The breakthrough required a thunderous artillery barrage augmented by naval guns and a heroic 800-yard sprint by Erskine's 3rd Division to flank Kuribayashi's rear.

While Marines continued to push the Japanese into the northern sector of the island, Seabees cleared Airfield No. 1 for landings. Marine Corsairs flew in from Agana, followed by Torpedo-Bombing Squadron 242 and the AAF's VII Fighter Group, whose pilots soon acquired the art of close air support. Before fighting for control of the island ended on March 24—the day General Kuribayashi committed *hara-kiri*—damaged B-29s returning from bombing missions over Japan were already making emergency landings on the airfield. By war's end, 24,761 flyers from 2,251 B-24s and B-29s had reason to thank the Marines for capturing Iwo Jima.

The butcher's bill came high. While nobody had believed Holland Smith when he predicted 15,000 casualties, the general's estimate fell lamentably short. The V Amphibious Corps counted 25,851 casualties, including 5,931 dead. Out of more than 20,000 Japanese on the island, only 216 surrendered. Twenty-two Marines were awarded the Medal of Honor, twelve of them posthumously. Smith called Iwo Jima the toughest fight "we've run across in 168 years." The battle nearly decimated three Marine divisions.

On March 26, 1945, two days after securing Iwo Jima, the pre-invasion bombardment of Okinawa began.

RIGHT: Artillery from the 4th Marine Division shell enemy positions in the hills flanking the northern end of Iwo Jima's Airfield No. 2, which is covered over with the debris and litter of bitter fighting.

BELOW: Navy Chaplain Lieutenant (jg) John H. Galbreath (center), who is attached to the 5th Marine Division, kneels beside a wounded leatherneck who has just been brought to the aid station from an artillery battery fifty yards away.

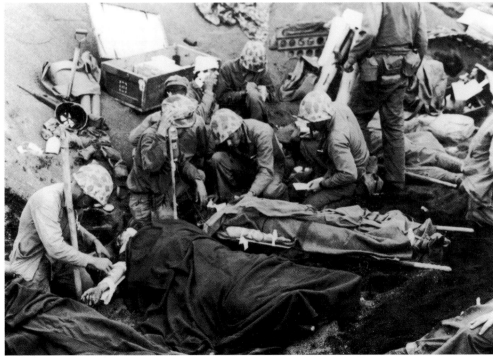

ABOVE: Wounded Marines on Iwo Jima assist navy corpsmen who are bringing the more seriously wounded to first aid stations set up short distances behind the front lines.

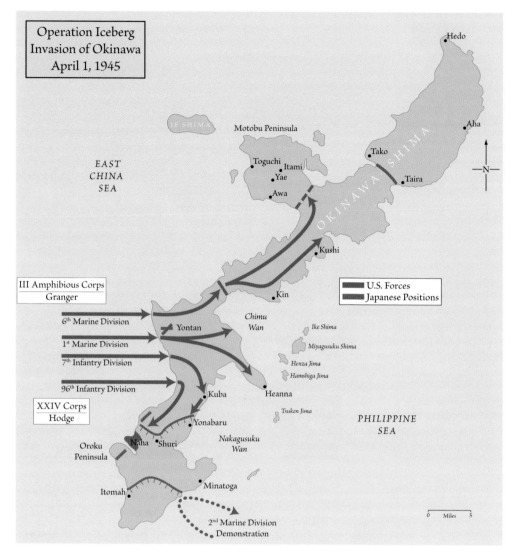

Operation Iceberg
Invasion of Okinawa
April 1, 1945

EAST
CHINA
SEA

Hedo

IE SHIMA

Motobu Peninsula

Toguchi
Itami
Yae
Awa

Tako

Taira

Aha

OKINAWA SHIMA

N

Kushi

III Amphibious Corps
Granger

Kin

U.S. Forces
Japanese Positions

6th Marine Division

1st Marine Division

7th Infantry Division

96th Infantry Division

XXIV Corps
Hodge

Yontan

Kuba

Yonabaru

Naha Shuri

Oroku
Peninsula

Itomah

Minatoga

Chimu
Wan

Ike Shima

Miyagusuku Shima

Henza Jima

Hamshiga Jima

Heanna

Tsuken Jima

Nakagusuku
Wan

PHILIPPINE
SEA

0   Miles   5

2nd Marine Division
Demonstration

ABOVE: The Japanese fielded 100,000 men on Okinawa, and most of them occupied defensive positions south of Yontan airfield. When the assault began on April 1, 1945, it marked the first operation in the Pacific not commanded by a Marine.

Okinawa—Operation Iceberg

Okinawa, in the Ryukyu Islands, lay 325 miles south of Kyushu, Japan, and provided an essential stepping stone for Allied forces assaulting the home islands. Imperial General Headquarters could not afford to lose Okinawa and poured more than 115,000 army and navy personnel into the defense of the island. Like Kuribayashi on Iwo Jima, Lieutenant General Mitsuru Ushijima believed that any attempt to destroy Americans on the beach was futile and the best way to defeat an assaulting force was to lure it into a heavily fortified defensive position branching across the southern sector of the island from Shuri. Ushijima also

TOP: Marines of Company A, 2nd Battalion, 5th Marines, discovered that the only way to root out Japanese lurking in tunnels was to blast them out with bazookas or flamethrowers.

ABOVE: Tired of being pinned down by snipers firing from caves, a demolition crew from the 6th Marine Division trigger a pack charge hurled into the tunnel's mouth.

ABOVE: Marines advancing along the Shuri defensive line are suddenly pinned downed as they attempt to move through and over a patch of ground called "Cemetery Ridge."

LEFT: A Marine from the 1st Division takes aim with his .45-caliber Thompson submachine gun on a sniper, covering a buddy who is moving forward in a crouch on Wana Ridge near Shuri, Okinawa.

counted on the Japanese navy and a thousand *kamikaze* suicide planes to destroy Spruance's Fifth Fleet, thereby denying Americans on the island naval or air support.

Being ignorant of Ushijima's game-plan, Lieutenant General Simon Bolivar Buckner, USA, and Spruance designed a typical king-sized beach assault involving 1,457 ships and more than 183,000 men. Buckner's Tenth Army consisted of General Geiger's III Amphibious Corps of 80,000 Marines and Major General John S. Hodge's XXIV Army Corps. Geiger's command consisted of the 1st, 2nd, and 6th Marine Divisions and the 2nd Marine Air Wing for close air support.

On April 1, 1945, after a furious week-long bombardment, the 1st Marine Division, commanded by Puerto Rico-born Naval Academy graduate Major General Pedro A. del Valle, went ashore near Yontan Airfield. The 6th Marine Division, commanded by Virginia Military Institute graduate Major General Lemuel C. Shepherd, Jr., went ashore beside the 1st Division to cover del Valle's right flank and the army's left flank. The 2nd Marine Division, Geiger's floating reserve, steamed around the tip of Okinawa and made a diversionary feint along the southeast coast. Ironically, the 1st and 6th Divisions went ashore against weak resistance, but the 2nd Division suffered the greater

ABOVE: During the fight for Shuri, a Marine dashes through Japanese machine gun fire while crossing a draw called Death Valley, where 125 American casualties occurred during a period of eight hours.

TOP: A Marine F4U Corsair performing close air support fires a broadside of eight five-inch rockets into a Japanese position on a ridge near Shuri. An army P-38, flying fifty feet off the Corsair's tail, snaps the photograph.

ABOVE: Artillerymen from the 15th Marines angle their 105mm howitzer into a new firing position on June 9, 1945. A Marine astride the barrel attempts to aid the move by functioning as a counterbalance.

casualties when their transports were hit by two *kamikazes*. Such *kamikaze* threats sent the floating 2nd Division back to Saipan.

The 6th Marine Division immediately overran Yontan, and by April 2 the 6th Engineer Battalion had the airfield in partial operating order. The 6th Division then wheeled north, toward the Motobu Peninsula, while the 1st Division mopped up the area. Hodge's army Corps turned south to assault the massive elevated enemy emplacements that began at Naha on the west coast and stretched through Shuri Castle to Yonabaru on Nagagusuku Bay on the east coast. The defenses resembled everything the Marines had experienced on Iwo Jima, but nobody in Hodge's XXIV Army Corps had been there. While the 6th Marine Division made steady progress on the Motobu Peninsula, Ushijima stopped Hodge's army Corps at the Shuri defensive line.

Geiger suggested an amphibious end run south of Shuri, but Buckner vetoed the movement as too risky. Instead, he brought the 6th Marine Division, already reduced by casualties, down from the Motobu Peninsula and joined it with the 1st Division, which Buckner had used sparingly. While the army held its position, the 6th Marine Division took heavy casualties securing three mutually supporting hills—Sugar Loaf, Horseshoe, and Half Moon—which anchored the western flank of the Shuri line. The veteran 1st Division, one of the toughest units of the war, took severe casualties overrunning Dakeshi Ridge, the key terrain feature obstructing Hodge's advance, and Wana Ridge, the most formidable eminence and worst deathtrap in Ushijima's defensive line.

After the 10th Infantry Division reached a stalemate against Ushijima's defenses on the Oroku Peninsula at Naha, Geiger convinced Buckner that the easiest way to break the bottleneck without heavy loss was to launch an amphibious assault in the rear of the enemy. Lieutenant Colonel Victor H. Krulak put the plan together in five days and on June 4 the 4th and 29th Marine Regiments landed from LVTs and LCTs and rapidly pushed inland. Joined by the 6th Division, the Marines squeezed the Japanese into a corner.

Peering from his command post on June 15, Ushijima wired Tokyo, "Enemy tanks are attacking our headquarters. The Naval Base Force is dying gloriously." Ushijima shut down radio communications and committed suicide. Three days later, during the final days of the Okinawa campaign, a wayward artillery shell killed Buckner. General Geiger took charge of the Tenth Army and became the only Marine to command a field army during the war. The army did not want a Marine in charge of their bailiwick, and pulled General Joseph W. Stilwell out of retirement to replace Geiger.

War's End

On May 7, 1945, during the battle for Okinawa, the war in Europe ended. The United States began moving more divisions to the Pacific for the invasion of Japan. On August 6, more than 300,000 troops were being trained on Okinawa. On that day, a B-29 named *Enola Gay* flew over Honshu and dropped the first atomic bomb on Hiroshima, killing 80,000 inhabitants in a city of 500,000. Three days later the air force dropped a second atomic bomb, on Nagasaki, a seaport on Kyushu, and killed 20,000 more. On August 14 Japan surrendered unconditionally. The following day every American, whether on Okinawa or in Peoria, Illinois, celebrated V-J Day.

On September 2, Japanese officials signed the instrument of surrender on the battleship *Missouri* (BB-63) in Tokyo Bay. MacArthur signed for the Allied powers and Nimitz for the United States. During the ceremony, Geiger represented the Marine Corps. He also represented the 86,940 leathernecks who had died during an unbroken series of victories in the Pacific. Eighty Marines were awarded Medals of Honor.

The Corps' six divisions made fifteen major

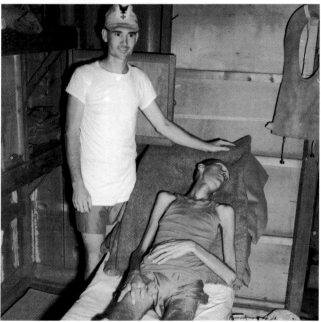

ABOVE: A few days after the first atomic bomb leveled Hiroshima, a Japanese soldier surveys the desolation from a distance, perhaps lamenting his nation's decision to go to war with America.

LEFT: On August 15, 1945, Marine, air force, and navy personnel arrive at Atsugi airfield and the search begins for American and British prisoners. In a mission headed by Commander Roger Simpson and Commander Harold Grassen into the wretched Aomori camp near Tokyo, the first of the near-dead prisoners are carried away on litters for medical treatment.

amphibious landings, and its air arm destroyed 2,355 enemy aircraft. Growing from a force of 70,000 in December 1941, some 670,000 men and women served the Corps during World War II. On V-J Day, the Corps still numbered 458,000 officers and enlisted personnel. Then suddenly, once again, the future of the Corps faced another threat to its existence.

COLD WAR: KOREA 1945–1960

After World War II, the Marines had many daunting tasks to perform, including the demobilization of 500,000 officers and enlisted personnel. General Schmidt's V Amphibious Corps (2nd and 5th Marine Divisions) had been training to assault Kyushu when Japan surrendered. After V-J Day, Commandant Vandegrift deployed the two divisions as the occupying force. In December 1945, the 5th Division went stateside for disbandment. Seven months later the 2nd Division followed but remained active as the Fleet Marine Force, Atlantic.

In September 1945, Vandegrift sent Major General Keller Rockey's III Amphibious Corps (1st and 6th Marine Divisions) into China to disarm 630,000 Japanese troops. Rockey had a second mission: to stabilize the country and prevent it from falling under the influence of Soviet and Chinese communists. Russia's leader Stalin had declared war on Japan two days after the atomic bomb fell on Hiroshima, for the sole purpose of expanding communism in the Far East. Marines tutored the Chinese in warfare, unaware that

> [A new military philosophy] consists of thinking in terms of the next war instead of the last. This means starting with ideas, when you have nothing more tangible, and developing them into concepts, procedures, and weapons of the future.
>
> *Victor Krulak, in* First to Fight.

communists would soon turn the training against American troops. During mid-1946, finding no more employment for his Marines, Vandegrift disbanded the 3rd, 4th, and 6th Divisions and reduced the Corps to 100,000 officers and enlisted. The 1st Division remained active and became the Fleet Marine Force, Pacific.

The Collins Plan

Ever since the Holland Smith/Ralph Smith imbroglio during the 1944 Saipan campaign, certain well-placed generals in the army seemed unduly obsessed to get even, or so it seemed two years later when Lieutenant General J. Lawton Collins, working on behalf of General George C. Marshall, produced a proposal that threatened to diminish the navy and eliminate the Marine Corps as an amphibious ground force. Part of Collins's proposal included General Carl W. Spaatz's effort to separate the AAF from the army and create the U.S. Air force (USAF) on the premise that all future wars would be mainly atomic and dependent upon air power. Secretary of the Navy James Forrestal did not know the details of the "Collins Plan" until he presented the role of the postwar Marine Corps to President Truman and discovered that, according to the army plan, Marines would never again be required except "in minor shore combat operations in which the Navy alone is interested." In addition, Collins proposed that the Corps be limited to no more than 60,000 men, with no expansion during war, and that the Marine Corps Reserve be abolished. Marine pilots would be assimilated into the USAF or the navy, and the soldiers

would no longer be fighters, acting only as landing craft crews and beach labor parties.

Collins further recommended the establishment of a secretary of defense with power to determine the roles and missions of the armed services without congressional oversight. The arrangement would remove the Marine Corps from the protection of Congress and enable Collins, a staff officer to Eisenhower, to superimpose the whims of the war department over all other branches of the service and, in particular, the navy. Secretary of the Navy Forrestal, who had stood on the bloody sands of Iwo Jima in 1945 and said that the Marine Corps had earned its future for the next 500 years, now faced a dilemma.

On May 6, 1946, while Forrestal searched for solutions, 59-year-old Commandant Vandegrift took the issue before the Senate Naval Affairs Committee. While his listeners fixed their eyes on the old hero's Medal of Honor ribbon, Vandegrift stoutly faced each senator and explained why the Collins Plan "spelled extinction for the Marine Corps." He did not ask any concessions, nor did he come "on bended knee," but he convinced the committee that the Corps had "earned the right to have its future decided by the legislative body that created it" in 1798. During the height of the controversy, President Truman took Vandegrift aside and during a private conversation said, "You Marines don't trust anybody, do you?" The president was right.

On July 26, 1947, President Truman signed the National Security Act, creating the post of secretary of

ABOVE: Instead of going home in 1945, the III Amphibious Corps went to China to accept the surrender of Japanese forces and attempt to prevent a takeover by communist forces. As part of one of the many liberation parades, Chinese citizens at Tsingtao stand curbside to watch as a Marine truck tows a 105mm howitzer through the street.

General Clifton Bledsoe Cates (1893–1970)

Clifton Cates fought in both world wars. In 1918 he distinguished himself at Belleau Wood, Saint-Miheil, and Meuse-Argonne (where he was gassed and wounded), and again during 1942–1945 at Guadalcanal, Saipan-Tinian, and Iwo Jima. Before becoming the 19th commandant on January 1, 1948, he fought another battle before the House Armed Services Committee during the writing of the National Security Act of 1947. His testimony contributed to the defeat of the "Collins Plan" to abolish the Marine Corps as an amphibious ready-force. In 1948, the Corps still had the same old enemies—the army, the air corps, and the president.

Although the National Security Act of 1947 preserved the traditional role for Marines, Cates fought old enemies on one hand while with the other hand he crafted new concepts. With the development of helicopters, he envisioned using rotary-wing aircraft on carriers instead of landing craft for assaults. Cates's landing-from-the-air proposal eliminated dangers from reefs, beach defenses, tides, or surf during amphibious landings. At the time, Cates had only five two-passenger helicopters, no aircraft carriers for experimentation, and many doubters in the navy.

Ignoring scoffers, Cates added "Employment of Helicopters" to the Marine Corps Schools' curriculum and borrowed the USS Palau, an old jeep carrier, from the navy as a practice ship. Encouraged by Cates, helicopter manufacturers took an interest in the Marine program. They began improving rotary-wing aircraft, and the Piasecki HRP-1 "Flying Banana" became the world's largest wingless aircraft of its time.

In March 1949, during helicopter development, Louis A. Johnson became secretary of defense and attempted to undo everything Forrestal had accomplished while serving as the first secretary. Johnson did not have the authority to eliminate the Corps, but he could reduce its size and did. Cates fought back and was still sparring with Johnson when the Korean War began.

Cates also never got along with Truman. A few days before the Inchon landing in September 1950, Congress suggested that a Marine be added to the Joint Chiefs of Staff. Truman retorted, "For your information the Marine Corps is the Navy's police force and as long as I am President that is what it will remain." After being thrashed by the press, Truman apologized to Cates for the outburst. Cates accepted the apology with grace, but after returning to his office he turned the picture of Truman to the wall and kept it that way.

ABOVE LEFT: Marines wounded at Kari San Mountain, Korea, are treated by navy corpsmen and carried to a waiting helicopter for evacuation to a field hospital.

ABOVE: General Clifton B. Cates had served as an officer in the Marine Corps since 1917. As commandant in 1948, he opposed the unification of the armed forces and attempts to diminish the Corps.

defense and establishing the USAF as a separate service, much as Collins had recommended, but the document also contained a sentence preserving the Marine Corps exactly as Vandegrift defined it:

As for the Marines, you know what Marines are. They are a small, fouled-up Army talking Navy lingo. We are going to put those Marines in the regular Army and make efficient soldiers out of them.

Brigadier General Frank Armstrong to the Saturday Evening Post, *February 5, 1949.*

"The Marine Corps shall be organized, trained and equipped to provide fleet Marine forces of combined arms, together with supporting air components, for service with the fleet in the seizure or defense of advanced naval bases and for the conduct of such land operations as may be essential to the prosecution of a naval campaign."

Forrestal became the first secretary of defense, Marines went about the business of preparing for the next emergency, and in January 1948 General Clifton B. Cates became the nineteenth commandant of the Marine Corps.

North Korea Attacks the South

Secretary of Defense Louis Johnson could not have reduced the Marine Corps at a worse time. By 1950 he had whittled the Corps back to 78,000 men, but Cates still had 90,000 reservists from World War II. Every year the reserves received two weeks training in the field. The average Marine regiment, however, had been shrunk to battalion size, and the average company consisted of barely enough men to fill two platoons.

On June 25, 1950, several months after General MacArthur, Commander-in-Chief, Far East, pulled the last American troops out of South Korea, six North Korean People's Army (NKPA) divisions and three Border Constabulary brigades, supported by 100 Russian T-34 tanks and flocks of Yak fighter aircraft, advanced across the 38th parallel and streamed southward.

After waiting two days, Truman authorized MacArthur to use American air and naval forces to support South Korea, but he waited until the NKPA captured Seoul before authorizing MacArthur to use ground forces. On June 30, MacArthur began airlifting to South Korea the only force in Japan—flaccid occupation troops from the 24th Army Division. By then the NKPA blitzkrieg had gathered momentum, rolling over lightly armed and ineffectual Republic of Korea (ROK) forces.

During the six days Truman temporized over the Korean situation, General Cates, on his own responsibility, ordered the 1st Marine Division to get ready for war. In Washington, while Truman and the JCS viewed the Korean conflict as a "police action," Cates went to Admiral Forrest Sherman, Chief of Naval Operations, and offered a full brigade on short notice. Sherman asked, "How soon?" Cates replied, "Two weeks." Sherman sent a private message to MacArthur asking if the general wanted a full brigade of Marines complete with air. MacArthur still had the 7th and 25th Infantry Divisions in Japan, but they were understrength, poorly equipped, and lax in training. On July 2, MacArthur

LEFT: In a jeep en route to Yang Yang headquarters, South Korea, seated left to right are Lieutenant General Matthew B. Ridgway, Major General Doyle Hickey, and General Douglas MacArthur, who eight days later (April 11, 1951) was relieved as commander of U.N. forces in Korea.

LEFT: A leatherneck machine gun crew from the 2nd Battalion, 5th Marines, dig in during the night of August 17, 1950, along the Naktong bulge sector of the Pusan perimeter, in support of the 24th Army Infantry Division.

radioed the JCS asking that the Marines be sent at once. When the JCS convened to consider MacArthur's request, Cates showed up uninvited. Trapped by their own ill-conceived policies, the JCS approved Cates's offer because the Marines represented, as they had for 171 years, the only force in America ready to fight.

Five days later Brigadier General Edward A. Craig's First Provisional Brigade, built around Lieutenant Colonel Raymond L. Murray's 5th Marines and Brigadier General Thomas J. Cushman's MAG-33, began assembling at Camp Pendleton, California. On July 12, as the 6,534-man brigade embarked at San Diego, Cates sent them off, saying, "You boys clean this up in a couple of months, or I'll be over to see you."

With the First Provisional Brigade en route to Pusan, General Shepherd flew to Tokyo and met privately with MacArthur. During the conference, MacArthur walked Shepherd to a map of Korea and poked the stem of his pipe at the city of Inchon. "If I only had the 1st Marine Division under my command," he said, "I would land them here and cut the North Korean armies attacking the Pusan perimeter from their logistic support and cause their withdrawal and elimination." Shepherd replied that he would have the division ready by September 1 if MacArthur would inform the JCS he wanted it. Sherman drew up the request, and MacArthur signed and forwarded it to Washington. With some hesitation, the JCS approved the request, and Cates went to work mobilizing the 1st Marine Division.

The Pusan Perimeter

On August 3, 1950, General Craig's First Provisional Brigade disembarked at Pusan and moved into the shrinking perimeter, where poorly equipped ROK units backed by the 24th Army Division had been fighting against heavy odds. NKPA divisions pressed against a broad arc from the ports of Chindong-ni in the south to Pohang in the east. Within hours, Marine F4U-4 Corsair pilots from VMF-214—the old "Black Sheep Squadron"—flew off the USS *Sicily* (CVE-118) and scored the first Yak kills.

On August 7, after relieving the 27th Army Regiment at Chindong-ni, the first major engagement between American and North Korean forces occurred when the NKPA launched a pre-dawn assault against a 5th Marines battalion. After stopping the enemy thrust, the Marines counterattacked and, in temperatures exceeding 100 degrees, captured the NKPA hill position. Two days later the entire brigade, supported by Corsairs from the USS *Badoeng Strait* (CVE-116), drove the enemy thirty miles beyond the perimeter and captured NKPA headquarters at Chinju.

TOP: During the early weeks of the Korean War and prior to the first appearance of jet aircraft, Vought F4U-5N Corsairs piloted by Marines provided extremely effective close air support day or night.

ABOVE: During the fighting along the 38th parallel in March 1951, men from the 1st Marine Division capture a group of communist Chinese infantry defending the southern edge of the Iron Triangle.

Helicopters—A New Evolving Doctrine

During July 1946 General Geiger, commanding the Fleet Marine Force, Pacific, witnessed test atomic explosions at Bikini Atoll and immediately afterwards wrote Commandant Vandegrift urging a complete review of amphibious concepts. Vandegrift formed a board, essentially asking how Marines could achieve the surprise, speed, and dispersion needed to survive on a potentially atomic battlefield. The board replied, "vertical envelopment"—which meant that instead of assaulting a beachhead frontally in concentrated, slow-moving waves of landing craft, Marines should leapfrog the beach using carrier-based helicopters.

In 1948, Colonel Edward C. Dyer formed Marine Helicopter Squadron I and began training at Quantico using Sikorsky helicopters, which then could lift only two combat-equipped Marines. Colonels Merrill B. Twining and Victor H. Krulak began pulling together the first manual (Phib-31) of helicopter amphibious doctrine. In August the squadron received its first Piasecki HRP-1 helicopters, which could carry six combat-ready Marines.

Twining and Krulak kept pushing for better rotary-wing aircraft, and in 1950 the first Sikorsky HO2S-1 helicopters became available for reconnaissance. A year later, transport helicopter squadron HMR-161 arrived in Korea with larger Sikorsky HRS-1s for troop- and supply-carrying operations. The HRS-1 became the first helicopter capable of operating without an airfield.

During the next two years in Korea, HRS-1s and HO2S-1s airlifted more than 60,000 men, 7.5 million tons of cargo, and evacuated 9,815 wounded.

LEFT: A Sikorsky HRS-1 Chickasaw helicopter hovers close to the ground as Marines hook a cargo net filled with 1,000 pounds of supplies and ammunition for airlifting to the front lines twelve miles away.

On August 12, as the brigade pushed toward Sachon, the 3rd Battalion, 5th Marines, received an urgent call to plug a gap twenty-five miles away where 2,000 enemy troops had infiltrated the perimeter and overrun two army artillery battalions. Helicopters delivered the 3rd Battalion to the site, and the infiltration ended in disaster for the NKPA.

During six days of fighting, two Marine fighter-bomber squadrons, night-fighter squadron VMF(N)-513, and observation squadron VMO-6, using helicopters and light planes, joined ground forces and supplied direct support. Before Marines could completely rid the area of the enemy, the 4th NKPA Division crossed the Naktong River thirty miles to the north, pushed back the 24th Infantry Division, and compelled General Craig to plug another hole.

In a series of fiercely fought battles along the Naktong River, Marines blasted T-34 tanks with rockets, fought off repeated infiltrations, recovered the dominating ridges, and on August 18 began smashing one NKPA position after the other. The enemy, completely routed, streamed back across the Naktong to regroup. Every plane from MAG-33 and VFM(N)-513 clobbered the river crossings. The rapid destruction of T-34 tanks so impressed General Collins that he sought and obtained a letter from General Craig explaining how the Marines did it.

MacArthur wanted Craig's brigade for the Inchon landing and on September 5 the 2nd Army Division relieved the Marines. The First Provisional Brigade marched back to Pusan, heads held high, and joined the 1st Marine Division. Craig's tactics added a new chapter to modern warfare, marking the first time that air and ground elements, task-organized under a single commander, engaged in combat. At a cost of 902 casualties, including 172 killed, Marines had covered 380 miles in thirty-eight days and fought three major battles without one leatherneck becoming a prisoner. MAG-33 flew 1,500 sorties, 1,000 in close air support over ground units, and, for the first time in war, Marines used helicopters in combat.

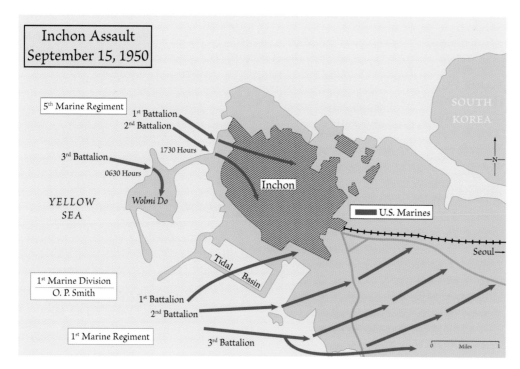

Inchon Assault
September 15, 1950

5th Marine Regiment — 1st Battalion — 2nd Battalion

3rd Battalion — 1730 Hours

0630 Hours

YELLOW SEA — Wolmi Do

Inchon

SOUTH KOREA

—N—

U.S. Marines

Seoul→

Tidal Basin

1st Marine Division
O. P. Smith — 1st Battalion — 2nd Battalion

1st Marine Regiment — 3rd Battalion

0 Miles 1

ABOVE: General MacArthur made the right decision when he chose the 1st Marine Division to spearhead the assault at Inchon. The Marines captured every objective on schedule and opened the way for the X Army Corps. In tribute, MacArthur said, "The Navy and the Marines have never shone more brightly . . ."

ABOVE RIGHT: Carrying ladders to scale the high seawalls surrounding Inchon, the 5th Marines head for shore on September 15, 1950, to execute one of the greatest tactical assaults in the history of warfare.

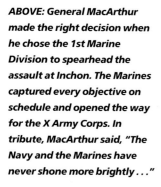

We shall land at Inchon and we shall crush them.
General MacArthur to his planning staff.

Planning Inchon

The JCS did not believe that Cates could have the 1st Marine Division ready for the Inchon assault in accordance with MacArthur's timetable, and exacerbated the problem by not immediately giving the operation the green light. MacArthur made three requests to the JCS before they released the division. Cates put the JCS straight by guaranteeing that the unit would be ready for the Inchon assault.

Cates could not keep his promise without mobilizing the reserves, which he promptly did with Truman's unenthusiastic approval. To assemble the men needed, Cates borrowed 6,800 troops from the 2nd Division on the East Coast and transported them to Camp Pendleton. He pulled the 3rd Battalion, 6th Marines, from the Mediterranean Sixth Fleet and sent them through the Suez Canal to Japan. He drew another 4,500 men from posts around the world. By adding Craig's brigade, already in Korea, Cates assembled in fifty-three days 24,000 Marines for a reinforced war-strength division and 4,000 more to fill the air wing.

On August 22, 1950, when division commander Major General Oliver P. Smith, USMC, arrived in Tokyo with his planning staff, he did not know that MacArthur had already set September 15 as D-Day, Inchon. He learned that to float an amphibious force up to the seawalls encasing Inchon required a thirty-three-foot tide, which occurred only on September 15 and again in mid-October. Smith doubted whether he could complete the planning in the time allotted, but MacArthur insisted he must. He expected Smith's 1st Marine Division to spearhead the assault, followed by Major General Edward M. Almond's X Corps and the army's 7th Infantry Division.

Neither Smith nor the JCS agreed with MacArthur's risky Inchon-Seoul operation. Even Seventh Fleet commander Admiral Arthur D. Struble had his doubts. But Smith had no say in the decision, and the JCS merely voiced their objections and let MacArthur have his way.

MacArthur's plan involved four steps: an amphibious landing at Inchon; the capture of Seoul and Kimpo Airfield twenty miles to the east; cutting

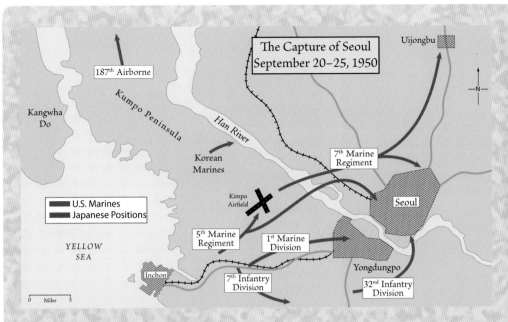

The Capture of Seoul
September 20–25, 1950

The Inchon-Seoul Assault

At 5:45 a.m., September 15, 1950, naval guns fell silent after softening-up enemy fortifications on Wolmi-do. Minutes later, landing craft containing Lieutenant Colonel Robert D. Taplett's 3rd Battalion, 5th Marines, chugged toward shore. Corsair squadrons VMF-214 and VMF-323, fresh from Pusan, swooped overhead providing air cover. At 6:15 air attacks ceased, giving way to a blanket salvo of 5-inch rockets launched from three rocket ships. Fifteen minutes later Marines scrambled ashore on Wolmi-do and overran the enemy's defenses. At 7:00 a.m., as MacArthur watched from the deck of the command ship Mount McKinley (AGC-7), Taplett broke out the colors on Radio Hill. Turning to his fellow officers, MacArthur said, "That's it. Let's get a cup of coffee." The 3rd Battalion mopped up the island and by noon had knocked out every enemy position covering the main landing approaches to Inchon.

Naval guns and air strikes continued to pummel Inchon throughout the day, and at 5:30 p.m. the 1st and 2nd Battalions, 5th Marines, reached the high seawall rimming the city. Using scaling ladders to get over the wall, the regiment advanced against light resistance, moving steadily toward the main road to Seoul.

On the far right flank and covered by another naval bombardment, Colonel Lewis B. Puller's 1st Marine Regiment landed south of Inchon. Puller swung the regiment north to the railroad and highway to cut off the approach of enemy reinforcements. By the following afternoon, the assault phase of the operation concluded in total success with only twenty-two Marines killed and 174 wounded.

General Smith deposited Korean marines in the rear to mop up Inchon, and pushed on to Seoul. On September 17, the 3rd Battalion, 5th Marines, captured

Kimpo Airfield, located midway between Inchon and Seoul. At nightfall, the first Marine helicopter landed with General Shepherd and Colonel Krulak. Two days later MAG-33 landed at Kimpo and began flying air support for Almond's X Army Corps.

Puller's 1st Marines pushed along the Inchon-Seoul highway towards Yongdung-po, brushing off the first of several NKPA counterattacks. On September 21, Puller found the enemy massed, with Soviet tanks, on Seoul's outskirts. While Company A worked around the enemy's flanks, the rest of the regiment blasted the tanks, routed the force in front, and walked into Yongdung-po in the morning. The 1st and 5th Marines then crossed the Han River and, joined by the 7th Marines and the 7th Infantry Division, pushed into Seoul. After a pitched house-to-house battle that lasted three days, the X Corps mopped up the city and secured Seoul.

TOP LEFT: After assaulting Inchon, Marines led the X Army Corps down the main road, capturing Kimpo Airfield and the capital city of Seoul, thus making it possible for the South Korean government to return from Pusan.

TOP: The hardest fighting through the streets of Seoul fell to the 1st Marines, who entered the city on September 20, 1950, and spent the next five days battling North Korean snipers lurking in buildings or behind barricades.

ABOVE: While fighting raged around Seoul, Marine Pfc Luther Leguire climbed to the roof of the U.S. consulate compound on September 27, 1950, and raised the Stars and Stripes.

ABOVE: At 6:30 a.m. on D-Day, following a heavy naval bombardment, landing craft head filled with Lieutenant Colonel R. D. Taplett's 3rd Battalion, 5th Marines, head for the smoking beaches at Wolmi-do.

ABOVE RIGHT: After the round-up of North Korean troops on September 26, 1950, a Marine tank guards a column of prisoners being escorted through a village street in the suburbs of Seoul.

NKPA supply lines across the Korean peninsula; and then crushing the NKPA in a vise between Almond's X Corps and Lieutenant General Walton H. Walker's Eighth Army, which would advance north from the Pusan perimeter. Opposition to the plan came from Collins and General Omar Bradley, both of whom scorned amphibious operations, but MacArthur believed in them, provided that Marines led the way.

A complicated chain of command threatened to muddle the plan of assault. The vital working parts involved Smith's 1st Marine Division as the assault force, and Rear Admiral James H. Doyle's Amphibious Group One as the naval support force. Superimposed over this team was General Almond, MacArthur's chief of staff, an irritating and conservative army officer who objected to assaulting a defended city against unknown odds and unpredictable tides. There were better places along the Korean coast to land an amphibious force, but none so close to the capital of Seoul and the airfield at Kimpo. As events later proved, MacArthur would have been better served by leaving Almond on staff and giving full command to Smith, but putting a Marine

general in charge of an army Corps would have upset the JCS.

Inchon's obstacles were daunting. Eight-knot tidal currents swept in and out of the channel. Seaward approaches contained bottomless flats and mounds of mud interposed by hazardous islets. During high tide, water flooded the shore and came partway up the granite walls of the city. Jutting into the sea, the fortified and cave-pocked island of Wolmi-do, connected by a 600-foot causeway to Inchon, defended the approaches to Inchon's harbor. Before an amphibious force could get to the city, the 3rd Battalion, 5th Marines, had to assault and neutralize Wolmi-do on the morning tide so that the 1st Marine Division could assault the city on the evening tide: the window of opportunity being thirty minutes on either side of 7:00 a.m. and 5:15 p.m. The 7th Marines had not arrived, nor would it in time for the assault, and although the enemy had only 2,200 troops at Inchon, there were more than 21,000 in the Seoul-Kimpo area. General Almond continued to complain about the planning and the unlikelihood of success, but even though two typhoons threatened to disperse the transports and delay the operation, MacArthur tenaciously maintained his timetable.

Applying the Vise

Although many military experts opposed the Inchon assault, it developed into a brilliant success that undoubtedly exceeded MacArthur's own expectations. General Walker's Eighth Army broke out of the Pusan perimeter, closed the vise on the NKPA, and with the X Army Corps finished the emasculation of the enemy. During the campaign, the Marines alone captured 4,700 prisoners, inflicted 13,700 casualties, and destroyed forty-four enemy tanks without losing one of their own. MAG-33 flew 2,500 sorties, mostly in close air support. Marine casualties numbered 2,774, including 457 killed.

Riding high on his accomplishments, MacArthur obtained approval from Truman and the United Nations to conduct operations above the 38th parallel and gave the task of capturing Pyongyang, the North Korean capital, to the Eighth Army. Smith's 1st Marine Division fell under the jurisdiction of X Corps commander General Almond, which immediately resulted in a dispute. Almond wanted Smith to launch an amphibious assault on Wonsan, located on the east coast, but Smith said he could get to Wonsan faster by hiking overland. Smith lost the argument because Almond insisted that an amphibious landing would be "cheaper."

On October 12 the 1st Marine Division sailed to Wonsan, but the navy found the harbor seeded with thousands of Soviet mines and the Marines spent a week cruising about the Sea of Japan while minesweepers cleared the harbor. When Marines finally disembarked at Wonsan, they found the ROK army in possession of the city and Bob Hope's USO entourage entertaining the troops.

On October 20, after Walker's Eighth Army captured Pyongyang, MacArthur decided to push up the peninsula to the Yalu River, which separated North

TOP: Not all close air support operations were flown from airfields: on November 10, 1951, ordnance crews fuse 500-pound and 100-pound bombs on board the carrier Bon Homme Richard for missions against North Korean forces.

ABOVE LEFT: A Marine patrol closes on a Korean hut in a village a few miles north of the 38th parallel, where a Chinese sniper has been pestering operations near the front lines.

ABOVE: In a pre-battle engagement near Yang-gu in central Korea, a heavy machine gun crew from the 1st Marine Division riddles an enemy emplacement ahead of advancing infantry.

We are not re-treating. We are just attacking in a different direction.

General Oliver P. Smith, quoted in The New Breed, *by Andrew Geer.*

Korea from Manchuria. Almond split the X Army Corps and sent it up the eastern side of the peninsula, the 1st Marine Division on the left, the 7th Army Infantry Division on the right, and with the 3rd Army Infantry Division in reserve. At Hungnam, the Marines advanced up the western side of the Chosin Reservoir while the 7th Infantry Division and the I ROK Corps took the eastern side of the reservoir. On November 24, three days after forward elements from the 7th Infantry Division reached Hyesasnjin on the Manchurian border, 300,000 Chinese troops crossed the border into North Korea, with another 400,000 on the way.

ABOVE RIGHT: Leathernecks from the 1st Marine Division fight along a front reminiscent of a World War I "no man's land." Charges planted in a bunker explode and strew debris all over the landscape while a Marine waits with his rifle to eliminate any survivors.

RIGHT: Supported by Marine air strikes, the 7th Marines wearing and carrying cold weather equipment pass through Hamhung on November 1, 1950, and begin the ill-fated trek towards the Chosin Reservoir.

RIGHT: Stopped by Chinese forces at Yudam-ni, west of the Chosin Reservoir, the 5th and 7th Marine regiments begin pulling back to the command post at Koto-ri on the morning of November 28, 1950.

The Chosin Reservoir

On November 17, 1950, the 7th Marine Regiment reached Hagaru-ri, located on the lower end of the Chosin Reservoir, and waited for Smith to bring up the rest of the division. MacArthur had promised to "bring the boys home for Christmas," and no troops were more anxious to get the Korean business finished than the 1st Marine Division. General Smith pushed hard to get the men to the Yalu River, and during a blizzard on November 27 moved two regiments up to Yudam-ni. That night, with the mercury registering -20 degrees F and the wind howling, elements from three Chinese divisions under the command of General Shih-lun Sung struck the two Marine regiments at Yudam-ni. Sung planned to isolate the Marines by using a fourth division to cut the road to Smith's headquarters at Hagaru. For two days Marines held their position against eight Chinese divisions while in western Korea Walker's Eighth Army reeled back from the Yalu in a massive retreat. Almond immediately panicked and ordered the 1st Marine Division and army units east of the Chosin Reservoir to fall back to the port of Hungnam on the Sea of Japan. The 7th Infantry Division and the I ROK Corps responded to the order with alacrity, but the Marines regrouped at Hagaru because General Smith decided upon a different plan.

By November 29, Chinese Communist Forces (CCF) had completely encircled the 1st Marine Division near the Chosin Reservoir. Although Almond disagreed with Smith's plan for a fighting withdrawal, he nevertheless turned the 7th Infantry and I ROK divisions, which were being encircled on the opposite side of the reservoir, over to Smith as the only way of possibly rescuing them. Smith sent Brigadier General Puller to open the road to Hagaru for the withdrawal. Puller's force attacked the enemy, opened the only available road to Hagaru, and formed a stubborn perimeter. At nightfall, December 3, after a five-day battle, the 5th and 7th Marines stumbled into Hagaru from Yudam-ni singing "The Marine Hymn." They brought all their weapons, serviceable equipment, and 1,500 wounded. Smith held the Hagaru road for three days, enabling Marine R4Ds and USAF C-47s to fly in and evacuate more than 4,400 Marines and infantry.

On December 6, Smith used the 1st Marine Division to spearhead the withdrawal through Koto-ri along a single narrow supply road that stretched fifty-six miles back to Hamhung. Close air support provided by land- and carrier-based aircraft covered the fighting withdrawal. On the first ten-mile leg, Smith's 14,000 Marines and infantry fought off four CCF divisions, losing only 100 killed, 500 wounded, and seven

missing. Five miles south of Koto-ri lay Funchilin Pass, a ten-mile frozen corridor where the Chinese had concentrated the bulk of their forces. Although the CCF blew up roads, hillsides, and bridges in an effort to trap Marines in pockets, Smith used an emergency airstrip laid down at Koto-ri to bring in bridge spans and other equipment to keep the road open. Fierce fighting continued all the way to Hamhung, where Smith found reinforcements waiting from Almond's X Corps.

ABOVE: When the 5th and 7th Marines withdrew from the Chosin River, they fought their way back to Koto-ri. Some of the men fell in behind a pair of M26 Pershing tanks that had kept the road open.

LEFT: During the consolidation and withdrawal of army and Marine forces at Hagaru-ri, Marine F4U Corsairs flying close air support bombed and strafed Chinese forces night and day for more than three weeks.

ABOVE LEFT: Following the bloody breakout from the Chosin Reservoir in December 1950, leathernecks pay their respects to fallen buddies during memorial services at the 1st Marine Division's cemetery at Hamhung.

ABOVE: *Flying an F9F Panther armed with four napalm bombs, a pilot targets on a troop billeting and supply center near Pyongyang. Ninety-two planes follow, armed with fragmentary bombs and napalm.*

A War of Politics

On January 1, 1951, the CCF launched a 500,000-man offensive against Allied forces formed along the 38th parallel, and three days later recaptured Seoul. Lieutenant General Matthew B. Ridgway took command of the Eighth Army, assumed control of all land operations, and posted the 1st Marine Division in reserve. With no more amphibious operations planned, Ridgway incorporated Marine air units into the USAF. Like it or not, the Marines found themselves shackled to the army and air force in a war of attrition.

The situation changed little until February 24, when the commander of the IX Army Corps died of a heart attack. Ridgway put General Smith in charge of the corps, and General Puller assumed command of the 1st Marine Division. Ridgway then decided upon a counteroffensive spearheaded by Marines. On March 14 Marines drove the CCF out of Seoul, and Ridgway's counteroffensive sent the enemy reeling back to the 38th parallel.

MacArthur now had a clear victory, and he wanted to destroy the bridges over the Yalu River to prevent the CCF from bringing more troops and supplies into Korea. Fearful of a broader war, President Truman and the United Nations scotched the proposal. MacArthur

BELOW: *General Lewis B. Puller (1898–1971) joined the Marines in 1918 and established a record as a front line commander. In Korea he won his fifth Navy Cross, the most awarded in Marine Corps history.*

During the "attack in a different direction" to Hamhung, Smith's unified Marine-army-ROK units fought fourteen divisions from four CCF army groups and inflicted 38,000 casualties. Since landing at Wonsan, the Marines had suffered 4,400 battle casualties, including 718 dead, 192 missing, and hundreds of cases of untreated frostbite. They left nothing behind but a battlefield strewn with Chinese corpses and useless equipment.

By December 10, 1950, Marines were the only American division north of the 38th parallel with the capability and the will to fight. Smith began withdrawing through Hungnam only after receiving direct orders from MacArthur. On that day, Admiral Doyle's task force began embarking 105,000 U.S. and ROK troops, 91,000 civilians, and 350,000 tons of supplies. The evacuation took two weeks. Relieved to see the leathernecks go, General Sung did not interfere.

ABOVE: *During operations along the 38th parallel in 1951, Marines launch a 4.5-inch rocket barrage against Red Chinese forces preparing an assault that collapsed before it got underway.*

continued to argue forcibly for an all-out bombing campaign against Manchuria's airfields and industrial sites. Truman lost patience with him. He recalled MacArthur and replaced him with Ridgway, who agreed with Truman's views. On April 14, Lieutenant General James A. Van Fleet arrived to command U.N. ground forces. One week later the CCF launched a 700,000-strong spring offensive.

During a Chinese night attack on April 22, Puller had posted the 1st Marine Division in the Iron Triangle, about thirty miles north of the 38th parallel. The CCF caromed off the left flank of the Marines and shattered the 6th ROK Division. By daylight the CCF had driven ten miles deep and ten miles wide, but the Marines had not budged an inch. With other elements of the IX Corps in jeopardy, Smith ordered Puller to pull back to the main line. Puller fought a vicious withdrawal, saving several IX Corps units from destruction.

Though the CCF lost 70,000 men during the offensive, on May 15 they tried again, this time on the eastern side of the peninsula. The Eighth Army counterattacked and pushed the Chinese back over the

38th parallel. The 1st Marine Division kept going and occupied the "Punchbowl," a volcanic area twenty-five miles above the parallel. Puller did not know the first ceasefire had been proposed. Though the first talks failed, the Korean War began resolving itself around the 38th parallel and possession of territory became politically important. When the CCF attempted to force the 1st Marine Division out of the Punchbowl, leathernecks experienced the most vicious fighting of the war but held the position. Puller used close air

ABOVE: After peace talks began to drag during the spring of 1953, the 1st Rocket Battery, 11th Marines, launched a midnight barrage against Chinese forces attempting to breach the regiment's perimeter.

LEFT: Marine infantry take cover behind an M26 Pershing tank during a May 22, 1951, assault on the highly contested ground around Hongchon, which lay a few miles south of the 38th parallel.

LEFT: On an airfield south of Seoul, F9F Panther jets rearm with rockets for another close air sortie against Chinese forces spilling across the 38th parallel during the spring of 1951.

LEFT: Panther jets made their combat debut in Korea. Because of soil conditions, once a jet landed it had to be towed to the assembly area to prevent dust from clogging the engines of other jets.

ABOVE: Helicopters from VMO-6 made their first appearance in Korea as observation aircraft, but the choppers soon proved their versatility by removing wounded or flying combat insertion and extraction missions.

support and Sikorsky HRS-1 helicopters for hit-and-run missions, reinforcing actions, evacuations, and logistics to hold a section of the Eighth Army's Main Line of Resistance, which angled across the peninsula from the Yellow Sea to the Sea of Japan until the July 27, 1953, the day of the armistice.

Marine Jets

Had it not been for the Korean War, Marines might still be flying a modern version of the popular propeller-driven F4U-4 Corsairs. But in Korea, the introduction of Soviet MiG fighters put Marines into jets. In April 1951 the navy staged the first bombing attacks using Grumman F9F Panther jets against CCF supply lines. Leatherneck flyers quickly shifted from the faithful Corsair to jet-powered Grumman F9F-2 Panthers and McDonnell F2H-2 Banshees. For air-ground operations, tactics quickly changed to accommodate the greater speed (575mph+) and ceiling (44,000 feet) of jet fighter-bombers, which offered a sturdier platform for guns, bombs, and rockets. After jets arrived, the casualty rate for pilots flying close air support dropped by half. Marine pilots began thumbing their noses at the MiGs. New squadrons of Marine jet night-fighters became the escorts for USAF B-29 bombers, whose crews specifically asked for Marine cover.

Major General Clayton C. Jerome, commanding Marine air in Korea, settled a dispute between the army and the USAF by providing air cover for the Eighth Army. When the recent separation of the two services threatened to interfere with operations on the ground, Jerome volunteered to use Marine pilots to protect the army's ground troops, and his flyers eventually became the tactical air force for the Eighth Army.

Marine air in Korea also marked another first. During October 1952, 2nd Lieutenant Frank E. Petersen completed his flight training and became the Marine Corps' first African-American pilot. Petersen went on to fly 350 combat missions in two wars, using Corsairs in Korea and F-4D Phantoms in Vietnam.

Between August 1950 and July 1953, the 1st Marine Air Wing flew more than 118,000 sorties, 40,000 of which were in close air support. Korea proved the versatility of Marine pilots. They could fly day or night from carriers or airfields and operate every type of aircraft from a helicopter to a jet fighter-bomber. Marines used the experience to revise the future doctrine of the Fleet Marine Force and study new ways to expand their niche in the armed services, all of which steadily evolved in later decades.

Marine Operations—Korean War	
Pusan Perimeter	August–September 1950
Inchon-Seoul Assault	September–October 1950
Chosin Reservoir Campaign	November–December 1950
U.N. Counteroffensive	March 1651
Chinese Counteroffensive	April–May 1951
Eastern Korea-Punchbowl	May 1951–March 1952
Main Line of Resistance	March 1952–July 1953
Post-Armistice duty of DMZ	July 1953–April 1955

"We Fight Our Country's Battles"

During the Korean War, forty-two Marines were awarded the Medal of Honor for heroism. All but sixteen were granted posthumously. On March 25, 1953, South Korean President Syngman Rhee awarded the entire 1st Marine Division the Korean Presidential Citation. After General Ridgway came to Korea, he quickly learned what MacArthur already knew, and used the 1st Marine Division to spearhead his assaults. Despite differences in doctrine, army generals discovered that Marines were the best-trained, -equipped, and -disciplined, and most tenacious fighters in the world. They would not fall back nor give an inch unless ordered, and then only grudgingly. MacArthur's demand for more Marines led to the passage of Public Law 416, the so-called Marine Corps

Bill, which expanded the Corps to three divisions, thus opening the way for Marines to become the nation's amphibious force in readiness around the world.

On January 1, 1952, when General Shepherd replaced Cates and became the 20th commandant of the Marine Corps, he moved from Washington to Quantico to head the Marine Corps Schools. Shepherd reorganized Marine Corps Headquarters along lines similar to the army's general staff. He redefined the Corps' responsibility, and as a sitting member of the JCS, began weaving recent air and weapons technology into new Marine doctrine.

The days of the old, under-appreciated Marine Corps had ended. Now with three permanent divisions, the rebuilding process could begin once more.

ABOVE: When the first round of cease-fire talks began at Panmunjon on October 11, 1951, they were led by Colonel James Murray, Jr., USMC, and Colonel Chang Chun San, of the North Korean Communist Army. The discussions involved the demarcation zone between the two Koreas. When no agreement was reached, talks continued off and on until the signing of the Korean armistice on July 23, 1953, which reestablished the separation line at the 38th parallel.

COLD WAR: VIETNAM 1961–1975

RIGHT: *France decided in 1946 to re-establish its colonial control over Indo-China and sent 40,000 troops to occupy the southern portion of the country and Cambodia. Eight years later France was still at war with Ho Chi Minh's Vietminh. During Operation Camargue on August 25, 1953, French and Indo-Chinese troops advance inland from the coast of central Vietnam.*

American involvement in Vietnam began on a very small scale in 1946 after France attempted to recover its former colony of Indo-China where, after the defeat of Japan, Ho Chi Minh began reorganizing the country under communist rule. President Truman took notice, but did not interfere. In 1950, after Mao Tse-tung defeated Chiang Kai-shek's Nationalists and took control of China, Truman did interfere with communist goals when he involved America in the Korean War. He also began supplying France with weapons, equipment, and military assistance with which to combat Ho's Vietminh. In 1953, when General Eisenhower succeeded Truman as president, he continued the policy of supporting France while avoiding direct involvement.

In 1954, the Vietminh trapped 12,000 French troops at Dienbienphu. Eisenhower's advisors urged

> First there was the Old Corps, then there was the New Corps. And now there's this god-damned thing.
> *Charles Coe,* Young Man in Vietnam.

him to intervene, and some advocated using nuclear weapons. Not wanting to involve Americans in another "hot war" while fighting a "cold war," Eisenhower declined. In July 1954, following a negotiated ceasefire, France signed an agreement dividing the former Indo-China at the 17th parallel into what became North Vietnam, controlled by Ho Chi Minh's communists, and South Vietnam, led by President Ngo Dinh Diem, a French-educated aristocrat and ardent anti-communist Catholic. Eisenhower promised economic and military assistance to Diem's government, and on August 2, 1954, Marine Lieutenant Colonel Victor Croizant arrived at Saigon as part of the Military Assistance and Advisory Group (MAAG), which by the end of Eisenhower's administration had grown to 685 advisors.

Diem proved to be incapable of leading South Vietnam. His corrupt and repressive government alienated the enormous working class. The Vietminh organized guerrilla operations to attack Diem's government. Despite disillusionment with Diem, Eisenhower continued to modestly support him.

TOP: During a ceremony in Hanoi for North Vietnam's political and military leadership, communist functionaries join an aging Ho Chi Minh, third from right, and General Vo Nguyen Giap, extreme left.

ABOVE: Mekong Delta villagers in the black pajamas of Viet Cong guerrillas file down a beaten path armed with Soviet-designed weapons.

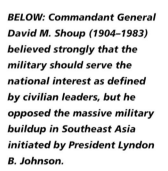

General Shoup's Marine Corps

Eisenhower had always been more interested in building the North Atlantic Treaty Organization (NATO) to buffer communism in Western Europe, and opposed struggling with problems in the Far East. He was also more interested in maintaining a strong army and saw little need for a Marine Corps. When Commandant General Randolph McCall Pate retired on December 31, 1959, Eisenhower searched the Marine Corps seniority list for a man who he thought would agree with his policies, and on January 1, 1960, he named 56-year-old Major General David Monroe Shoup commandant. Shoup had always been an independent and outspoken maverick officer who in 1926 slipped into the Corps through the ROTC program at DePauw University. He had also earned the Medal of Honor at Tarawa and became the first such recipient to sit with the JCS. The president's choice drove several senior Marine lieutenant generals into retirement, but Shoup proved to be a thorough Marine and a far better political tactician than Eisenhower anticipated.

Instead of reducing the three Marine divisions to regiment-size units, as Eisenhower proposed, Shoup expanded the Corps along with its capabilities. He replaced battle-tested M1 rifles with new M14 7.62mm rifles and exchanged the old reliable BARs with M60 machine guns. In 1960 he expanded the aviation cadet program and put Marines into the cockpits of F-4B Phantom jets, which came equipped with the latest weapons systems. While Marine air officers steadily improved the Corps' doctrine of readiness with better aircraft, other planners worked on improving the tactics of vertical assault.

Shoup also concentrated on improving the quality of volunteers entering the Corps. He expanded General Pate's "Devil Pup" program, which enabled teenagers to spend a few weeks training each summer at a Marine base, into a Physical Testing Program offered by Marines as a public service to the nation's high schools. The program nurtured self-esteem and enhanced the Corps' image as a civic force as well as a fighting force.

In one year, Shoup changed Eisenhower's mind about the Marine Corps. Before leaving office in 1961, Eisenhower submitted a budget for a Corps of three full divisions, three air wings, and 175,000 personnel.

Vietnam—A Boiling Pot

In 1961, President John F. Kennedy beefed up the Seventh Fleet with more Marines and sent them into the South China Sea. On April 12, 1962, some of those Marines landed in Thailand to help curb North Vietnamese incursions into Laos. During the same period, Marine Medium Helicopter Squadron 362 flew into the Mekong Delta near Saigon to support South Vietnamese Army (ARVN) troops fighting Viet Cong (VC). In 1962, Kennedy increased the number of American military advisors in South Vietnam to 4,000, including 600 Marines.

During 1962–1963, communist activities threatened to spread far beyond the shores of Vietnam, with ten major or potentially critical situations occurring in Germany, Taiwan, Laos, Cambodia, Cuba, Panama Canal Zone, Cyprus, Haiti, South America, and Zanzibar. The problems in Vietnam continued to escalate as each month passed.

On November 1, 1963, South Vietnamese generals, with support of the Kennedy administration, assassinated President Diem. Three weeks later in Dallas, Texas, an assassin killed President Kennedy. Lyndon B. Johnson assumed the presidency and watched as the government of South Vietnam changed nine times in eighteen months. On August 5, 1964, using the controversial Tonkin Gulf incident to rally American support, Johnson ordered carrier air strikes on North Vietnamese naval bases and oil depots. Two days later, Congress empowered Johnson to "take all necessary measures to repel any armed attack against the forces of the United States . . ." Having been given the authority to "Americanize" the war, Johnson increased U.S. military strength in Vietnam from 4,000 in 1962 to 23,000 in 1964.

Marine Commandants and the Vietnam War

During the early 1960s, Commandant General David M. Shoup had doggedly and openly opposed sending ground forces to Vietnam. For the four years Shoup served as commandant, General Greene had been his chief of staff. A brusque and no-nonsense Vermonter, Greene became the first Naval Academy graduate (1930) to serve as commandant of the Marine Corps. Unlike Shoup, he believed that the Vietnam War could be won if fought properly, which meant taking the war to North Vietnam, blockading and mining the port of Haiphong, blowing up the dikes and dams along the Red River supply line, and making an Inchon-like amphibious landing to capture Hanoi and remove Ho's government. Instead, Greene spent four years as commandant constantly frustrated by the weak and wavering policies of the president and his secretary of defense, Robert S. McNamara.

When Greene's term ended on December 31, 1967, Johnson replaced him with General Leonard Fielding Chapman, who one day later became the Corps' 24th commandant. Johnson believed that Chapman would be a more pliable team player than two better-qualified candidates—Lewis W. Walt, hero of three wars, and Victor H. Krulak, the brilliant commanding general of the Fleet Marine Force. Johnson soon discovered that his meandering warfighting policies displeased Chapman as much as they had annoyed Shoup and Greene.

After being named commandant, Chapman flew to Vietnam to evaluate conditions on the ground and arrived during the Tet Offensive (January 30–31, 1968). While there, Marines recaptured Hue and defended the combat base at Khe Sanh against the North Vietnamese army (NVA). Chapman knew the moment had come to mop up the severely weakened enemy and win the war, but Johnson balked. Chapman returned to Washington flabbergasted by the president's personal involvement in the small details of running the war. He observed many opportunities where a decision from Johnson or McNamara could have turned the tide. Completely disenchanted by executive interference, Chapman undertook a personal objective to get the Marines out of Vietnam in the best possible condition. Before turning his office over to Robert E. Cushman on January 1, 1972, Chapman told Marines in Vietnam to not "leave anything behind worth more than five dollars."

TOP: General Wallace M. Greene became commandant in 1964 and while in office advised that U.S. military power and credibility had become too committed to Vietnam to allow withdrawal without victory.

CENTER: General Leonard F. Fielding, Jr., became commandant in 1968 with the chore of systematically withdrawing 300,000 Marines from Vietnam.

LEFT: Robert E. Cushman, Jr., became commandant in 1972, after commanding the III Marine Amphibious Force in Vietnam. He clashed regularly with General William Westmoreland over the mismanagement of Marine assets.

Johnson's strategy for fighting the war became challenged by men who understood war, and nobody became more frustrated by the president's policies than General Wallace Martin Greene, Jr., who on January 1, 1964, became the Marine Corps' 23rd commandant.

ABOVE: As U.S. military presence increased, Viet Cong terrorist attacks escalated. The U.S. embassy in Saigon became one of the principal targets and was severely damaged in 1965 by a VC bomb.

BELOW: Major General Lewis W. Walt (1913–1989) commanded the 3rd Marine Division and the III Marine Amphibious Force in Vietnam from 1965 to 1967. Walt placed more emphasis on small-unit operations and pacification than did General Westmoreland.

How Not to Fight a War

President Johnson was a political heavyweight, not a military man. Secretary of Defense McNamara was a Ford Motor Company executive, also not a military man. But Johnson and McNamara decided how the war would be fought and made the mistake of trying to micromanage air and ground operations from Washington.

On February 7, 1965, when VC attacked an American barracks, killed eight servicemen, and wounded 126 others, Johnson approved Flaming Dart I: the bombing of Dong Hoi, a North Vietnamese port north of the DMZ. Three days later the VC struck back and bombed another barracks and a helicopter base at Qui Nhon. In reprisal, Johnson authorized Flaming Dart II, and U.S. carrier aircraft dropped bombs on Chan Hoa. When more VC reprisals followed, Johnson escalated the bombing campaign and authorized Rolling Thunder. The operation became a playground for McNamara's "Whiz Kids," who believed that incremental pressure on North Vietnam would eventually touch Ho Chi Minh's "ouch level" and induce peace talks. The enemy's "ouch level" remained untouched until December 1972, when President Richard M. Nixon authorized Linebacker II in an effort to blast North Vietnam to the negotiating table. During the in-between years, America fought its most unpopular war.

Marines at Danang

In March 1965, following the president's authorization of Rolling Thunder, Brigadier General Frederick J. Karch's 2nd and 3rd Battalion, Ninth Marine Expeditionary Brigade (MEB), trudged ashore to provide security for the airbase at Danang—the only airfield north of Saigon capable of handling jets. A gathering of garland-bearing Vietnamese schoolchildren and sightseers greeted the Marines on the beach. Four American soldiers based in Danang carried a sign: "Welcome Gallant Marines."

Karch's MEB represented the first commitment of combat troops to Vietnam. The battalions had been languishing on ships offshore for two months, waiting for orders. Lieutenant General Krulak had trained the brigade in counterinsurgency tactics against both large combat units and guerrillas. Danang's mayor and his staff registered shock after witnessing the businesslike landings. They had not expected Marines to arrive with tanks, artillery, and a pair of nuclear-capable 8-inch guns. A few days later Karch's 3rd Battalion arrived from Okinawa on KC-130 transports. As the planes approached Danang's 10,000-foot runway, VC greeted them with ground fire.

General Krulak exploded on learning that army General William C. Westmoreland, commanding American forces in Vietnam, had restricted Karch's combat-trained Marines to protecting Danang's airbase, which was surrounded by a fence in a city of 200,000 people, some of them hostile. Despite Westmoreland's orders, the 9th MEB made helicopter sorties into trouble spots outside Danang, and on one occasion defeated, without loss, a large VC force attempting to breach the airfield.

On April 10, VFMA-531 arrived with a squadron of F-4B Phantoms. By mid-1965 two fixed-wing and two rotary-wing Marine Air Groups (MAG 11, 12, 16, and 36) began operating in Vietnam.

During early May 1965, Danang officially became Marine headquarters when Major General William R.

Collins arrived with the 3rd Marine Division and rolled all units, including air groups, into the 9,000-man III Marine Amphibious Force (III MAF). Collins became immensely annoyed when General Nguyen Chanh Thi, the local ARNV commander, refused to give the Marines an expanded role by insisting that they continue to guard the airfield.

On May 5, Lieutenant General Lewis W. Walt arrived and assumed command of the III MAF. He wore two Navy Crosses and soon became the most widely admired Marine general in Vietnam. Meanwhile, Westmoreland had temporarily convinced President Johnson that "only American offensive operations could save Vietnam . . . from a VC military victory." With presidential permission, Westmoreland divided South Vietnam into four military districts. Walt's sector became the I Corps Tactical Zone headquartered at Danang. The zone encompassed five provinces consisting of 10,000 square miles running between the DMZ and the II Corps' sector to the south. The Annamite Mountains formed a topographical barrier separating the two corps.

General Thi—known in Saigon as the "Warlord of the North"—commanded 30,000 ARNV troops and 23,000 militiamen of the so-called Popular Forces. Thi insisted that the ARNV control the rural and inland areas, though most of his troops seldom strayed from Danang. The Popular Forces were to act as security for the hamlets and villages, but many of the men were VC. Thi expected the Marines to continue guarding the airfield, but Walt now had enough men to do as he pleased. He wanted more control over the 2.6 million people who lived in the provinces of his military district, and launched his own program.

Expanding Air Operations

Walt demanded more airfields in the northern provinces and did not wait for concessions from General Thi to build them. On May 7, 1965, General

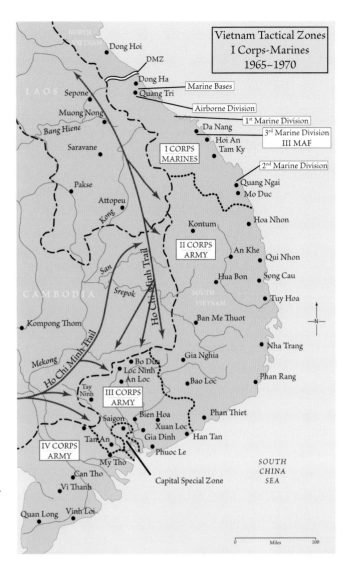

Vietnam Tactical Zones
I Corps-Marines
1965–1970

LEFT: Operations in South Vietnam were divided into four sectors, each with a Corps. The I Corps consisted mostly of Marines who militarily controlled the five provinces between the DMZ and the northern sector of the II Corps.

BELOW LEFT: When the 3rd Marine Division landed at Danang on August 3, 1965, many of the young volunteers looked like naïve boys out of high school without the slightest idea of the task before them.

BELOW: During August 1865 a gunner in a Sikorsky CH-34 Choctaw helicopter opens on Viet Cong in the Elephant Valley northwest of Danang while Marine medevacs in other helicopters begin disembarking to extract severely wounded men.

ABOVE: Two McDonnell Douglas F-4B Phantoms from VMFA-542, Marine Aircraft Group 2 (MAG-2), 1st Marine Aircraft Wing out of Danang, prepare to support Marines battling an NVA division assaulting the Khe Sanh firebase during January 1968.

ABOVE RIGHT: A Douglas A-4E Skyhawk of VMFA-211, 1st Marine Air Wing, with a payload of fragmentary bombs prepares to take off in 1967 from Chu Lai's improvised airbase during operations in Quang Ngai Province.

RIGHT: Chairman Nguyen Van Thieu, President Lyndon B. Johnson, and Prime Minister Nguyen Cau Ky salute during the playing of the U.S. and Vietnamese National Anthems during welcoming ceremonies at Guam's International Airport at Agana on March 20, 1967.

Krulak put the 1st and 2nd Battalion, 4th Marines, and several hundred Seabees on a beach in Quang Tin Province, fifty-five miles south of Danang. The site had no name, so Krulak called it Chu Lai, his own name in Mandarin Chinese. While Marines established a perimeter, Seabees built the first Short Airfield for Tactical Support. On June 1, the first Marine A-4 Skyhawks flew in from the Philippines and landed on a 4,000-foot strip of aluminum matting. The new airfield resembled the deck of an aircraft carrier, complete with arrester wires. Flyers called it the "tinfoil strip" and used jet-assisted take-off (JATO) bottles to get airborne. Chu Lai's Skyhawks and helicopters became immediately involved in reconnaissance and combat operations.

By 1968, the I Corps operated thirteen tactical airstrips and two jet operational airfields, one at Danang and one at Chu Lai. Westmoreland attempted to transfer Walt's F-4 Phantoms and RF-8A Crusader squadrons to Major General Joseph H. Moore's USAF command but lost the battle. Westmoreland became so impressed with Marine tactical air support that he asked the navy to attach more squadrons to carriers posted offshore.

Johnson Takes the Offensive

On July 1, 1965, VC guerillas broke through General Thi's ill-prepared ARNV guards, attacked the Danang airbase, reached the runway, destroyed three planes, and damaged three others. After leathernecks mopped up the guerrillas, Walt confronted Thi on his policy of restricting Marines to the airbase, and the general relented. The attack also induced President Johnson to up the ante. On a nationally televised address on July 28, 1965, the president increased the commitment

of U.S. forces from 75,000 to 125,000. The announcement added 55,000 men to the Marine Corps. Johnson now had his war, and having made the commitment, he continued to throw more units into Vietnam, eventually expanding the Marine Corps to 280,000.

Operation Starlite

By mid-August 1965, the Marines had four regiments and four air groups scattered among the I Corps sector. General Walt again complained to Westmoreland, citing Thi's inability to suppress VC operations in rural areas outside Danang. During the same period, President Johnson modified his policy of restraint and secretly authorized Westmoreland to engage in counterinsurgency combat operations. Walt responded immediately. He sent patrols fifty miles beyond Danang to break up heavy concentrations of VC.

Walt's ability to operate with less restraint resulted in Operation Starlite, an amphibious assault against the 1st Viet Cong Regiment camped on the Van Tuong Peninsula, which lay fifteen miles south of Chu Lai. On August 18, 1965, supported by air and naval gunfire, 4,000 Marines from Walt's Regimental Landing Team 7 went ashore and engaged in the first major ground action between U.S. and VC troops. Other elements, transported by helicopters from the *Iwo Jima* (LPH-2), landed inland. At a cost of forty-five Marines, the six-day battle wiped out the VC regiment, killing 964 and capturing 125. VC survivors learned a harsh lesson. They could not win a head-to-head battle with Marines.

Two months passed before the VC struck again. On October 27-28, using tactics of surprise and self-preservation, VC sappers struck the Marble Mountain Marine base near Danang and destroyed or damaged forty-seven helicopters. At Chu Lai, another raiding party damaged eight A-4 Skyhawks. The VC attacked swiftly and dissolved into nearby villages. The raids

ABOVE: In the aftermath of Operation Starlite—a search and destroy mission south of Chu Lai in August 1965—Marines killed 599 Viet Cong but captured only six, who sit silently on the ground, waiting to be embarked on a CH-34 helicopter in the background.

marked the beginning of lightning attacks on Marine outposts by VC hiding among the civilian population.

Viet Cong guerrillas proved to be well trained, adept, and stealthy fighters. They carried modern weapons, were well fed and clothed, deeply indoctrinated in communist dogma, and willing by the thousands to sacrifice their lives to unify the country under Ho's regime. Marines discovered that VC had infiltrated General Thi's ARNV to the extent that Walt began to question the loyalty of some of the officers in South Vietnam's army.

Strategy and Escalation

In December 1965, as monsoon rains turned red earthen roads to muck and low clouds charged with moisture obscured ground targets from air attacks, President Johnson called a bombing halt, thinking that doing so might encourage peace talks. The effort failed

TOP: A Marine Rifleman from Company H in Lieutenant Colonel Hal. L. Coffman's 2nd Battalion, 5th Marines, leaps across a break in a rice paddy during a search and destroy mission in Quang Tin Province during Operation Colorado on August 15, 1966.

RIGHT: During Operation Hastings, which ended on August 3, 1966, Marines of Company H, 2nd Battalion, 4th Marines, wade quietly down a creek toward a suspected enemy position near the DMZ at Dong Ha.

Battalion, 1st Marines, and the 2nd Battalion, 4th Marines, went ashore near Thach Tru. The following day, the 2nd Battalion, 3rd Marines, flew in by helicopter and landed five miles west of the beach. The 2nd Battalion, 9th Marines, advanced from Quang Ngai's airstrip and moved into the mountain fringes northwest of the beach. A series of firefights ensued, during which the NVA withdrew into the Que Son Valley. During the fighting, Marines grappled for the first time with hardened NVA regulars armed with Soviet weapons: AK-47 assault rifles, heavy machine guns and mortars, and deadly B-40 rocket-propelled grenades. Marines punished the NVA, but casualty counts were about equal.

During March 1966, the 1st Marine Division arrived and joined the 3rd Division, marking the first time since World War II that two Marine divisions had been committed to the same war zone. The 1st Division, after sending two regiments to Chu Lai, settled into Danang, and the 3rd Division moved fifty miles north to Hue. By then the Marines had conceived a new strategy—pacification.

Pacification—Winning Hearts and Minds

The concept of pacification traced back to the summer of 1965 when Generals Walt and Krulak decided to use Marine patrols circulating through Danang's countryside to treat villagers with kindness while rooting out VC "sleepers." Although autumn operations netted about 400 VC guerrillas living in sundry villages, Marines paid a heavy toll in casualties. Nevertheless, the program worked quite well in some districts, and in 1966 Walt and Krulak believed that welfare work and civic action would eventually "win the hearts and the minds" of the Vietnamese. Marines modified the slogan: "Grab them by the balls and their hearts and minds will follow."

The program started off well. Companies composed of a squad of Marines with local volunteers circulated

but gave the VC more than a month to reorganize and rearm. When scattered fighting resumed in February, Marines discovered large North Vietnamese army units assembling in the Annemite Mountains between the I and II Corps' Tactical Zones.

Walt did not wait to be attacked, and combined four Marine battalions with the army's 1st Air Cavalry Division for an assault against the 325A NVA Division in Quang Ngai Province. On January 28, 1966, in the largest Vietnam amphibious operation to date, the 3rd through villages cleaning out VC on one hand while distributing food and aid with the other. Medical teams followed and set up tents. Villagers soon appeared in droves to receive treatment and returned home with medicine, disinfectants, soap, and bandages.

Where Marines established safe zones, volunteers built schools and orphanages, dug wells, improved sanitation, opened markets, and distributed food provided by CARE. As the program progressed, villages near Danang asked the 9th Marines to provide protection during the months of harvest. Walt organized Operation Golden Fleece, and safeguarding the harvest became an annual event. Pacification in Quang Nam Province worked so well that Walt organized a Joint Coordinating Council of Marines and Vietnamese volunteers to expand the program.

As pacification spread to other provinces, Walt and Krulak became concerned that humanitarianism efforts would have little lasting effect unless villagers received permanent protection. In early 1966 the two generals initiated Operation County Fair, using combined Marine/Vietnamese forces augmented by civic action groups to root out VC agents hiding in the communities. County Fair participants made every effort to prevent VC counteraction that might turn the village into a battleground and civilians into unintended targets.

The pacification strategy, though never free of problems, worked successfully in areas controlled by Marines. The army remained skeptical. In an unauthorized action on March 16, 1968, the army severely damaged the success of pacification efforts

All of this has meaning only if you are going to stay. Are you going to stay?
District Chief of Le My to General Krulak,
quoted from Krulak, First to Fight.

The Vietnam Marine

In addition to mud, Marines lugged a mix of weapons and equipment. Riflemen carried an M16 gas-operated, automatic rifle capable of firing 800 rounds a minute, at least 150 rounds of ammunition, and two grenades. In addition to firearms, machine gun crews draped themselves with belts of 1,200 linked cartridges, and 3.5-inch rocket-launcher teams carried five high explosive and five white phosphorous rockets. Everyone carried a backpack, canteen, steel helmet, flak jacket, first-aid supplies, and rations. If grenadiers joined the patrol, they carried twenty-eight 40mm shells for their stubby M79s. Riflemen often added portable antitank weapons to their normal load. To aggravate the misery of carrying eighty pounds of gear through rice patties, elephant grass, and jungles, temperatures often exceeded 105 degrees, with high humidity and no shade or breeze.

TOP: During a Viet Cong ambush at An Hoa in 1967, a Marine M29 mortar team sets up behind a barricade during the firefight and drops 81mm shells on buildings sheltering the enemy.

ABOVE: An exhausted young Marine returns from patrol near Gio Linh on March 25, 1967, carrying a standard issue M14 7.62mm rifle with a 20-round magazine. His M14 is capable of semiautomatic and automatic fire.

ABOVE: During Operation New Castle on March 26, 1967, Marines locate a Viet Cong conclave in a hamlet deep in the jungle. After dealing with the enemy, a Marine with a flamethrower incinerates the huts and renders the area unserviceable.

During the spring of 1966, the NVA showed signs of becoming more active in South Vietnam. To defend against a possible invasion, Major General Lewis J. Fields distributed the 1st Marine Division through the southern provinces of Quang Nam, Quang Tin, and Quang Ngai. Major General Wood B. Kyle's 3rd Marine Division covered the upper two provinces from Danang to the DMZ. In July, Walt learned that the 324B NVA Division had crossed the DMZ and moved into the northern-most province of Quang Tri. He now had a war on two fronts plus an infiltration of VC raising havoc with the rice harvest.

On July 15, 1966, Walt launched Operation Hastings—8,000 men from the III MAF and 3,000 ARNV troops—in a sweep through Quang Tri Province to clear out the enemy. Supported by ground-directed bombing, Marines captured the 700-foot hill called the "Rockpile" from which they could observe and target enemy movements. After two weeks of fighting, a thousand NVA troops lay dead in the bamboo stands and elephant grass, but thousands more dissolved into the jungle and continued to fight. Walt dedicated three battalions to root out the survivors, and the hunt continued for nine more months.

The enemy discovered they could not win battles fighting Marines, so they resorted to other tactics. They set punji bear-traps in the jungle, an ancient device consisting of two boards with spikes. When stepped on, the boards sprung like jaws and drove spikes into the leg. VC also laid trip wires connected to grenades, and Marines learned to walk cautiously during combat patrols. The VC also coaxed Marines into minefields and then disappeared into the jungle. They mined rice patties, especially during the planting and harvest season, forcing Marines to use amphibious vehicles to detonate the devices. Each Marine collected about twenty pounds of mud as he slogged behind an amtrac, adding extra weight to an already heavy load.

when Lieutenant William Calley, leading an inexperienced and poorly disciplined platoon from the 23rd Infantry Division, panicked and massacred 347 Vietnamese civilians at My Lai.

A War on Many Fronts

In March 1966, Marines launched two offenses with the ARNV to rescue South Vietnamese troops surrounded by VC outside the town of An Hoa, located thirty-five miles south of Danang. The operation wiped out the VC, but a Buddhist uprising against the government in Saigon overshadowed the victory. The political disturbance affected Buddhist ARVN soldiers cooperating with the Marines. Some became rebellious and joined the enemy. General Walt restored order with a minimum of bloodshed, but the action weakened pacification. VC capitalized on the turmoil and infiltrated previously "sanitized" villages.

Operations on the DMZ

With the incursion of more NVA units, the DMZ became a hotbed of activity. To disrupt infiltration, Major Bernard Trainor (later lieutenant general) developed seven-man Sting Ray reconnaissance teams to patrol the DMZ and the Laotian border, to interdict enemy supply routes. Helicopters inserted Sting Ray teams, often behind enemy lines, and later extracted them. After spotting enemy activity, the team called in fire coordinates for artillery, napalm-carrying fighter-bombers, and helicopter gunship assaults. No team went behind enemy lines without having at least two artillery pieces dedicated as direct support somewhere in the rear. The insertions became extremely valuable for destroying and keeping tabs on the enemy.

Oddly enough, because of the rising toll of American casualties, President Johnson demanded daily data on enemy body counts. When one company commander asked for a body count from a returning patrol, the team's feisty gunnery sergeant replied, "Let the stupid son-of-a-bitch come to Nam and count his own goddamned gooks. Who the hell has time for that?"

From August 1966 to May 1967, the Marines conducted four "Operation Prairie" search-and-destroy missions between the DMZ and Route 9, and during ten months of fighting lost 525 killed and 3,167 wounded. Prairie operations ranged from seven-man patrols to pitched battles involving up to seven Marine and three ARNV battalions facing off against reinforced NVA divisions straight through the monsoon season.

In conjunction with Prairie, the Marines established an air and combat base on the Khe Sanh plateau near the Laotian border, fourteen miles south of the DMZ. Jungles and hills surrounded the base. On April 24, 1967, the 325C NVA Division pushed regiments onto the hills surrounding the base and ambushed Company B, 9th Marines. General Walt airlifted reinforcements

LEFT: After being helicoptered in to reinforce the Khe Sanh firebase in July 1967, a lone Marine from Lieutenant Commander McElroy's 3rd Battalion, 26th Marines, stands watch in a tower while a Marine chaplain holds mass on Hill 950.

ABOVE: Positioned for defense against possible attack from North Vietnam, Hawk antiaircraft missiles stand ready on July 9, 1967, near the Danang airbase as part of Battery C, 2nd Light AA Missile Battalion, 1st Marine Aircraft Wing.

and after fierce fighting drove the North Vietnamese back. During the battle, another NVA unit attacked Marine bases to the east and occupied Route 9, thereby isolating Khe Sanh and rendering the garrison entirely dependent on air support.

On June 1, 1967, Lieutenant General Robert E. Cushman, Jr., replaced Walt, who for two years had commanded the III MAF. During the same period, Major General Norman J. Anderson replaced Major General Louis B. Robertshaw as commander of the 1st Marine Aircraft Wing. Both men took charge of their

LEFT: Two McDonnell Douglas F-4B Phantoms from VMFA-542 based at Danang answer the call for close air support of ground troops fighting North Vietnamese forces in the hills surrounding Khe Sanh.

posts during Operations Cimarron and Buffalo, a concentrated and unsuccessful effort by Marines to clean NVA units out of Quang Tri Province. Although the 11th Engineer Battalion cut a "firebreak" 600 yards wide and nine miles long near the edge of the DMZ, stripping it of vegetation and filling it with barbed wire, minefields, sensors, watchtowers, and fortifications, enemy operations merely edged westward and towards Khe Sanh.

During 1967, Marines experienced some of the heaviest fighting of the war, mostly against NVA units near the DMZ. Though Marine ground and air forces had maintained control over the northern border of South Vietnam, the effort cost the Corps 3,452 killed and 25,944 wounded. Of 81,249 Marines in Vietnam, 77,696 were with the III MAF in the northern provinces of the I Corps. Also stationed in Vietnam were fourteen of the thirty-three Marine fixed-wing squadrons and thirteen of the twenty-four helicopter squadrons. The entire I Corps consisted of twenty-one Marine battalions, most of the air wing, 3,436 navy personnel, thirty-one ARNV battalions, fifteen army battalions, and four battalions of Korean marines. Going into 1968, every man would be required.

Marine Aircraft

In 1965, Major General Paul J. Fontana's 1st MAW arrived in Vietnam. Fontana's aircrews never anticipated a seven-year fighting assignment. Two helicopter squadrons flying Sikorsky UH-34Ds were already present and operating out of Danang, as were MAG-12s Douglas A-4 Skyhawks. On April 10 the first Marine fixed-wing fighter squadron (VMFA-531) arrived with F-4B Phantom IIs, by most accounts the most successful fighter produced during the Vietnam War.

Marine fixed-wing aircraft performed specific roles. Phantoms and Skyhawks flew close air support: Grumman A-6 Intruders made deep interdiction bombing runs: Chance-Vought F-8 Crusader fighter-bombers performed multiple missions. Often called "the last of the gunfighters," the Crusader was a superb fighter and "MiG Master," but was poorly configured for ground attack missions.

Helicopters performed combat assault, resupply, medical evacuation, liaison, transport, and observation tasks. Eventually, Bell UH-1 Hueys and Boeing Vertol CH-46 Sea Knights replaced the venerable UH-34 Seahorses. Sikorsky CH-53 Sea Knights became the heavy lifters and Bell AH-1 Cobras the dreaded gunships.

Marines also used the four-engine Lockheed KC-130 Hercules for aerial refueling and forward base supply, and the two-engine North American OV-10 Bronco for aerial observation and light utility chores.

At peak strength, the 1st MAW consisted of six aircraft groups comprised of twenty-six squadrons flying 242 fixed-wing aircraft and 186 helicopters. American withdrawals from Vietnam began in 1969, and most Marine air units were stateside by 1971. A few squadrons were rushed back to Vietnam during the NVA Easter offensive in 1972.

Khe Sanh and the Tet Offensive

In April 1967, NVA units cut Route 9 and isolated Colonel David E. Lownds' 26th Marines (3,500 men) holding Khe Sanh's combat base. General Walt reinforced the garrison and airlifted additional 105mm batteries for base defense. On January 20, 1968, ten days before the Tet Offensive, 20,000 troops from two NVA divisions surrounded the 6,000-man Khe Sanh firebase. General Cushman admitted the situation bore a worrisome resemblance to the French disaster at Dienbienphu in 1954. For several months the key difference had been, and would continue to be, air power.

When on January 21 NVA artillery opened and the siege of Khe Sanh began in earnest, President Johnson panicked and demanded hourly situational reports. Nine days later the Tet Offensive erupted and another 60,000 enemy troops struck every important American base and all of the principal cities from one end of South Vietnam to the other, including the U.S. embassy in Saigon. The Tet Offensive quickly fizzled out, but not the siege of Khe Sanh.

Although Marines warded off daily attacks and kept Khe Sanh's airfield in service, the Tet Offensive dramatically undermined American homeland support for the war. The communist offensive had been destroyed, but nobody stateside any longer believed military reports out of Vietnam. On March 1, 1968, Clark Clifford replaced McNamara, who had been the chief architect of the war, as secretary of defense. Three weeks later Johnson unexpectedly recalled Westmoreland and replaced him with General Creighton W. Abrams, Jr. Westmoreland had severely weakened the enemy and believed that with 206,000 reinforcements he could win the war. Johnson, however, was confronted with weekly death tolls averaging 500 Americans and ordered a gradual pullout. Nine days later he halted the bombing of North Vietnam—except near the DMZ—urged peace talks, and withdrew from the 1968 presidential campaign. In March, while Johnson deliberated over

political options, Marines continued to fight for their lives at Khe Sanh. On May 13, preliminary talks began in Paris, but without result.

Marine tenacity and air power made the difference. The NVA never succeeded in closing the airfield. During the siege, transports flew in supplies, with only four aircraft being lost. Aided by USAF B-52 bombers

ABOVE: Colonel David E. Lownd's 3rd Battalion, 26th Marines, fight to oust a North Vietnamese battalion entrenched between Hills 881 North and 881 South near the Khe Sanh firebase on January 20, 1968.

LEFT: During Operation Lancaster II in 1968, a Marine from Company E, 2nd Battalion, 3rd Marines, is silhouetted against a cloudy sky north of Dong Ha as the company fights its way up Mutter's Ridge near the DMZ.

RIGHT: In a desperate attack against the base at Khe Sanh, the North Vietnamese army attempts to weaken resistance with another pulverizing rocket attack on February 21, 1968, but Marines once again repulse the ensuing ground assault.

BELOW: During the Tet Offensive, which began on January 31, 1968, Marines reacted with alacrity and repulsed the Viet Cong assault on Hamo village in Quang Nam Province, at heavy cost to the enemy.

and Seventh Fleet F-4 fighter-bombers, which together dropped 100 tons of bombs and napalm on enemy positions, Marines repulsed every attack. On April 12, the 1st Air Cavalry Division and a South Vietnamese airborne battalion established overland contact with Khe Sanh and reopened Route 9. Two days later the North Vietnamese withdrew after suffering more than 9,000 casualties. During the seventy-seven-day siege, the Marines lost 205 killed and 800 wounded.

During the defense of Khe Sanh, a battalion of the 5th Marines had also assisted the South Vietnamese in the recapture of the ancient holy city of Hue, the only other communist carryover from the Tet Offensive. Had President Johnson not decided to exit from Vietnam after the Tet Offensive, during which the enemy lost more than 400,000 men, the outcome of the war would likely have been much different.

LEFT: *One of the roughest fights during the Vietnam War occurred in the holy city of Hue during the Tet Offensive. During the battle on February 6, 1968, navy Corpsman D. R. Howe treats Pfc. D. A. Crum of "H" Company, 2nd Battalion, 5th Marines, for shrapnel wounds.*

Perspectives from "Marineland"

U.S. officials and army officers working out of Saigon referred to the I Corps sector as "Marineland." Some believed Marines were in the wrong place. Efforts were made to move units into the Mekong Delta, south of Saigon, but Marines did not want to be controlled by the army and stayed where they were. On January 5, 1967, the Seventh Fleet's Special Landing Force (1st Battalion, 9th Marines) made one helicopter insertion six miles south of Saigon (Operation Deckhouse V) to place U.S. combat troops in the Mekong Delta. During the balance of 1967, the Special Landing Force made twenty-two more landings, all of them in "Marineland."

In easing away from the war, General Abrams gave special attention to the I Corps sector, where Marines had severely bloodied several NVA divisions. He ordered the impregnable Khe Sanh combat base dismantled and troops moved back to Route 9. The action baffled the Marines because the withdrawal reopened the corridor for NVA infiltration into South Vietnam. Abrams then stopped search-and-destroy missions and used helicopter-borne forces to make piecemeal stabs at enemy positions. He also abandoned pacified villages and hamlets and concentrated Marine forces around populous cities. Encouraged by the American pullback, guerrilla attacks intensified, fueling the American press with more horror stories.

Marines slugging it out in the field could not comprehend this loathsome form of warfare. From Danang and the DMZ, they could not see the corrosive effect of the Vietnam War on Americans or the disturbing images spun by news correspondents circulating in the rear. Nor could they see the home

ABOVE: An M48A3 Patton tank was the mainstay of Marine mechanized battalions in Vietnam. A flamethrower variant could spray napalm up to 150 yards. Some 370 Patton tanks served in Vietnam during 1969.

LEFT: A platoon from Company B, 4th Marines, 3rd Marine Division, crosses a creek in December 1969 while on a search and destroy mission in the Scotland II area east of Vandegrift Combat Base.

front, where politicians took cover from the press and blamed the generals for mishandling the war. Marines believed they were winning the war against North Vietnam and could not understand why politicians insisted on losing it.

Getting Out

On October 21, 1968, President Johnson discontinued Rolling Thunder, thereby enabling the North Vietnamese to rearm and reorganize. Two weeks later Richard M. Nixon won the national presidential election by pledging to end American involvement in Vietnam. The election of Nixon ended the "Americanization" of South Vietnam, and "Vietnamization" became the president's new policy. Still, the Marines kept fighting a war nobody else wanted to win.

On March 26, 1969, Lieutenant General Herman Nickerson, Jr., arrived at Danang and relieved General Cushman as commander of the III MAF. Cushman still believed in winning the war: Nickerson came to end it. Nickerson used the III MAF to train South Vietnamese marines in amphibious operations, but nobody explained how the trainees could conduct amphibious landings without a navy. In October 1969, the 3rd Marine Division went home. The 1st Marine Division soon followed, along with the air wings. On March 30, 1972, when North Vietnam began an Easter offensive, there were only 500 Marines in South Vietnam.

When Saigon fell on April 30, 1975, a few Marines posted on the roof of the U.S. embassy occupied some of the best seats in town. During a span of eighteen hours, navy and Marine helicopters evacuated 1,373 American citizens, 6,422 civilians, and 989 Marines who had been specially inserted to cover the withdrawal. The last Marines departed on flights made from the rooftop of the embassy. As the helicopters flew from the city, Marines watched from the windows as North Vietnamese tanks rolled into the city.

ABOVE: *During the early Vietnamization of the war, Lance Corporal Larry W. Elam instructs an ARVN marine in the setup and firing of an M60 general purpose machine gun, which can also be fired from the shoulder or a tripod.*

The Final Tally

During fourteen years of war (1962–1975) the Marines lost 13,067 killed and 88,633 wounded. The casualties exceeded the Marines' losses in World War II. Only thirty-eight Marines were captured during the Vietnam War. Eight died in captivity, and forty-nine remained missing in action. Marine air lost 252 helicopters and 173 fixed-wing aircraft, mostly during combat operations.

Fifty-seven Marines were awarded the Medal of Honor, forty-six of them posthumously. During the Vietnam War the Marine Corps became entirely integrated. There were no black or white Marines: just "green Marines," all wearing combat green. Of the 448,000 Marines serving in Vietnam, 41,000 were African-Americans. Of the latter, five won Medals of Honor for falling on exploding enemy grenades, giving their lives to save others.

Marines came home disgusted. As one gunny sergeant declared, "To win the war in the field and lose it in Washington damn near kicked the guts out of the Corps."

On July 1, 1975, General Louis H. Wilson, Jr., became the 26th commandant of the Marine Corps. A Medal of Honor recipient for heroism during the Iwo Jima campaign and a veteran of Vietnam, Wilson understood the plight of the Corps and vowed to maintain its image, despite Vietnam. On November 10, 1975, he staged a huge ceremony to celebrate the 200th birthday of the Corps. With America weakened by its involvement in Vietnam, Wilson spent the next four years preparing the men and women of the Corps for the next national crisis. What the Marines needed was another war, but not another Vietnam.

Above: African American Marines from Company E, 2nd Battalion, 3rd Marines, fighting on Mutter's Ridge, north of Dong Ha, during Operation Thor. Sergeant Rufus Patterson tosses a grenade while Sergeant Anthony Carter, seated, watches the man on his left. "There were no black Marines or white Marines. Just [Green] Marines."

ENEMIES OLD AND NEW
1961–2006

CHAPTER 8

ABOVE: During boot camp operations at Quantico, Virginia, three drill instructors (DIs) demonstrate the proper technique of crawling under barbed wire to a platoon of October 1989 recruits about to enter the base infiltration course.

ABOVE RIGHT: Marine Corps drill instructor Staff Sergeant Schliesman of "H" Company, 2nd Battalion, works enlistees on a horizontal bar to do dead hang pull-ups at the recruit depot at Parris Island, South Carolina. Grimacing faces suggest that some recruits will have to work harder to make the grade.

In early 1946, before the Korean and the Vietnam Wars, the Soviet "Iron Curtain" descended across Eastern Europe and marked the beginning of the Cold War. Three years later, on September 23, 1949, the Soviet Union exploded its first atomic bomb and ended America's nuclear monopoly. Three months later Mao Tse-tung's armies drove the Nationalists out of Mainland China, and the most populous nation in the world became communist. For more than five decades

> The Marine Corps is in the best condition of readiness that I have seen in my thirty-seven years of naval service.
> *Commandant General Wallace Greene to House of Representatives, 1965.*

the United States would be confronted with constant threats from communists and/or terrorists, and the Marines would provide the ready force to intervene wherever American interests were threatened.

The New Marine Corps

In 1960 Commandant General David M. Shoup launched a campaign to keep the Marine Corps from becoming "soft." At the time, Shoup did not know he would need platoon and company officers for the Vietnam War. At Quantico, Virginia, he began putting all applicants for Officers Candidate (OCS) through the same arduous testing regimen imposed on enlistees, but made it a longer and more grueling course. More than 30 of the candidates washed-out because of physical injury, or choice. There was no secret formula for success, just hard endurance work and perseverance. As one instructor declared: "If a young man is physically fit and has the right mental attitude, he'll make it. That also goes for women, who do the same training as the men with modified physical test requirements."

Those who survived fitness training were not finished with "boot camp" until they worked through a 1,200-yard labyrinth resembling the World War I battlefield of Belleau Wood but with walls to scale, ditches to leap, barbed wire to crawl under, two-plank bridges to cross, a water-filled drainage pipe to navigate, and an enemy bunker to attack. After that, steadfast men and women entered The Basic School as second lieutenants and spent the next twenty-three weeks learning leadership skills, battlefield tactics, firing and care of infantry weapons, marksmanship, land navigation, and more physical fitness work.

The Mixed Breed

Training of enlistees also began to change. The men who joined the Corps during the previous world wars came mostly from farms and were already physically strong. After the Korean War, and especially during the Vietnam War, society drastically changed. The "Old Breed" and the "New Breed" gave way to a mixed breed of less compliant draftees. Roughneck drill instructors (DIs) faced new challenges. Combat training did not change, but hazing, maltreatment, and random brutality did. Fifty push-ups, an elbow in the gut, extra duty punishment, and various threats that once worked wonders on shirkers ended. Today a DI is not permitted to touch a recruit except to adjust his uniform.

When the Marine Corps celebrated its 200th birthday on November 10, 1975, many changes had occurred. Although the nation's culture had become far more permissive, the Marines still wanted men and women who could be shaped into the high standards of the traditional Corps. The DI's methodical

indoctrination into the fundamentals of military life still came as a shock to most enlistees. He began stripping away civilian habits on the day the recruits arrived. He paid ruthless attention to details of dress and kit maintenance, and he administered his instructions in loud nose-to-nose verbal assaults that sometimes humiliated or flabbergasted the recipient and made him or her madder than hell.

After hours of drilling and torturous conditioning exercises, rifle maintenance and training began on the firing range. With fifty rounds, each worth five points, a Rifleman had to score at least 190 to qualify as "marksman," 210 as "sharpshooter," and 220 as "expert." When platoons engaged in competition, Riflemen scoring less than 190 points suffered the penalty of wearing their shooting jackets backwards. DIs encouraged competition between platoons because it inspired teamwork.

ABOVE: "In your face" verbal pressure has long been used by Drill Instructors in their attempts to toughen up, mentally and physically, recruits who in the future may go into combat for their nation. Today's DI is more restricted in the way that he can cajole best efforts from a rooky recruit. Here, at the Marine Corps Recruit Center in San Diego, California, DIs impress on recruits the correct way to perform stretching exercises and limber up before the more strenuous activity of the day begins.

Marine Operations (1958–1990)

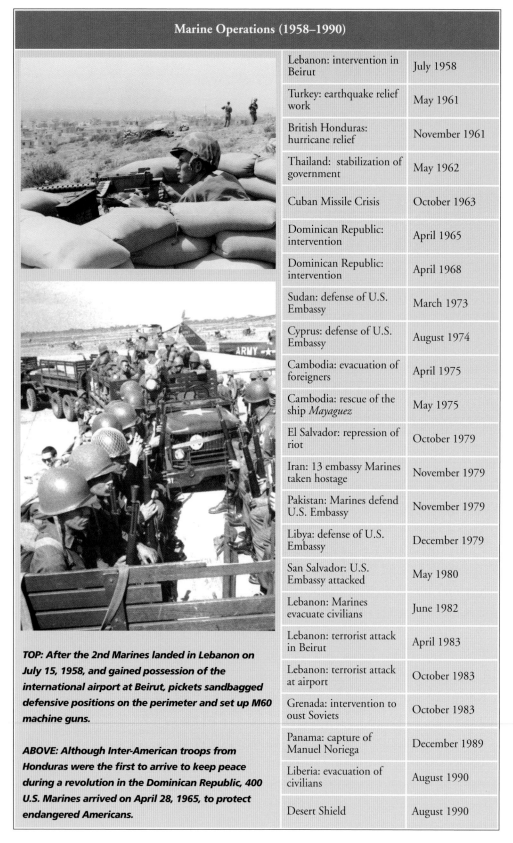

Lebanon: intervention in Beirut	July 1958
Turkey: earthquake relief work	May 1961
British Honduras: hurricane relief	November 1961
Thailand: stabilization of government	May 1962
Cuban Missile Crisis	October 1963
Dominican Republic: intervention	April 1965
Dominican Republic: intervention	April 1968
Sudan: defense of U.S. Embassy	March 1973
Cyprus: defense of U.S. Embassy	August 1974
Cambodia: evacuation of foreigners	April 1975
Cambodia: rescue of the ship *Mayaguez*	May 1975
El Salvador: repression of riot	October 1979
Iran: 13 embassy Marines taken hostage	November 1979
Pakistan: Marines defend U.S. Embassy	November 1979
Libya: defense of U.S. Embassy	December 1979
San Salvador: U.S. Embassy attacked	May 1980
Lebanon: Marines evacuate civilians	June 1982
Lebanon: terrorist attack in Beirut	April 1983
Lebanon: terrorist attack at airport	October 1983
Grenada: intervention to oust Soviets	October 1983
Panama: capture of Manuel Noriega	December 1989
Liberia: evacuation of civilians	August 1990
Desert Shield	August 1990

TOP: After the 2nd Marines landed in Lebanon on July 15, 1958, and gained possession of the international airport at Beirut, pickets sandbagged defensive positions on the perimeter and set up M60 machine guns.

ABOVE: Although Inter-American troops from Honduras were the first to arrive to keep peace during a revolution in the Dominican Republic, 400 U.S. Marines arrived on April 28, 1965, to protect endangered Americans.

ABOVE: At Twenty-nine Palms, California, student Marines enrolled in the Infantry Officers Course dismount a pair of Assault Amphibian Vehicle Personnel (AAV7A1) carriers at the Marine Air Ground Task Force training center.

During the final days of training, enlistees confronted the Confidence Course, an assault area designed to test the individual's strength, agility, and physical courage. Afterwards, recruits prepared for a series of written exams, followed by one last physical fitness test and a series of drill competitions judged by senior NCOs. The best platoon became the honor platoon on graduation day. Family and friends received invitations to witness the ceremony: a distinct difference from the 1950s when Marines, after completing their training, were routinely shuttled off to their assigned unit.

Young Marines eventually realized that their DIs cared for them. Before leaving boot camp, a Marine knew something about fighting, survival, and readiness. With a Cold War and terrorism spreading across the world, those talents would be needed anywhere and everywhere. There is not a man in the Marine Corps, regardless of his age, who does not remember the name of his drill instructor.

The Cuban Missile Crisis

On October 14, 1962, two years before the official beginning of the Vietnam War, an American U-2 reconnaissance plane photographed Soviet missile sites under construction in western Cuba. Photographs taken two days later revealed Soviet Il-28 bombers being assembled on Cuban airfields. President John F. Kennedy spent six days deliberating before deciding on October 22 to order a naval "quarantine" of Cuba. Two days later the U.S. Second Fleet sailed toward Cuba with two aircraft carriers and the II Marine Expeditionary Force (MEF). Four hundred Marine aircraft prepared to fly an aerial umbrella over Guantánamo Bay and provide close air support for an amphibious assault on Cuba. In eight days, Marines assembled a task force of 40,000 men, the largest amphibious gathering since Okinawa. Had an assault been ordered, the II MEB would have led it. Instead, President Kennedy and Soviet Premier Nikita Khrushchev reached a mutually face-saving compromise. After Kennedy promised not to overthrow dictator Fidel Castro's communist government, and Khrushchev agreed to remove Soviet missiles and bombers from Cuba, the II MEF returned home.

General Shoup expressed his gratification to the men and women of the Fleet Marine Force because they had achieved the Joint Forces Strike Command's criteria for operational responsiveness. Although Shoup always sought improvement, the very readiness of the Fleet Marine Force proved that the "Flexible Response" doctrine of the Corps could deter war as well as fight one.

The Dominican Republic's Revolution

In 1961, trouble began in the Dominican Republic following the assassination of pro-U.S. dictator Rafael Trujillo. The U.S remained watchful while the Dominican Republic attempted to reestablish a stable government.

No longer fearing invasion by the United States, Fidel Castro supported a communist effort to gain control of the Dominican Republic. Four years passed, during which assassins took the life of President Kennedy and President Lyndon B. Johnson became mired in the Vietnam War. As Americans focused on the emerging conflict in Southeast Asia, street fighting between Santo Domingo's new military junta and leftist insurgents threatened to spark civil war in the Dominican Republic.

On April 25, 1965, President Johnson ordered the navy's six-ship Caribbean Ready Group to Santo Domingo to evacuate American citizens. The following day the 6th Marine Expeditionary Unit (MEU), which consisted of the 3rd Battalion, 6th Marines, and the Marine Medium Helicopter Squadron HMM-264, arrived off Haina, a naval base west of Santo Domingo. By then, leftist rebels controlled the capital's streets, and Reid Cabral, the president, had resigned and gone into hiding.

BELOW: *During the intervention at Santo Domingo, Dominican Republic, the 1st Battalion, 8th Marines, move up to the safety zone established in the city on May 8, 1985, to relieve men from the 3rd Battalion, 6th Marines.*

ABOVE: On May 8, 1965, Marine interpreters from Company K, 6th Marines, discuss operations with Dominican soldiers in an effort to coordinate an assault on rebel positions in Santo Domingo.

While American citizens began embarking on two navy ships docked at Haina, others assembled at the Embajador Hotel in Santo Domingo, from where Marine helicopters airlifted them to ships waiting offshore. Orderly evacuations ended on April 28 when Dominican police and Colonel Pedro Bartolome Benoit of the military junta asked for military assistance from the 82nd Airborne Division. In the meantime, snipers in Santo Domingo began firing on Marines at the American embassy. On April 29, 1,500 Marines from the 6th MEU came ashore.

On May 1, Marines linked with the army's 82nd Airborne and formed an international security zone between the combatants. At first, Marines could not distinguish between the good guys and the bad guys. Advancing with care, they isolated the rebels and began mopping-up the city in house-to-house street fighting. To prevent a communist coup, the U.S. eventually poured 32,000 troops into Santo Domingo, including 8,000 Marines from four battalions, two helicopter

squadrons, and two fighter squadrons.

Marines lost nine killed and thirty wounded in a peacekeeping mission that quashed communist expansion in the Dominican Republic and adjoining Haiti. During the formation of a stable government, Marines provided a constabulary force and remained in Santo Domingo until June.

The *Mayaguez* Incident

On May 12, 1975, two weeks after the evacuation of Saigon, a gunboat from the Cambodian Khmer Rouge regime seized the *Mayaguez*, an old American container ship en route to Thailand. President Gerald Ford, having succeeded Richard Nixon, decided to use the ship's capture as an opportunity to prove to the world that the United States, despite losing Vietnam, was not a "paper tiger." He warned that "serious consequences" would follow if Cambodia did not release the ship unharmed.

On May 15, after nothing happened, a battalion of Marines flew from Okinawa to Thailand to mount a rescue operation. While planes from the *Coral Sea* (CVA-43) bombed air and naval bases in Cambodia, sixty Marines and sailors from the *Harold E. Holt* (DE-1074) boarded the *Mayaguez* eighteenth-century-style and found it deserted. During the operation, Company G, 4th Marines, landed by helicopter on the island of Koh Tang to rescue the *Mayaguez* crew. The Khmer Rouge had released the crew two hours prior to the attack and the men were already back on the ship, but the Americans landing on Koh Tong ran into a hornet's nest and lost forty-one killed, fifty wounded, and five helicopters.

Marine Security Guard Battalion

Since the nineteenth century, Marines had been posted around the world guarding American consulates and embassies, but not until 1967 were they formed into the Marine Security Guard Battalion. The men (and at times a few women Marines) carried only pistols, shotguns, and tear gas and were under the direct control of the state department official in charge of the embassy.

Exactly when terrorist attacks began can be argued, but in 1971 a Marine sergeant lost his life while defending the embassy in Cambodia. Two years later another Marine died defending the embassy at Khartoum after Palestinian terrorists abducted and murdered the ambassador. In August 1974, Marines defended the embassy at Nicosia, Cyprus, while Greeks and Turks battled each other for control of the island. On November 21, 1979, a seven-man detachment in Islamabad, Pakistan, used nothing but tear gas to hold off a mob of Muslims that eventually burned down the U.S. embassy. On the same day, Pakistanis stormed the American consulate at Karachi, where two women Marines, Corporals Vicki Lee Gaglia and Betty Jo Rankin, appeared in helmets, flak jackets, and weapons, to stand fast with their male counterparts. Similar problems occurred in Central America when

on October 30, 1979, more than 200 leftists attacked the U.S. embassy in San Salvador and were repulsed by Marines using tear gas. Such incidents, once considered anomalies, had now became commonplace.

The most notorious episode occurred in Tehran in 1979 after the shah abdicated. Ayatollah Khomeini returned from exile in France to lead an Islamic fundamentalist revolution and take control of the government. Encouraged by Khomeini, 400 militant students stormed the U.S. embassy and on November 4 seized sixty-five Americans, including fourteen Marine guards. Eight more Marines were taken from other buildings. Among the leaders of the assailants was Mahmoud Ahmadinejad, currently president of Iran. Thirteen Marines were eventually released, but nine others, along with thirty-nine men and two women embassy employees remained Khomeini's hostages for 444 days. Hostage-taking in Tehran, and the lack of American response, stimulated militant elements in Pakistan and Libya to emulate Iran.

ABOVE: Marines boarding the captured American container ship Mayaguez found it deserted when they rushed to Cambodia to retake it, but another group flown in from Okinawa ran into a hornet's nest on May 15, 1975, when they assaulted the Cambodian island of Koh Tang.

Rapid Deployment Joint Task Force (RDF)

On March 1, 1980, after the hostage-taking episode in Tehran and the Soviet invasion of Afghanistan, President Carter authorized an interservice Rapid Deployment Joint Task Force. The assignment went to 51-year-old Lieutenant General Paul X. "P.X." Kelley— "P.X." being the abbreviation for a military "Post Exchange." A hard-nosed graduate of Villanova University, Kelley understood rapid deployment the Marine way. He had served with the Fleet Marine Force, Atlantic and the British Royal Marines

Commandos in the Middle East, and had earned a Silver Star while commanding Marines in Vietnam.

Kelley formed the RDF to serve mainly in the Persian Gulf and Arabian Sea. The system bogged down for two reasons: the Marine Corps already considered themselves a rapid deployment force, and the new setup produced interservice rivalry. Kelley wanted the RDF to be an all-Marine operation. Instead, the unit was transferred to an army lieutenant general and eventually became part of Central

Command (CENTCOM), which encompassed most of the Middle East and northeastern Africa.

Kelley was determined to revitalize the Corps' sense of mission. Promoted to general in 1981, he became the assistant commandant of the Marine Corps, and two years later replaced General Robert H. Barrow as commandant. Kelley immediately began developing his own all-Marine "rapid response" force. Although President Carter drastically cut the number of naval ships on active duty, Kelley developed a prepositioning squadron to provide rapid response. The force required three sets of four or five prepositioned ships, each set having equipment for a 16,500-man brigade and the capability of moving rapidly into troubled areas. Though the system lacked forcible-entry capability, it reduced the time required to move Marines into battle.

Operation Blue Light—Desert One

On April 7, 1980, President Carter severed diplomatic relations with Iran and authorized Operation Blue Light, the rescue of American hostages. Army Colonel Charles Beckwith, commanding the 1st Special Forces Operational (Delta) Detachment, drew the assignment and attempted to organize the first "unofficial" RDF interservice operation. He slung together a mixed force of troop-carrying Lockheed MC-130 Hercules transports flying out of Egypt and eight old Sikorsky RH-53D Sea Stallion navy helicopters flown by Marines from the carrier *Nimitz* (CVAN-68). Beckwith intended to load a ninety-man Delta force from Egypt onto Sea Stallions at Desert One, a staging-area hide-site 200 miles south of Tehran. From there, Beckwith planned to launch a complicated hostage-freeing operation supported by aerial firepower. Marine-piloted Sea Stallions would drop into designated areas to extract the hostages and, with the Delta assault team, ferry them to Manzariyeh Airfield, thirty-five miles south of Tehran. There a force of U.S. Rangers would be waiting with a flight of Lockheed C-114 StarLifter transports to fly everyone out of Iran.

Beckwith launched Blue Light on April 24. The operation began to unravel when two helicopters

The Reagan administration [did] an awful lot, but what changed our whole outlook came in 1979 when [Carter's Secretary of Defense] Harold Brown gave us the maritime prepositioning ship concept. That poured money into our coffers that gave us a whole new base line. It included money for ships and an awful lot of money for equipment. Then, when Reagan came in, we took off.

Commandant Kelley quoted in J. Robert Moskin, The U.S. Marine Corps Story, *754.*

ABOVE: Before dawn on April 24, 1980, Marines begin revving the engines on eight old Sikorsky RH-53D Sea Stallions on the carrier Nimitz **in preparation for Operation Blue Light, the ill-fated attempt to rescue Iranian-held American hostages in Tehran.**

developed mechanical trouble during a dust storm and returned to the *Nimitz*. After reaching Desert One, a third chopper broke down. Without six helicopters, Beckwith could not complete the mission, so he cancelled it. As the helicopters lifted off, one collided with a C-130 on the ground, setting off Redeye missiles. Both aircraft burst into flames. The troops inside the C-130 made a miraculous escape, but the five-man aircrew and the three Marines in the Sea Stallion lost their lives. Beckwith abandoned the four remaining helicopters and the eight charred bodies of the flyers and departed on the transports.

President Carter remained distressed over the incident for the remainder of his term. He even increased the military budget after having reduced it. After holding the hostages for 444 days, Iran made an undignified gesture toward the Carter administration by releasing the hostages on January 20, 1981, the day Ronald Reagan became president.

Marine Corps Budget $ billions	
Jimmy Carter (1978)	4.6
Ronald Reagan (1986)	14.8
George H.W. Bush (1991)	9.6

ABOVE: Marines stand guard outside the U.S. embassy in Beirut after a Syrian-sponsored terrorist exploded a truck bomb on April 18, 1983, killing sixty-one persons. One Marine lost his life. Eight others suffered wounds.

Terrorism in Lebanon

Since the 1950s, Marines had been involved in constant clashes between Christian and Islamic factions in the Middle East. The Israeli wars made the problem worse by driving most of the Palestinians into Lebanon, where in 1975 the Palestine Liberation Organization (PLO) increased the country's instability by promoting civil war over religious differences.

On June 6, 1982, Israeli forces invaded Lebanon with the objective of eliminating the PLO. The action forced the U.S. Navy and Marines to evacuate 600 American and foreign citizens from Juniyah, near Beirut. On August 25, Colonel James M. Mead landed a peacekeeping force of 800 Marines from the 32nd Marine Amphibious Unit at Beirut to assist in the evacuation of 12,000 Palestinians. On September 10, the Marines completed the evacuation and departed. Three days later Syrian-sponsored assassins murdered Lebanon's newly elected Maronite Christian president, Bashir Gemayel. On September 29, President Reagan sent Mead and 1,200 Marines back into Lebanon as part of a multi-national peacekeeping force.

Marines moved to the Beirut airport for what developed into a long and arduous stay. They patrolled the streets, against what or who they were never certain. They took casualties without knowing who shot at them. Every few months they rotated, relieved by another amphibious unit. The situation in Beirut began to stabilize when suddenly, on April 18, 1983, terrorists exploded a truck bomb outside the U.S. embassy, killing sixty-one persons: among them eighteen Americans, including one Marine. Eight others suffered wounds.

On May 17 Israel agreed to withdraw from Lebanon, but Syria, having moved sizeable forces into the country, refused to budge. So Israeli troops stayed to keep watch on Syrian forces. Peacekeepers got in the way and suffered casualties attempting to keep the two rivals at bay. The presence of a Christian peacekeeping force only made matters worse. On August 29, two Marines died when Syrian artillery, mortars, and rockets struck the Marine perimeter at the airfield. The frigate USS *Bowen* (FF-1079) moved inshore and battered Syrian artillery positions in the hills above Beirut.

Operation Urgent Fury
Grenada
October 25–27, 1983

Cattle I.

London Bridge I.

—N—

CARIBBEAN SEA

Sauteurs

Victoria

USS Guam

22nd Marines
Amphibious Unit

Gouyave

USS Independence

Grand Roy

GRENADA

Pearls Airport
Paradise

Grenville

22nd Marines
Amphibious Unit

82nd Airborne

Saint George's

Gov't House
Fort Frederick

Navy SEALs

Corinth

ATLANTIC OCEAN

Calivigny

Point Salines
Airport

75th Rangers

17th Infantry Rangers

0   Miles   6

LEFT: After the Caribbean island of Grenada became involved in a Soviet-sponsored attempt by Cubans to overthrow the government, President Reagan dispatched 500 Marines, 500 rangers, and 5,000 paratroops to oust the communists.

Operation Urgent Fury—Grenada

On October 19, 1983, four days before the Beirut bombing, a Soviet-sponsored coup overthrew the government of the 133-square-mile, eastern Caribbean island of Grenada, a former British colony and Commonwealth nation. Extreme leftist Bernard Coard took control of the government and ordered the execution by firing squad of Maurice Bishop, the prime minister. Coard's action, coupled with military construction financed by the Soviets, spurred official concern in Washington over the safety of some 1,000 Americans on the island, mostly students at St. George's University Medical School. President Reagan concluded that Moscow intended to use Grenada as a springboard for spreading communism among the eastern islands of the Caribbean and considered the military buildup as just as dangerous to American security as the Cuban missile crisis of 1962.

Using the safety of American lives as a pretext for intervention, Reagan diverted to Grenada a task force of twelve ships with 1,900 men of the 22nd Marine Amphibious Unit then at sea and en route to Lebanon. The JCS augmented the force with 500 rangers from the 75th Infantry Regiment, 5,000 paratroopers from the 82nd Airborne Division, and navy SEALs. On October 22 the Organization of Eastern Caribbean States, fearing that Grenada would become a Cuban-Soviet base for communist mischief,

officially asked the United States to intervene. Reagan gave the green light, and Vice Admiral Joseph Metcalf III, the mission commander, launched Operation Urgent Fury. Had it not been for the 1986 movie "Heartbreak Ridge," starring Clint Eastwood, the intervention in Grenada may have passed into the oblivion of a few sound bites from major news networks.

Before dawn on October 25, Metcalf sent SEALs ashore to infiltrate St. George's, the island's capital, and secure the Government House, where Governor General Sir Paul Scoon and thirty-two other government officials were being held. At 5:36 a.m., 400 Marines from the amphibious assault ship Guam (LPH-9) went ashore at Pearls Airport and Grenville and seized the only operational airfield on the island. Thirty minutes later USAF transports from Barbados airdropped rangers on the partially completed 9,000-foot jet airfield being constructed at Point Salinas. Cuban troops, numbering about 800, staged a stiff resistance, but by mid-morning Marines had secured Pearls Airport, moved across the island, and taken possession of the medical school's campus.

During the evening another detachment of 250 Marines with five tanks made an amphibious landing at Fort Rupert, north of St. George's. On the morning of the 26th they reached Fort Frederick and Richmond Hill, where

they reinforced SEALs besieged by Cubans. Marines pushed the Cubans aside, reached the Government House, rescued the governor and his officials, and airlifted the Grenadan government to the Guam.

After giving students at the medical school's True Blue campus time to pack personal belongings, Marines transported them to the Point Salinas airport. Cuban troops, supported by an unknown number of Grenadan troops, attempted to interfere with the evacuation but were either killed or captured before harming any students.

By October 27, American forces had secured every military objective and captured more than 600 Cubans. Marines and rangers mopped up pockets of resistance, and by nightfall, fighting ceased. Of eighteen Americans killed and 116 wounded, Marines lost three killed and fifteen wounded.

In the roundup of prisoners, American forces found forty-nine Russian, twenty-four North Korean, and thirteen Eastern European diplomats and advisors engaged in converting the island into a fortified Cuban-controlled military base. Marines also found warehouses crammed with Soviet weapons and plans for providing a 7,000-man Cuban garrison. Though a few Grenadans had cast their lot with the Cubans, the majority of the inhabitants greeted the Americans as liberators.

ABOVE: Although certain sections of Panama City were set afire by street fighting during Operation Just Cause on December 20–21, 1990, only one Marine from Task Force Semper Fidelis lost his life during a skirmish in the suburbs.

RIGHT: Marines of Company D, 2nd Light Armored Infantry Battalion, stand guard with their LAV-25 light armored vehicles outside a destroyed Panamanian Defense Force building near the Bridge of the Americas on December 20, 1990, the first day of Operation Just Cause.

At 6:25 a.m. on Sunday, October 23, 1983, a Muslim suicide bomber driving a yellow Mercedes five-ton open-bed truck packed with 2,000 pounds of high explosives crashed through wire barricades outside the four-story concrete Marine headquarters building. After penetrating the lobby, the suicide-driver detonated the equivalent of six tons of TNT, killing 241 Americans, 220 of them Marines, and wounding seventy others. Minutes later, a second suicide truck rammed into French headquarters and killed another fifty-eight peacekeepers. Iranian-backed Shiite Hezbollah, representing themselves as enemies of "The Great Satan," meaning the United States, claimed credit for the bombings.

Fighting in Lebanon immediately escalated, drawing America closer to war in the Middle East. On February 7, 1984, President Reagan opted out of the mess and ordered the Marines back to their ships. The loss of so many men in Lebanon marked one of the darkest days in Marine history. From Commandant Kelley's perspective, if Marines were not permitted to fight, he did not want them there.

Panama—Operation Just Cause

Communism was not the only threat to the United States during the final decades of the 20th century. An equally insidious activity developed when a seemingly unstoppable flow of Colombian narcotics passed through the hands of Panamanian strongman General Manuel Antonio Noriega into the United States. In February 1988, federal grand juries in Miami and Tampa, Florida, indicted Noriega on charges of drug running. The action merely destabilized the Panamanian government and made Noriega stronger, after which President Reagan increased the company-sized Marine Corps Security Force in Panama City to a full battalion.

On December 16, 1989, four unarmed American officers dressed in civilian clothes lost their way while driving to a restaurant and were stopped by Noriega's Panamanian Defense Force (PDF). Confronted by a hostile group, the officers attempted to drive off. The PDF opened fire, mortally wounding Marine Lieutenant Robert Paz and injuring a second officer. Secretary of Defense Richard B. Cheney put the 12,000 soldiers guarding the Panama Canal on heightened alert, and President George H. W. Bush considered the incident provocative enough to justify Operation Just Cause, the capture and extradition of Noriega to Florida for trial.

Modernization of the Corps

In 1986, Commandant Kelley replaced the Corps' mixture of amphibious ground-air units of various strengths with a permanent Marine Air-Ground Task Force (MAGTF) concept, all made possible by President Reagan's increase in military expenditures. Kelley created fourteen permanently manned headquarters to command three amphibious forces, six amphibious brigades, and five amphibious units. Three of the amphibious brigades evolved into the Maritime Positioning Squadron (MPS). By 1986 the MPS program had in place thirteen ships with one squadron located in the eastern Atlantic, one at Diego Garcia in the Indian Ocean, and one at Guam in the western Pacific. During the 1990–1991 Persian Gulf War, the MPS program would prove its effectiveness by delivering well-supplied Marines on call. "The troops merely had to fly in," said Kelley.

For tactical ability on the battlefield, Kelley added a variety of new vehicles, beginning with M1A1 Abrams main battle tanks to replace the M60A1s. New trucks appeared, including eight-wheeled Light Armored Vehicles (LAV-25) and High-Mobility Multipurpose Wheeled Vehicles (HMMWV), or "Hummers," which replaced the traditional jeeps.

Kelley also beefed up tactical air wings. In 1985 the 26th MEU had been the first to fly Harriers after the Department of Defense introduced the unique British vertical-short-take-off-landing (VSTOL) jet into the American arsenal. Marine Attack Squadron 331 immediately adopted and became the first to fly the AV-8B Harrier II, a second-generation VSTOL. By 1986 the

Marines had four active squadrons with twelve planned, each with Harriers and twelve F/A-18 Hornets to replace the aging A-4 Skyhawks and F-4 Phantoms. Marines also operated the improved EA-6B Prowler variants, which provided surveillance, intelligence gathering, targeting, and a multitude of other functions. Prowlers carried precision-guided munitions, usually laser-guided glide bombs and HARM anti-radiation missiles for suppressing enemy air defenses.

Cobra attack helicopters were also upgraded. AH-W SuperCobras had TOW missile handling capability, and the AH-1J Cobras were fitted with Hellfire missiles. The MV-22A Osprey, a fixed-wing, tilt-rotor aircraft also went into development to replace the Vietnam-vintage medium CH-46E helicopter. Kelley called the Osprey "the most revolutionary advance in aircraft since the jet engine," but the unique aircraft had problems and remained in development for more than a decade.

Kelley also equipped the Corps with vastly improved

ground weapons. The 15-round 9mm Beretta pistol replaced the venerable M1911 Colt 45. Marines began carrying the M16A2 5.56mm rifle, the M249 5.56mm Belgian-made squad automatic weapon (SAW), the 83mm antitank rocket launcher (SMAW), the M60E3 7.62mm light machine gun, the Mark 19 40mm machine gun, and the improved M224 60mm mortar.

ABOVE LEFT: An AH-1W SeaCobra from Marine Utility/Attack Helicopter Squadron comes in to land on the flight deck of the amphibious assault ship USS Nassau during the commencement of Desert Storm.

ABOVE: A Marine Corps AV-8B Harrier takes off from the flight deck of the amphibious assault ship USS Nassau during Desert Shield. Parked on deck are CH-46E Sea Knights, AH-1T SeaCobras, and UH-1N Iroquois helicopters.

At 1:00 a.m. December 20, armored vehicles and helicopters moved out from the Canal Zone and headed into Panama City. C-130 and C-141 transports flew another 7,000 troops from the army's 82nd Airborne and the 7th Light Infantry Division from the states. Panama City and its environs had been divided into four tactical areas, the southwest sector having been assigned to Task Force Semper Fidelis, 700 Marines commanded by Colonel Charles E. Richardson. The colonel had two missions: one to secure the Bridge of the Americas, the principal causeway over the canal, and the other to capture the suburban PDF outpost at Arraijan, both of which he

did. During the Arraijan operation Corporal Garreth C. Isaak became the first (and the only Marine) member of the operation to be killed. The action lasted two days, during which the Marines rounded up 1,500 PDF prisoners.

On December 24, after an extensive search, U.S. forces found Noriega hiding in the Vatican embassy. On January 3, 1990, after being coaxed to surrender by papal officials, Noriega landed in Florida that night and was arraigned the following day in Miami on drug trafficking charges. Operation Just Cause put Noriega out of business, but not the Colombian cartels.

RIGHT: M60 main battle tanks disembark from a utility landing craft as the 4th Marine Expeditionary Brigade performs a beach assault exercise in the Persian Gulf during Operation Desert Shield. Considered obsolete by some, the M60 proved more than a match for Soviet-built Iraqi tanks in Desert Storm.

I need $30 billion and if they don't give it to me, I'm going to take it from them.

Saddam Hussein, 1990.

Trouble in the Persian Gulf

Throughout the 1980s the situation in the Persian Gulf remained unsettled partly because of Soviet intervention in Afghanistan but mainly because of the eight-year Iran-Iraq war. During the latter, the U.S. Navy became involved in protecting oil tankers and sweeping Soviet-made mines planted in the gulf. On August 20, 1988, the war finally ended when Iran accepted a U.N.-sponsored cease-fire.

Saddam Hussein, who in 1979 had risen to power in Iraq, had spent $500 billion on the war and gained nothing. During 1989 he added another $80 billion to Iraq's national debt by becoming the world's largest arms importer. With one million troops, he also fielded the world's fourth largest military force. Needing cash, he decided to use his army to alleviate Iraq's debt by demanding funds from his oil-rich Persian Gulf neighbors.

At 2:00 a.m. on August 2, 1990, after accusing Kuwait of pumping oil from Iraqi territory, Hussein sent 100,000 Republican Guard troops, supported by tanks, jets, and helicopters, across the Kuwaiti border. Kuwait's ruling family fled in limousines to Saudi Arabia, and six days later Hussein annexed the emirate to Iraq.

President Bush promptly responded, "This will not stand!" On August 7, he announced Operation Desert Shield and ordered JCS chairman General Colin Powell to perfect the plans necessary to protect Saudi Arabia from invasion and oust Iraqi troops from Kuwait. Desert Shield, followed by Desert Storm, became one of the most remarkable campaigns in modern warfare.

Operation Desert Shield

Marines were first to respond. On August 15, 1990, one week after the announcement of Operation Desert Shield, 15,000 men and women from the 7th Marine Expeditionary Brigade (MEB) began landing at Al-Jubayl, Saudi Arabia, from giant C-5A Galaxy transports. A few days later the brigade's combat equipment arrived by ship: 123 tanks, 425 artillery pieces, and 124 tactical aircraft. By August 22 three Maritime Position Squadrons arrived in the Persian Gulf in ships, enabling CENTCOM commander General Norman Schwarzkopf to advise Powell that Marines were prepared to hold a line forty miles north of Al-Jabayl. Across the Saudi border from Al-Jubayl, the 7th MEB faced tens of thousands of Iraq's finest troops waiting for orders to invade Saudi Arabia. Despite a weakness in numbers, Marines arrived just in time to discourage Hussein from assaulting Saudi Arabia's economic centers along the gulf coast.

On August 21, as the 1st MEB arrived by air from Hawaii, Lieutenant General Walter A. Boomer, USMC, consolidated it with the 7th MEB and formed the powerful I Marine Expeditionary Force (MEF), which included Brigadier General James M. "Mike" Myatt's 1st Marine Division and the 1st Marine Aircraft Wing. By the beginning of November, Boomer had 42,000 Marines—a quarter of the Corps' active strength—in Saudi Arabia.

General Alfred M. Gray, Jr., who on July 1, 1987, became the Corps' 29th commandant, envisioned a

great opportunity to get his Marines into real combat again. He called up 23,000 reservists, fed most of them into Major General William M. Keys's 2nd Marine Division, added the 2nd Marine Aircraft Wing, and formed the II MEF. In December Gray shipped the II MEF to Saudi Arabia and a few weeks later added the 5th MEB. Gray then packed his bags and flew to Saudi Arabia to participate in Desert Storm.

Arriving at Riyadh, Gray went to CENTCOM with Boomer to become involved in planning Desert Storm. With Gray present, Schwarzkopf assigned Boomer's I MEF to spearhead a frontal assault against the Iraqi line while the bulk of U.S. and Coalition forces swung wide around the enemy's right flank. Schwarzkopf called it his "Hail Mary" assault, but the strategy looked more like a football offensive coach's "end run." Schwarzkopf also placed the 4th MEB at sea to stage a fake amphibious landing. Annoyed by the non-combatant assignment, Gray protested to Powell, and Boomer protested to Schwarzkopf. Both requests for more active combat participation were turned down because of "dangerous uncleared" minefields.

ABOVE: A partially camouflaged M109 launching station for the MIM104 Patriot missile stands ready in Saudi Arabia to intercept Iraqi Scud missiles aimed at airbases and military and civilian facilities.

LEFT: General Alfred M. Gray, commandant of the Marine Corps, briefs members of the 1st battalion, 5th Marines, during Operation Desert Shield. The general dearly wanted to become more involved in Desert Storm, but he lost the opportunity when he became commandant.

If the Iraqis are dumb enough to attack, they are going to pay a horrible price.
General H. Norman Schwarzkopf, August 27, 1990.

ABOVE: An F/A-18C Hornet strike-fighter from Marine Fighter-Attack Squadron 232 (VMFA-232) taxies on the runway before taking off for an air strike on Baghdad in support of Operation Desert Storm.

RIGHT: At 4:00 a.m. on February 24, 1991, the 1st and 2nd Marine Divisions spearhead a frontal attack against Iraqi forces in Kuwait that serves the double purpose of diverting the enemy's attention away from General Schwarzkopf's "end run" around the right flank of Saddam's Republican Guard.

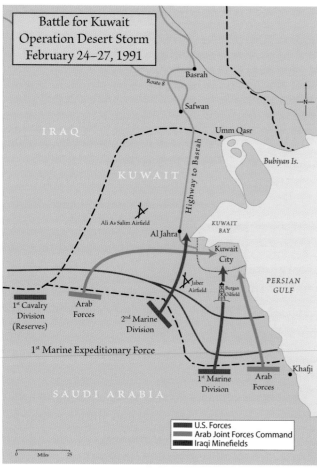

Battle for Kuwait
Operation Desert Storm
February 24–27, 1991

IRAQ

Route 8

Basrah

Safwan

Umm Qasr

KUWAIT

Bubiyan Is.

Highway to Basrah

Ali As Salim Airfield

KUWAIT BAY

Al Jahra

Kuwait City

PERSIAN GULF

Jaber Airfield

Burgan Oilfield

1st Cavalry Division (Reserves)

Arab Forces

2nd Marine Division

1st Marine Expeditionary Force

Khafji

1st Marine Division

Arab Forces

SAUDI ARABIA

- U.S. Forces
- Arab Joint Forces Command
- Iraqi Minefields

0   Miles   25

Desert Storm Preliminaries

Before dawn, January 16, 1991, the world watched as Desert Storm's aerial campaign burst in flashes of bright color over Baghdad. At 7:06 p.m. EST, Presidential Press Secretary Marlin Fitzwater announced, "The liberation of Kuwait has begun." Hussein also aired his thoughts, declaring, "The great duel, the mother of all battles, has begun."

Tracer bullets from Iraqi antiaircraft streaked through night skies at unseen targets as navy Tomahawk cruise missiles slammed into Baghdad communication and control centers. During the commotion, F/A-18 Hornets of the 1st MAW, flying about one-quarter of the fixed-wing aircraft in the Gulf, hit enemy communications and military targets on the ground. During the days that followed, Marine pilots from the 3rd MAW struck enemy positions located along the sector designated for assault by the I MEF. Desert Storm marked the debut of the Corps' new F/A-18D two-seat, all weather, night-attack fighter-bomber that eventually replaced the A6-E Intruder.

On the night of January 29, 1991, a bout of early ground fighting began when the Iraqi 5th Mechanized Division initiated the ground war by driving ten miles across the Saudi border and capturing Ras al Khafji, a coastal oil-processing town. The attack made little tactical sense but attracted the attention of a few Marines who were scouting and spotting for artillery. The Iraqi tanks approached with their turrets turned rearward, a gesture of surrender. On observing Saudi troops ahead, the turrets spun around and spat fire. Baghdad radio announced the attack as "a sign of the thunderous storm that would blow across the Arabian desert and destroy America." Iraqis held the unimportant town for thirty-six hours. Marine spotters called in artillery, Cobra helicopters, and F/A-18 and A-10 Warthog jets. After smashing twenty tanks, Marines stood aside and let Saudi and Qatari Coalition troops charge into Khafi to round up more than 400

ABOVE: A Marine M998 High-Mobility Multipurpose Wheeled Vehicle (HMMWV) leads a convoy of mechanized vehicles of the Headquarters Battalion, 2nd Marine Division, from Kuwait City to Jubail, Saudi Arabia, during Operation Desert Storm.

prisoners. After the fight, General Boomer observed that the Iraqis had lost only thirty killed and thirty-seven wounded, suggesting that perhaps Hussein's vaunted Republican Guard were not as tough and resolute as advertised.

Though greatly helped by Marines, the Saudis justifiably celebrated. They had won the first land battle in the modern history of their kingdom.

The 100-Hour War

The main event did not begin until 4:00 a.m. on February 24, 1991, when the first 155mm howitzer rounds screamed overhead and kicked off General Schwarzkopf's ground offensive. Hussein's "mother of all battles" had begun.

Boomer planned to have the 1st and 2nd Marine Divisions drive the Iraqis off the al-Wafrah oilfields and link up with a possible Marine amphibious landing near Kuwait City. Marines faced an Iraqi defensive line formed by huge rolls of barbed wire strung one on top of the other and rigged with mines and booby-traps. Behind the wire lay high barriers of sand, tank traps, trenches, and forts: the same obstacles that Iraq had used with effect against Iran.

Rain fell that morning, and when Marines crawled out of their holes to attack, massive black clouds overhead drenched them with saturated soot from oilfield fires ignited by Iraqis at al-Wafrah.

While tank-busting Cobra helicopters thrummed overhead, spitting rockets into enemy armor and artillery positions, engineers from the 2nd Marine Division cut passages through barbed wire, fired Mic-Lic rocket-propelled explosive charges, and cleared six lanes twelve feet wide and 300 feet long through thousands, some surrendering to television camera crews and unmanned drones. Marines moved straight through huge clumps of disarmed Iraqis on the burning oilfields and captured the Al-Jaber Airfield and Kuwait International Airport. On February 27 Marines stepped aside so that a composite Arab battalion could be the first to liberate Kuwait City.

Marines afloat worked their feint so effectively that they never had to come ashore, and the attack of the 1st and 2nd Marine Divisions completely distracted the Republican Guard from General Schwarzkopf's end-around flank attack. When Coalition ground and air forces struck the rear of the Republican Guard, the enemy line collapsed and the rout began.

ABOVE: Marines from Attack Squadron 331, stationed aboard the amphibious assault ship USS Nassau, load Mk82 500-pound bombs under the wings of an AV-8B Harrier fighter/attack aircraft in preparation for a mission during Operation Desert Storm.

The Iraqi forces are conducting the Mother of all Retreats.

Secretary of Defense Richard Cheney, February 27, 1991.

minefields. Abrams tanks fitted with plows, rakes, and rollers charged through the gaps, followed by 8,000 vehicles and more than 19,000 Marines.

At 9:30 a.m. the 1st and 2nd Marine Divisions linked with the army's 2nd Armored Division and pushed into Kuwait. As Abrams tanks pressed through the enemy's defenses, Iraqi soldiers fled from their posts and attempted to vanish in the smoke. "We just went up the battlefield and killed everything in our path," said one tank commander. The enemy stopped running, threw down their weapons, and surrendered. By nightfall, the 2nd Marine Division had destroyed four Iraqi brigades and captured 5,000 men. The 1st Marine Division battled through the al-Burgan oilfield south of Kuwait City, where fires from 500 oil wells set by the enemy made it difficult to see more than ten feet in any direction.

Along the Kuwaiti coast, Marines and Saudis repulsed three Iraqi counterattacks. With visibility slightly improved, A-10 ground-attack jets and AH-1W SeaCobras swooped overhead, chopped the counterattacks to pieces, and started another massive haul of prisoners. Iraqis threw down their arms by the

The Marine Record—Desert Storm

On February 27, 1991, President Bush announced a ceasefire. While General Schwarzkopf spent four days resolving the terms of surrender with Iraqi generals, 92,000 men and women of the Marine Corps waited for the final outcome. Desert Storm became the largest single operation in Marine Corps history, as well as the shortest. General Boomer commanded more Marines in Desert Storm than General Geiger had commanded at Okinawa.

As evidence of improvements in tactics, weaponry, equipment, and air assets, Marines lost only twenty-four killed, ninety-two wounded, and none missing in action. They destroyed 1,040 Iraqi tanks, 608 armored personnel carriers, 432 pieces of artillery, and 5 missile sites. During four days of combat, Marines killed 1,500 Iraqis and took 20,000 prisoners.

Not since World War II had America welcomed back combat troops with such patriotic enthusiasm. At San Diego, California, the 1st Marine Division paraded through the streets to the cheers of thousands. In Washington, D.C., the 2nd Marine Division marched between immense, densely compacted, flag-waving files of admirers. Commandant Gray watched with pride as his superbly trained Marines passed in review. On the

Marine Operations Beyond Desert Storm	
Somalia: Mogadishu evacuation	January 1991
Bangladesh: flood disaster relief	April 1991
Bosnia: ethnic cleansing prevention	July 1992
Somalia: humanitarian relief	August 1992
Somalia: armed intervention	December 1992
Haiti: stabilizing political unrest	January 1993
Bosnia: peacekeeping air umbrella	April 1993
Burundi: evacuation of foreigners	April 1994
Rwanda: humanitarian relief	July 1994
Haiti: intervention to stabilize	September 1994
Kuwait: rebuffing Iraqi threat	October 1994
Somalia: evacuation of troops	February 1995
Liberia: defending U.S. embassy	April 1996
Central African Republic: embassy evacuation	May 1996
Albania: embassy evacuation	March 1997
Sierra Leone: embassy evacuation	May 1997
Kenya: humanitarian relief	February 1998
Eritrea: evacuation of civilians	June 1998
Yugoslavia: air war with Serbia	March 1999
East Timor: stabilizing political upheaval	October 1999
Afghanistan: attack on Taliban	October 2001
Iraq: Operation Iraqi Freedom	April 2002

eve of leaving office he muttered one regret: letting General Boomer lead the Marines in Desert Storm instead of doing it himself.

Not all the Marines came home after the ceasefire. The Persian Gulf War developed into a relief and peacekeeping operation codenamed "Provide Comfort" to assist 750,000 displaced Kurds in northern Iraq. Five hundred miles from their ships, the 24th MEU remained behind to prevent Saddam Hussein from

continuing his ethnic cleansing campaign against Kurds. In a touching sobriquet, Kurdish children called the tough, war-hardened leathernecks "food soldiers." Such simple words expressed by children made a man proud to be a Marine.

Desert Storm marked the first major land operation since the Korean War without Soviet interference. The communist empire had been gradually eroding. On December 8, 1991, the final segmentation began, and two weeks later the former Soviet Union ceased to exist. After more than forty years of strife, the Cold War ended in a victory for the free world.

ABOVE: In the aftermath of Desert Storm, Marines participate in Operation Provide Comfort and in April 1991 enter northern Iraq in trucks and ambulances to give medical care and meals ready to eat (MREs) to Kurdish refugees suffering from years of mistreatment by Saddam Hussein.

ABOVE: During the U.S. intervention in Somalia in December 1992, a group of Marines, riding in an M998 series vehicle, patrol a near empty street in support of Operation Restore Hope, a multinational relief effort.

RIGHT: Trouble develops in Mogadishu during Operation Restore Hope, and Marines armed with M60 machine guns and M16A2 rifles begin a building-to-building sweep of the weapons cantonment area seized in an early morning raid on January 7, 1993.

Operation Restore Hope—Somalia

Problems in Somalia, East Africa, began on January 4, 1991, during the Persian Gulf War, and President Bush rushed Marine helicopters into the capital, Mogadishu, to evacuate 241 employees of the U.S. embassy. After Marines departed, fourteen clans competed for power and during the process inflicted death by starvation on more than 500,000 Somalis.

On August 18, 1992, Bush ordered 145,000 tons of food and medical supplies shipped to the starving population. On December 9, after warlords interfered with U.N. food distribution, recon Marines and SEALs, followed by elements from the 15th MEU(SOC), came ashore at Mogadishu and secured the port, airfield, and embassy. A few days later 17,000 Marines from the I MEF under Major General Charles Wilhelm disembarked and entered the city for Operation Restore Hope.

After President William J. Clinton took office in January 1993, what began as a peacekeeping and food distribution effort escalated into firefights with hit-and-run bandits. After snipers shot two Marines in Mogadishu, Clinton relinquished the peacekeeping task to the U.N., which included U.S. troops. In October, after more soldiers were killed, Clinton ordered the 26th MEU into Mogadishu to withdraw all American forces. The Marines performed the task, leaving food distribution to the U.N.

In early 1995, when Somali warlords struck U.N. forces in Mogadishu, Clinton received an urgent request for troops. Lieutenant General Anthony Zinni mounted Operation United Shield, which he called a "reverse amphibious landing" because the executed withdrawal required a relief-in-place extraction of one nationality at a time because of language differences. Over the course of seven days, Marines embarked every nationality, one by one, to waiting ships. During the withdrawal, Marines engaged in twenty-seven firefights against snipers armed with automatic weapons and rocket-propelled grenades. During a brief truce, warlords stopped fighting each other to drive out the peacekeepers.

On the night the 26th MEU attempted to disengage, they fought an armed mob on the beach. With Cobra gunships laying down a withering fire overhead, Marines backed their amphibious tractors into the sea. President Clinton's U.N.-sponsored nation-building effort collapsed in defeat, but leathernecks got away without losing a man.

The Bosnian Experience

The 1990s proved to be a hectic decade for the Marine Corps because of violence in Africa, Europe, Haiti, and the Middle East, but none of the missions was quite like the Bosnian experience. For four years, Commandant General Carl E. Mundy, Jr., had weathered the complicated task of peacekeeping in Bosnia, in the former Yugoslavia, where there was neither a civil war nor a purely ethnic or religious conflict, but a combination of all.

The war to restore Serbian hegemony began in June 1991, during the collapse of the Soviet Union. Slovenia and Croatia declared independence and revolted against Slobodan Milosevic's Serbia. The conflict drifted into Bosnia-Herzegovina, where Serbs comprised the majority population and Muslims the minority. To retain a grip on Bosnia, Milosevic put 70,000 Serbian regulars into the province for operations mainly against Muslims. During the five-year Bosnian mission, the U.S. flew 109,000 sorties, slightly fewer than Coalition forces had flown during the Persian Gulf War.

During the bombing campaign, a Serb SAM shot down USAF pilot Captain Scott O'Grady's F-16C Fighting Falcon over a mountainous section of Bosnia. Admiral Leighton Smith, commanding NATO forces in the area, suspected that O'Grady had bailed out. Marine Colonel Martin Berndt insisted that he could find O'Grady, but Admiral Smith referred the matter to Commandant Mundy, who approved the search and rescue mission. Before turning Berndt loose, Smith sent a message to Bosnian Serb commanders, warning, "I am coming to get him. Stay out of my way!" The Serbs replied that they had already captured O'Grady, but Smith said, "We didn't believe it."

At dark on June 7, 1995, Colonel Berndt loaded forty Marines from the 24th MEU(SOC) into two CH-53E Sea Stallions from the USS *Kearsarge* (LHD-3). For air cover, Berndt took along enough

firepower to discourage any Serbs who might have ignored Smith's message—AH-1 Cobra light-attack helicopters and AV-8 Harriers from the Amphibious Ready Group in the Adriatic. As Sea Stallions homed in on O'Grady's weak ground signal, Berndt's Marines dropped into a clearing and formed a perimeter. O'Grady stumbled out of the woods and grabbed Berndt's extended arm. "I just reached out," the colonel said, "and pulled him into the cockpit."

After midnight on June 8, Berndt deposited O'Grady on the deck of the *Kearsarge*. When Smith greeted the returning Marines, Berndt simply thanked him for letting him go after O'Grady. "These were boys," Smith said of the Marines, "but what guts, what training."

Shortly after the rescue of O'Grady, General Mundy retired and on July 30, 1995, Lieutenant General Charles C. Krulak, the youngest son of General Victor H. Krulak, became the 31st Commandant of the Marine Corps. Krulak stepped into a situation much different from the Persian Gulf War, where his stellar

ABOVE: Marines from Lima Battery, 3rd Battalion, 10th Marines, in support of Operation Joint Guardian, leave a staging area in Kosovo and head for the forward support base at Cernica with an M198 155mm medium howitzer towed by an M813 cargo truck.

ABOVE: Marines from the 2nd Light Armored Reconnaissance Battalion prepare for an urban patrol in Light Armored Vehicle-25s in the village of Zegra, Kosovo, during a peace and stability mission associated with Operation Joint Guardian.

RIGHT: Emergency crews respond to a terrorist attack after militant Muslims associated with al-Qaeda highjack a commercial jetliner on September 11, 2001, and fly it into the southwest corner of the Pentagon Building in Washington, D.C.

performance had jumped him from brigadier general to lieutenant general.

On August 30, after Serbs attacked safe areas in Sarajevo, NATO launched Operation Deliberate Force, a three-week bombing offensive that included Marine Corps aircraft operating out of Aviano, Italy. The air attacks led to the Dayton Accord, signed on December 14, 1995, that ended the fighting in Bosnia-Herzegovina,

but Krulak never got a breather. After a series of interventions into Liberia, Central African Republic, Albania, Sierra Leone, Kenya, and Eritrea, NATO initiated an air war against Yugoslavia and Serb units in Kosovo. The seventy-eight-day air campaign, which involved Marine F/A-18 Hornets from Aviano and security forces from the 26th MEU(SOC), eventually unseated strongman Milosevic and brought a semblance of peace to troubled Yugoslavia.

General Jones and Terrorism

On July 1, 1999, General James L. Jones became the 32nd commandant of the Marine Corps. Jones was no stranger to war. He had commanded a company in Vietnam, the 24th MEU during the Persian Gulf War, and became involved in peacekeeping operations in Bosnia-Herzegovina and Macedonia. By then, the world once again appeared to be stabilizing, except for an Arab named Osama bin Laden, who in the 1990s began to spread a new brand of terrorism driven by radical Muslim fundamentalists of many nationalities.

During the 1980s bin Laden organized a quasi-military organization called al-Qaeda (the Base). He deployed a $300 million bank account to drive Western influences out of the Middle East while mounting a war of terrorism against the United States. In 1993, the first year of Bill Clinton's presidency, one of bin Laden's cells attempted but failed to blow up the World Trade Center in New York City. Clinton referred to the incident as a civil crime rather than a terrorist act.

On September 11, 2001, during the first year of George W. Bush's presidency, bin Laden's terrorists succeeded, this time from the air. Two Boeing 757 jetliners, taken over by the terrorists, flew into the World Trade Center and brought it to the ground. Another jetliner crashed into the Pentagon. A fourth, having changed course to strike the White House, crashed to the ground in Pennsylvania after American passengers subdued the terrorists. More than 3,000 civilians died.

On September 12, Bush declared war on terrorism. He soon learned the terrorist attack had been arranged by bin Laden, who organized and directed his al-Qaeda operation from Taliban-controlled Afghanistan. Commandant Jones now had a new war to fight.

Afghanistan—Operation Enduring Freedom

During the days prior to October 7, 2001, the official beginning of Operation Enduring Freedom, General Tommy Franks, commanding Coalition forces in Afghanistan, rushed Special Forces from all the U.S. services into Pakistan and Uzbekistan for operations against Taliban fighters there. Helicopters inserted Marine units to gather intelligence and direct bombing sorties against a Taliban/al-Qaeda army estimated at 40,000 men. Meanwhile, the 15th MEU(SOC), commanded by Colonel Thomas D. Waldhauser in the USS *Peleliu* (LHA-5), and the 26th MEU(SOC), commanded by Colonel Andrew P. Flick in the USS *Bataan* (LHD-5), waited offshore in the Arabian Sea for operational assignments against al-Qaeda. They

were soon be joined by the 13th MEU(SOC) from the USS *Bonhomme Richard* (LHD-6).

In northern Afghanistan, Marine special operations detachments joined forces with the anti-Taliban Northern Alliance to fight a common enemy. Television camera crews soon provided pictures for national networks to show special operations detachments roving with Northern Alliance troops through rugged mountainous terrain on horseback.

Afghanistan had no border on the Arabian Sea, so the MEU(SOC) commands had to wait for orders to fly over Pakistan. There were no allies like the Northern Alliance in southern Afghanistan, only a few Pushtun tribes, and when Marines went in they would be on their own. While the fighting around Kabul in northeastern Afghanistan escalated, MEU(SOC) Marines never stopped training and waited each day to be summoned into action.

On November 14, two Pashtun tribal forces moved against Kandahar, the spiritual center of the Taliban regime, where there was an international airfield twelve miles south of the city. On November 25, after Pashtun forces began to fall back, helicopters from the 15th MEU(SOC) inserted more than 200 Marines to establish a forward operating base on a deserted airfield fifty-five miles south of Kandahar. By the end of the week, more than 1,000 Marines from the two MEUs began moving north from newly established Camp Rhino to interrupt Taliban communications with offensive ground and air patrols.

The presence of Marines advancing on Kandahar completely disrupted Taliban operations in the south and cleaned out pockets of resistance as far north as the mountains of Tora Bora, where 2,000 al-Qaeda Arab fighters eventually took refuge. On December 7, Taliban fighters in the stronghold at Kandahar surrendered their weapons and returned to their homes. During Operation Enduring Freedom, the largest American force operating in Afghanistan were Marines.

ABOVE: This propaganda poster of Osama bin Laden was found among valuable intelligence documents on al-Qaeda operations in the Zhawar Kili area of eastern Afghanistan during Operation Enduring Freedom.

LEFT: A CH-46 Sea Knight chopper from Marine Medium Helicopter Squadron 365 (HMM-365) inserts a special operations force from the 26th Marine Expeditionary Unit on an undisclosed mountaintop in Afghanistan during Operation Enduring Freedom.

We got shot at every night. It was small arms fire, usually from small groups and caravans. We could see muzzle flashes.

Sergeant Jennifer Austin, 22-year-old crew chief on a Super Stallion.

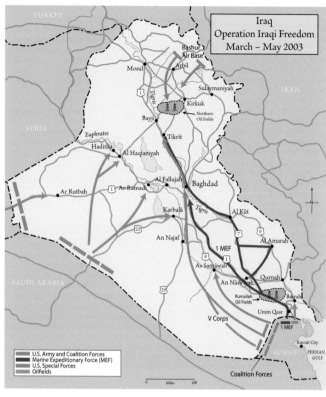

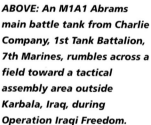

ABOVE: An M1A1 Abrams main battle tank from Charlie Company, 1st Tank Battalion, 7th Marines, rumbles across a field toward a tactical assembly area outside Karbala, Iraq, during Operation Iraqi Freedom.

ABOVE RIGHT: Some 60,000 Marines from the I MEF spearhead the opening attack during Operation Iraqi Freedom, and on March 21, 2003, cross the Kuwaiti border with the British First Armoured Division and roll north on the most direct route to Baghdad.

Ousting Saddam—Operation Iraqi Freedom

In March 2002, General Tommy Franks' CENTCOM planners went to work shaping the scope of a possible military operation to remove Iraqi dictator Saddam Hussein from power. An early rough sketch of the tactical plan never changed a great deal from the final plan. The problems faced were the building of a strong and capable Coalition, which proved troublesome, and verifying the existence of weapons of mass destruction (WMDs), which the CIA, Congress, and several Middle Eastern countries confirmed were there.

Commander of the I Marine Expeditionary Force (I MEF) Lieutenant General James T. Conway said the plan consisted of four distinct phases: a deployment phase, a shaping phase, a decisive operations phase, and a reconstruction phase. Conway's 60,000-man I MEF would share in every phase as part of the Third Army's V Corps ground force.

The V Corps became the main attack force with the I MEF sprinting north on the right flank, picking fights wherever one could be found, but always keeping abreast or slightly in advance of General Franks' main attack. After Turkey refused to cooperate, Franks added the entire 30,000-man British First Armored Division to the MEF, swelling Conway's command to nearly 90,000 Marines, sailors, and soldiers. Every American soldier conscious of stateside news banter asked the same question: "Is the country behind us?" Conway told every formation "not to worry about it" and to "just do their jobs."

On the evening of March 21, 2003, the "shock and awe" air campaign kicked off earlier than planned because on March 20 Saddam Hussein began destroying the Rumailah oilfields west of Basrah. At 9:30 p.m. the MEF crossed from Kuwait into Iraq where three Iraqi Corps—two regular army and one Republican Guard—lay waiting. Because the MEF expected to be hit with chemical weapons either as they crossed the Kuwaiti border or as they approached Republican Guard units near the Tigris River, they crossed the line of departure in bulky chemical suits and stayed in them for more than two weeks.

After Desert Storm, Commandants Mundy, Krulak, and Jones had shaped the Marine Corps into the deadliest killing machine on the battlefield. With air, ground, and logistics all integrated under a single commander, Conway delivered a punch that generated a speed and momentum that only a routed enemy could appreciate. He used 340 combat aircraft to deliver some 700 sorties a day on targets of choice. During Desert Storm, it took ten bombs to knock out a target. During Operation Iraqi Freedom, a single aircraft could destroy ten targets. An Iraqi tank commander later admitted making a forced eighty-mile retrograde movement to position his tanks east of Baghdad. He hid them in palm groves, thinking they would be safe. At 2:00 a.m. under the cover of darkness during the worst sandstorm in twenty years, Marine pilots began the systematic destruction of Iraqi tanks. After thirty had been ripped apart by pinpoint bombing, Iraqi troops abandoned the position and melted away.

After depositing British forces at Basrah, Marines worked through the Rumailah oilfields and in two columns—one taking Route 1, the other column Route 7—headed for the Tigris River and Baghdad. Iraqi formations crumbled. Some surrendered, others disappeared into the civilian population. After securing Baghdad, Conway sent a light armored column north to Tikrït to knock out any resistance around Hussein's birthplace. After securing Tikrït, Conway reviewed the assault and noted that the MEF had attacked farther and faster than any unit in U.S. history. He tried to convince his army boss, Lieutenant General David McKiernan, that "Marines are assault troops, we don't do nation-building," but lost the argument. The MEF spent the next five and a half months trying to conduct reconstruction efforts in cities like Najaf, Karbala, and Samawah, and finally returned to Southern California in September 2003.

Operation Iraqi Freedom succeeded in achieving every military goal, including the eventual capture of Saddam Hussein. The civilian planners in Washington, however, underestimated the problems of reconstruction, tribal hostility, religious rivalry, and the opposition of militant mercenaries from other Muslim countries. After five months in California, the I MEF was ordered back to Iraq by Secretary of Defense Donald Rumsfeld for Operation Iraqi Freedom II, which has evolved into a classic and troublesome insurgency that continues to take the lives of American troops and Iraqi civilians.

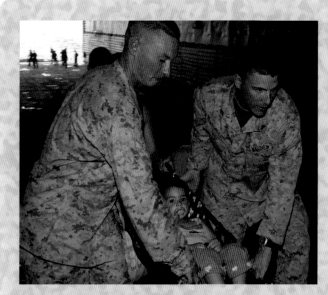

LEFT: During the fight between Syrian-backed Hezbollah militants and the Israeli army in July 2006, men from the 24th Marine Expeditionary Unit carry a child in a stroller to the USS Trenton during an evacuation of American and other foreign nationals from Beirut, Lebanon.

Lebanon Evacuation—2006

During July 2006, Hezbollah paramilitary troops from Lebanon crossed into Israel and captured two soldiers. After efforts failed to recover the illegally taken prisoners, war broke out between Israel and Hezbollah, the latter being for many years supported and armed by Iran and Syria. For thirty-four days Hezbollah rockets plunged into Israel's northern cities, while Israeli bombs and artillery blasted Lebanon's infrastructure.

Evacuees began piling up in Beirut. Marine Brigadier General Carl B. Jensen, commanding the newly established Expeditionary Strike Group (ESG), received a call from CENTCOM to handle the evacuation of Americans from Beirut. The new ESG concept contained an MEU, amphibious warfare ships, destroyers, frigates, and sometimes a subMarine. On July 15, Jensen arrived at Beirut ahead of the ships and began evacuating Americans using USAF MH-53 Pave Low helicopters and the cruise ship *Orient Queen*. A few days later

the *Iwo Jima* ESG arrived and evacuations began in earnest.

Based on early estimates, Jensen expected to extract about 1,500 Americans. On July 21 alone, the ESG moved 3,900 evacuees to waiting ships. By August 11 the number had grown to 14,500 American citizens. In addition to the *Iwo Jima* and the *Orient Queen* (which could take only about 1,200 passengers), Jensen brought in the *Nashville* and *Whidbey Island* from CENTCOM, and the *Trenton*, the *Berry*, and the *Gonzales* from the European command. On July 21, utility landing craft began picking up evacuees on the beach and transporting them to ships offshore.

Marines had not been in Lebanon since the 1983 terrorist bombing of the Beirut barracks. The site "is a sacred spot for the Marine Corps," Jensen recalled. Too many men had died, and in the war against terrorism, many more Marines will spill blood wherever terrorists threaten freedom.

INTO THE FUTURE

RIGHT: General Jones's detailed vision of the Marine Corps' future, proposed in November 2000, when he was commandant, called for widespread advances in weapons and equipment, and warfighting doctrine in land, sea, and air elements. At the heart of his proposals was the Marine Expeditionary Force.

FAR RIGHT: Rapid transportation of combat-ready Marines would include airlifting troops by air and sea. Here, Marines of the 3rd Battalion, 8th Marine Air Contingency Regiment from Camp Lejeune, catch some sleep on a C-17A Globemaster III cargo transport en route from Charleston Air Force Base, South Carolina, to Port-au-Prince, Haiti, on March 3, 2006,.

On November 3, 2000, General James L. Jones, Jr., the 32nd commandant, released *Strategy 21* and set the objectives for the future Marine Corps by providing "the vision, goals, and aims to support the development of future combat capabilities." Jones explained the strategy as building upon the Corps' "foundations of heritage, innovation, and excellence to move beyond the [status quo] and succeed on tomorrow's battlefields . . .

> . . . the strength of the Corps is the Marine, and the strength of the Marine is the Corps.
> *Commandant General James L. Jones, Jr., in* Marine Corps Strategy 21.

capitalizing on innovation, experimentation, and technology." In Jones's perspective, the signature characteristics of *Strategy 21* committed the Marine Corps to be the nation's premier expeditionary "Total Force in Readiness." He called for the 17,938 officers and 153,302 enlisted personnel to be "capable of a multitude of missions across the spectrum of conflict," while at the same time being nimble enough to "perform such other duties as the President may direct." Jones also envisioned the Corps as "scalable to meet combatant commanders' requirements" with the flexibility to participate in "joint, allied, and coalition operations."

The core became the Marine Expeditionary Force, which he divided into the four parts called the Marine Air-Ground Task Forces (MAGTF).

At the present time, elements from the MAGTF are posted around the world as a ready sea-based force against existing and potential threats.

Jones's *Marine Corps Strategy 21* proposed four distinct MAGTFs, all of which are connected directly to the navy, as follows.

ABOVE: The Wasp-*class amphibious assault ship USS* Kearsarge *passes through the Straits of Gibraltar on January 28, 2003, with the 2nd Marine Expeditionary Brigade during Operation Enduring Freedom.*

Marine Expeditionary Forces (MEFs) consist of up to 90,000 troops and are task-organized to fight in major theater wars. In addition to containing one or more Marine divisions, the MEF may often contain several MEB and MEU/SOC units.

Marine Expeditionary Brigades (MEBs) consist of up to 20,000 troops and are task-organized as a premier response force for smaller-scale actions. MEBs can also contain a number of MEU/SOC units.

Marine Expeditionary Units (Special Operations Capable)(MEU/SOCs) consist of 1,500 to 3,000 seabased troops task-organized to provide a first-on-the-scene, forward deployment presence with multiple capabilities. MEUs normally pave the way for MEF and MEB operations.

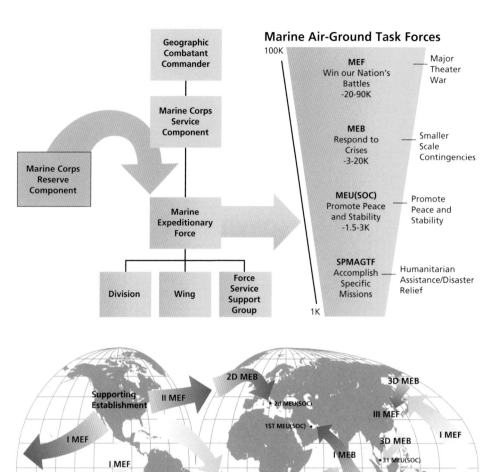

TOP: *In the current and future Marine Air-Ground Task Forces, forward deployed MEUs serve as advance echelons of MEBs, which in turn serve as advance echelons of MEFs.*

ABOVE: *Marine Expeditionary Forces (MEFs), Marine Expeditionary Brigades (MEBs), and Marine Expeditionary Units (Special Operations Capable) (MEU/SOCs) are currently posted around the world.*

Special Purpose MAGTFs (SPMAGTFs) of various size perform task-organized specific missions including humanitarian assistance, disaster relief, and peacetime engagement activities whether coming from amphibious ships, maritime prepositioning ships, or strategic airlift in response to terrorist attacks or other crisis-related matters.

ABOVE: General Michael W. Hagee (center), thirty-third commandant of the Marine Corps (2002–2006), listens attentively as Corporal Brad D. Widener of the 2nd Battalion, 5th Marines, 1st Marine Division, explains how his Trijicon TA31RCO-A4 advanced optical combat gunsight night vision system works with his M16A2 rifle and M203 grenade launcher attachment. At the time, Widener was engaged in Operation Iraqi Freedom security and stabilization operations in al Anbar Province.

General Jones designed the four basic MAGTFs to operate either independently or as part of a larger joint force. The MAGTF concept anticipates that during most operations forward-deployed MEU/SOCs will serve as advance echelons for MEBs, which in turn will serve either independently or as advance echelons for MEFs. As an example, the smaller MEU/SOC units flew into southern Afghanistan while larger MEBs formed the I MEF and played a principal combat role during Iraqi Freedom.

On July 1, 2003, Commandant Jones passed the baton to General Michael W. Hagee, the 33rd commandant of the Marine Corps. Unlike most outgoing commandants, Jones did not retire. He became the Supreme Allied Commander, Europe, and the

> Our *goal* is to capitalize on innovation, experimentation, and technology to prepare Marine Forces to succeed in the 21st century.
> *General James L. Jones, Jr., in* Marine Corps Strategy 21, *8.*

Commander of the United States European Command. Hagee stepped into the commandant's office at a time when the Corps had more than 39,000 Marines forward deployed or forward based against the "Global War on Terror." Like Jones, and the thirty-two commandants who preceded him, Hagee looked upon the Corps as "soldiers of the sea." Borrowing a concept from General Jones's *Strategy 21*, Hagee declared, "A guiding principle of the Marine Corps is that we fight as combined-armed teams, seamlessly integrating our ground, aviation, and logistics forces. We exploit the speed, flexibility, and agility inherent in our combined-arms approach to defeat traditional, terrorist, and emerging threats to our nation's security." (Quoted from Hagee, *USMC Concepts + Programs 2006*.)

When on July 1, 1920, General John A. Lejeune became the 13th commandant of the Marine Corps, he said: "Marine has come to signify all that is highest in military efficiency and soldierly virtue." Eighty-three years later, Commandant Hagee reminded the Corps of Lejeune's words, adding:

"I charge each and every Marine to join me in this challenging journey into the twenty-first century. Our tasks are before us—we will win the current battles and be ready to defeat the nation's future foes. Let us proceed with boldness, intellect, and confidence in each other, as we continue to forge the legacy of our great Corps and strive to take our rightful place in the 'long line' of Marines that 'have acquitted themselves with greatest distinction, winning new honors on each occasion.'" (Quoted from Commandant General Michael W. Hagee in *Commandant's Guidance*.)

Though engaged in a Global War on Terror (GWOT), it became Hagee's job to fuse the concepts, capabilities, and core competencies expressed in the U.S. Navy's vision document *Sea Power 21*, the Marine Corps' vision document *Marine Corps Strategy 21*, and the Marine Corps' capstone concept *Expeditionary*

Maneuver Warfare (EMW). Together, the three documents chart the future course of the Marine Corps.

Global War on Terror (GWOT)

The high operating tempo of GWOT and problems elsewhere compelled Commandants Jones and Hagee to reset the requirements for the Marine Corps. During recent operations in Afghanistan and Iraq, Marines reported equipment worth more than $180 million destroyed and $140 million damaged. Service life of many ground vehicles had been shaved from an expected life of more than twenty years to five, and the life of helicopters from twenty years to less than ten. The reasons need no elaboration. CH-46 helicopters assigned to GWOT currently fly at four times their planned utilization rate. To sustain operations in the Middle East, Marines have been forced to draw equipment from pre-positioning ships stationed elsewhere.

To reset force requirements, which include navy appropriations in support of the Marine Corps, General Hagee asked for $11.7 billion a year through 2020. The budget includes funds to re-establish capabilities impacted by GWOT operations in addition to funding for MAGTF modernizations and replacements of damaged or destroyed equipment.

The Marine Corps admits that the Global War on Terror could span decades. Seabasing, Expeditionary Maneuver Warfare, and Distributed Operations are the conceptual foundations of the 21st century Marine Corps. Expanded capabilities for forceful entry from the sea will be required. While the Marine Expeditionary Brigade provides the primary forcible entry force, the Marine Expeditionary Force will provide the principal contribution to the joint fight in major combat operations. Both the MEB and the MEF require Seabasing enhancements to provide combatant commanders with unprecedented versatility in operations ranging from cooperative security to major combat readiness.

Seabasing—The Maritime Prepositioning Force (MPF)

In conjunction with *Marine Corps Strategy 21*, the navy's future Maritime Prepositioning Force (MPF) will be the primary enabler of future sea-based operations. It will serve four functions: (1) at-sea arrival and assembly of units; (2) direct support of the assault echelon (the MEB); (3) indefinite sea-based support of the landing force; and (4), at-sea reconstitution and redeployment of the force. With Seabasing, no land base would be needed for follow-on forces to assemble and deploy, and no stationary target would exist for enemy ballistic missiles, cruise missiles, or weapons of mass destruction to target and strike.

The MPF provides all the elements for the Marine Air-Ground Task Forces, as well as the navy's Expeditionary Strike Force (ESG). The ESG contains not only a Maritime Prepositioning Force, but also cruisers, guided missile destroyers, frigates, and attack submarines. Yet a MEU(SOC) or a SPMAGTF, which are small components of the Marine Air-Ground Task Forces, also become components of the future MPF.

BELOW: Marines from the 26th MEU practice amphibious assault techniques on the beach at El Omayed, Egypt, during a multinational exercise involving more than 74,000 troops from forty-four countries that often partner with the United States in maintaining regional stability.

Expeditionary Maneuver Warfare (EMW)

As a part of *Sea Power 21*, *Naval Power 21*, and *Marine Corps Strategy 21*, Expeditionary Maneuver Warfare (EMW) becomes the capstone concept that determines how the Marine Corps will organize, deploy, employ, and sustain its forces today and in the future. It is the concept that capitalizes on the Marine Corps' philosophy of maneuver warfare and its expeditionary heritage as "soldiers of the sea." The EMW emphasizes agile and tactically flexible Marine Air-Ground Task Forces, with the operational reach to project power directly against critical points or threats in the littorals and beyond. EMW also moves the Marine Corps beyond traditional "amphibious operations" and toward "expeditionary warfare," which requires a broader range of operational capabilities and in turn expands organizational, deployment, employment, and sustainment methods. EMW relies on Seabasing and the Marine Air-Ground Task Forces as the central organizational concept and strengthens MAGTF capabilities with improved weaponry, technology, and warfighting doctrine.

Distributed Operations

The implementation of Distributed Operations is an extension of EMW that focuses on enhanced small units that are more autonomous, more lethal, and better able to operate across a wide spectrum of tasks. Distributed Operations can be widely dispersed Marines positioned in response to an enemy that does not attack in a conventional manner. Decision-making authority is pushed down the chain of command to younger, lower-ranking Marines operating on their own behind the lines or in areas where there are no lines. These are often forty-four-man platoon-sized operations resembling "boots-on-the-ground" tasks like those in Afghanistan and Iraq.

Distributed Operations often involve various tasks based on the mission, enemy dispositions, and the nature of the terrain. When pockets of the enemy are found, several distributed units will use swarming attacks bolstered by air attacks to defeat the enemy in detail. Marines have used the tactics with good results during the 2007 "surge" to stifle the activities of mercenaries and insurgents in Iraq.

Amphibious Ships

The total warfighting amphibious requirement for today's Marine Corps is two MEB Assault Echelons, which currently equates to thirty amphibious ships, including five large-deck LHA/LHD amphibious assault ships. *Strategy 21* increases MEB Assault Echelons to three. Today's navy cannot lift two MEB Assault Echelons, and to do so requires assistance from some of the ships comprising the Maritime Prepositioning

ABOVE: Today, Tarawa-class general-purpose assault ships (LHAs) form an integral part of eleven Amphibious Ready Groups, but the LHAs will reach the end their expected service lives by 2015.

BELOW: The Wasp-class amphibious assault ship USS Bataan gets underway with eight new MV-22 Osprey Marine tiltrotor aircraft for operational testing and evaluation of its package of advanced technology

Force. Currently, there are eleven large-deck amphibious assault ships (seven *Wasp*-class LHDs and four *Tarawa*-class LHAs) in service, with an eighth longer and wider *Wasp*-class LHD under construction.

To meet the objectives of the future MPF requires several improvements in amphibious ships. The five *Tarawa*-class amphibious assault ships will be replaced with the LHA(R) class, which are scheduled for delivery in 2013 and are part of the navy's *Seapower 21* program for supporting Sea Strike and Seabasing for MEBs. The new LHA(R)s will have three times the fuel capacity and are designed to carry either twenty-three F-35B Joint Strike Fighters (JSF) or twenty-eight MV-22A Osprey tiltrotors, or some of each. Helicopters will include a mix of CH-53E Sea Stallions, UH-1Y Hueys, AH-1Z Super Cobras, and MH-60 Seahawks. The new LHAs will carry a full brigade of 1,894 Marines.

The *San Antonio*-class Amphibious Transport Dock LPD-17 is currently replacing the *Austin*-class LPD-4.

TOP: Marines with full gear pile on board MV-22 Osprey vertical/short takeoff and landing multipurpose tactical aircraft during exercises. with the new MV-22 Osprey vertical/short takeoff and landing

ABOVE: A San Antonio-class Amphibious Transport Dock (LPD-17) pulls into port after returning to the United States as part of the 26th Marine Expeditionary Unit, Special Operations Capable, serving in Iraq.

The newly designed LPDs serve both the near- and far-term future of America's naval expeditionary forces. The *San Antonio*-class has a larger flight deck capable of launching or landing two MV-22 Ospreys or two CH-53E Super Stallion helicopters, or up to four CH-46 Sea Knight, AH-1, or UH-1Y helicopters. The LPD also has a well deck sized for two Landing Craft Air Cushion (LCAC) craft or one Landing Craft Utility (LCU). The ship also carries an embarked landing force of up to 800 Marines. The USS *San Antonio* went into commission in 2005. Four more from that class are currently in the construction schedule, with another four to follow.

Naval Surface Fire Support

Expeditionary operations depend on robust naval all-weather, round-the-clock, accurate sea-based fire support. The current Naval Surface Fire Support (NSFS) capability is inadequate in range, volume, and accuracy for supporting expeditionary operations over an extended battlefield. In order to engage targets from the sea in close support of maneuver forces with collateral damage concerns, the navy plans to field in 2011 the Extended Range Munition (ERM) on guided missile destroyers equipped with 5-inch/62-caliber guns. The ERM will enable MAGTF commanders to accurately engage targets with volumes of fire from GPS-guided precision weapons over the horizon, thereby extending the range from thirteen to sixty-three nautical miles, with multiple round impact of up to nine projectiles.

Beginning in 2014, the debut of the DD(X) Land Attack Destroyer will add a fully integrated, transformational fire support system of two 155mm Advance Gun Systems (AGS) with a 600-round magazine. The AGS, firing the Long Range Land Attack Projectile (LRLAP), will extend the lethal effects of fire support for MAGTF to 100 nautical miles.

Future fire support technologies include a Multipurpose Loitering Missile (MLM) and an Electro-

ABOVE: A Landing Craft Air Cushion (LCAC) is a high-speed, fully amphibious craft capable of carrying a 60-ton payload at speeds in excess of forty knots within a nominal range of 200 nautical miles.

magnetic Gun. The ship-launched MLM will be able to loiter over deep target areas to support long-range, tactical level operations. Battlefield commanders will also be able to harness the destructive power of Mach 7+ propelled projectiles using electromagnetic energy produced aboard the navy's future family of DD(X) and CG(X) all-electric destroyers and cruisers.

Landing Ships

The Landing Craft Air Cushion is a fully amphibious craft designed to carry a payload of more than 60 tons at 40 knots over a nominal range of 200 nautical miles. The LCAC's ability to ride on an air cushion allows it to operate directly from well decks on amphibious warships and to access more than 70 percent of the world's beaches, compared with 17 percent for conventional landing craft. Originally designed with a service life of thirty years, the craft is constantly being enhanced with command and control communications equipment, computers, navigation systems, and engine upgrades.

To address the Global War of Terror, a Joint Maritime Assault Connector (JMAC) is being explored to determine the feasibility of redesigning the LCAC to

ABOVE: The Marine Corps expects the first 40 knot-plus Joint High Speed Vessel (JHSV) to be funded in 2008. The ship will serve as a high-speed connector between sea-based operations and advanced follow-on operations ashore.

carry up to two M1A1 tanks and to have greater range to support sea bases operating twenty-five miles or more from the coast.

Two other high-speed connectors (HSCs) are also on the drawing board: the Joint High Speed Vessel (JHSV) and the Rapid Strategic Lift Ship (RSLS). The primary attributes of HSCs will be their capability to sustain high speeds over operational ranges while carrying significant payloads of personnel and equipment.

The JHSV, built with a draft of less than fifteen feet, will generate a speed of more than 40 knots. Unlike the LCAC with a range of 200 nautical miles, the JHSV will self-deploy from the continental United States or from forward basing sites. Once in a theater, the JHSV will play a crucial role in transporting a force from advanced bases to the sea base. Once within the sea base, the JHSV will support the transfer of personnel, supplies, and equipment to platforms of the Expeditionary Strike Group (ESG), thereby providing enhanced striking capability during forcible entry operations.

The Rapid Strategic Lift Ship (RSLS) will be designed along the lines of the JHSV but will be configured to deliver additional equipment, such as

non-self-deploying aircraft, to other land-based prepositioned sites in the Joint Operating Area.

Triad of Ground Fire

With the increased range and speed of Expeditionary Fighting Vehicles (which are currently in the concept stage to replace both light armored vehicles and M1A1 tanks) and the MV-22 Osprey tilt-rotor aircraft, access to the breadth and depth of the battlefield is rapidly increasing. To keep pace with increased maneuver technologies, the Marines are preparing a triad of new ground weapons.

The M777A1 lightweight 155mm towed howitzer began replacing the M198 standard howitzer in 2005. At 9,800 pounds, the new howitzer is 6,200 pounds lighter than the M198. The weapon has a range of fifteen miles using unassisted projectiles, or eighteen miles when firing assisted projectiles. A new Modular Artillery Charge System will reduce the number of propellant types used, and Multi-Option Fuze Artillery will reduce the number of fuzes in use.

BELOW: The High Mobility Artillery Rocket System (HIMARS) is an air-transportable, wheeled, indirect-fire, rocket/missile system capable of firing all types of rockets and missiles in the current and future Multiple Launch Rocket System family of munitions.

BELOW: The joint effort (Army and Marines) M777A1 Lightweight 155mm towed howitzer began replacing the M198 howitzer in 2005.

LEFT: A Marine Corps Osprey with rotors at full tilt practices touch and go landings on the flight deck of the multipurpose amphibious assault ship USS Wasp (LHD 1) during deck landing qualifications on December 6, 2006.

MV-22 Osprey

The MV-22 Osprey is neither a fixed-wing nor a rotary-wing aircraft. It is an advanced vertical/short takeoff and landing, multi-purpose tactical aircraft, designed with tilt-rotors. In forthcoming years, it will replace the weary fleet of Vietnam-era CH-46E and CH-53D helicopters currently in service. The MV-22 will join Marine amphibious assault ships in the MAGTF and become an integral part of Seabasing, along with Expeditionary Fighting Vehicles and LCACs. Marine pilots will fly MV-22s on a variety of missions, including expeditionary assault from land or sea, raid operations, medium cargo lift, tactical recovery of aircraft and personnel, and fleet logistic support.

The MV-22's 38-foot prop-motor system and engine/transmission nacelle mounted on each wing tip permit it to operate as a helicopter for take off and landing. Once airborne, the nacelles rotate forward 90 degrees, converting the aircraft to a high-speed, high-altitude, fuel-efficient turbo-prop aircraft. The Osprey has a 350 nautical mile combat radius and is capable of carrying twenty-four fully equipped Marines or a 10,000-pound load.

Marine Tiltrotor Operational Test and Evaluation Squadron Twenty-Two (VMX-22) began testing the tilt-rotor concept in 2003 and completed operational evaluation in June 2005. In September, after additional testing on the USS Bataan (LHD-5), the Defense Acquisition Board authorized full production of the Osprey. Twenty-nine Ospreys have already been delivered for training purposes to the Marine airbase at New River, North Carolina. The first deployment of the MV-22, planned for the fall of 2007, will begin replacing CH-46E Sea Knight and CH-53D Super Stallion helicopter squadrons at the rate of two per year.

The forthcoming High Mobility Artillery Rocket System (HIMARS) is designed to deliver high volumes of long-range rocket artillery in support of ground maneuver. HIMARS will fire a family of munitions for both precision and area operations, and will be capable of striking targets at distances of thirty-six miles in all weather conditions.

The Expeditionary Fire Support System (EFSS) is designed to accompany the Marine Air-Ground Task Force in any of its four modes of operation. It will be the primary indirect fire system for the vertical assault element of the ship-to-objective maneuver force. The system will be internally transported by CH-53 helicopters or MV-22 Ospreys to allow the greatest range and flexibility of employment.

In addition to the triad group, the Marine Corps also is developing enhancements to fire support platforms. The program includes a family of sensors, including the Ground Weapons Locating Radar, the Target Location Designation Handoff System, and the Common Laser Range Finder.

Rotary-wing Aircraft

The MV-22 Osprey program may never replace all helicopters, which is the reason rotary-wing aircraft continue to be upgraded. Although the CH-46 Sea Knight traces back to the Vietnam War, the newest version, the CH-46E, has been much improved. During Operation Iraqi Freedom, Sea Knights performed medium lift combat missions and still do. The platform meets the current Marine Air-Ground Task Forces joint warfighting requirements and will do so for at least another ten years. Operational power margins have been improved with increased engine reliability, and antiquated engine control systems have been simplified and replaced. New Aircraft Survivability Equipment Systems have also being installed, which include improved missile warning systems and infrared missile jamming systems. Lightweight ceramic armor has replaced the original steel armor, thereby increasing the helicopter's carrying capacity by 1,000 pounds.

The Sikorsky CH-53E Super Stallion has also been around since Vietnam. The three-engine, long-range, heavy-lift helicopter supports assault operations. Heavy work in the Global War on Terror has reduced the fatigue life of the helicopter to the end of this decade, and structural modifications will be required to keep the aircraft in service. Currently, there are no new CH-53Es in the building schedule.

Over the next fifteen years, a new model known only as the Heavy Lift Replacement (HLR) will eventually eliminate the Super Stallion. The HLR will have a maximum range of 480 nautical miles and the capability of externally lifting 27,876 pounds. The new helicopter is needed to meet the joint warfighting requirements of the MAGTF and will come with an Integrated Mechanical Diagnostic System, a T-64 Engine Reliability Improvement Program, a Helicopter Night Vision System, and missile warning systems, missile countermeasures, small arms protection, and self-defense weapons.

ABOVE: An AH-1W Cobra from Marine Light Attack Helicopter Squadron-167 prepares to land at al Asad Air Base, Iraq, following a March 5, 2007, Operation Iraqi Freedom mission.

Also to meet MAGTF requirements, 180 Bell AH-1W SuperCobra attack helicopters, scheduled to become AH-1Zs, and 100 Bell UH-1Y utility helicopters will undergo upgrades. An H-1 Upgrade Program is being implemented to reduce life-cycle costs of both helicopters and significantly improve operational capabilities. With changes, both aircraft can be operated and supported in the new squadron structure. Two-bladed rotors will be replaced with new, four-bladed, all-composite rotor systems. The helicopters will carry a more lethal weapons platform, and an integrated glass cockpit will be upgraded with modern digital avionics systems. Eighty-four percent of the components will be interchangeable between the two aircraft. Operational

enhancements include dramatic increases in speed, range, payload, and lethality in both aircraft. Super Cobras will be able to carry twice the current load of precision-guided munitions (2,500 pounds). The "build new" strategy for the UH-1Y kicked off in 2006, with the AH-1Z to follow.

TOP: U.S. Army troops board a Marine CH-46 Sea Knight on January 31, 2007, at Camp Hit, Iraq, to return home after the conclusion of their deployment.

ABOVE: To ensure that Marine have the best rotary-wing attack and utility support, the H-1-type helicopter shown will be upgraded with 100 UH-1Ys and 180 AH-1Zs for warfighting.

ABOVE LEFT: A CH-53E Super Stallion lifts pallets of meals ready to eat (MREs) from the amphibious assault ship USS Bataan on February 21, 2007.

Tactical Aircraft

The Tactical Aircraft Integration (TAI) plan to marry the navy's tactical aircraft with the Marine Corps has been a work-in-process for many years. Since early 2004, five of the Corps' eight F/A-18A Hornet squadrons have been operating from aircraft carriers. The first navy F/A-18 squadron deployed to the Marine air station at Iwakuni, Japan, in 2004. Integrating both services achieves two important purposes: it provides a smaller, yet more capable and affordable joint tactical air force and provides increased combat capability in forward areas, which fits nicely into the concept of forward Seabasing.

McDonnell Douglas F/A-18A/C/D Hornets have been around for many years. They are constantly being upgraded with avionics and hardware to make them capable of carrying all current and programmed future weapons. Upgraded models, referred to as "A+" aircraft, will remain in active inventory until 2015. As existing models are decommissioned, Marine Corps pilots will begin shifting to F/A-18E/F Super Hornets in the navy's inventory.

The more recent F/A-18D has been upgraded to carry the Advanced Tactical Airborne Reconnaissance System (ATARS), which provides broad battlefield reconnaissance for Marine Air-Ground Task Forces. Eighteen ATARS sensor suites with digital solid-state recording systems are now operational in all six Marine F/A-18D squadrons.

Marine F/A-18s are 56 feet in length, 15 feet 4 inches high, and have a wingspan of 40 feet 5 inches. They depend on two F404-GE-402 enhanced performance turbofan engines for thrust to push them along at speeds approaching Mach 2 at 50,000 feet. A, C, and E models are single-seat; B, D, and F models

LEFT: Marine Helicopter Squadron One (HMX-1) provides safe and timely transportation for the president and vice president. The current helicopters, a VH-3D (shown) and a VH-60N, are aging designs scheduled for replacement in October 2009 by Lockheed Martin's 14-passenger VH-71A, which will have a 350 nautical mile range and an airspeed of 140 knots.

The President's Helicopter

Marine Helicopter Squadron One (HMX-1), which was first organized in December 1947, provides safe and timely transportation for the president, the vice president, foreign heads of state, and others as directed by the White House Military Office. HMX-1 operates two types of aircraft, the Lockheed Martin VH-3D and the VH-60N. When the president is on board Marine One, the aircraft becomes the commander-in-chief's primary command and control platform and provides him with the flexibility and capabilities necessary to execute the duties of his office. The nature of presidential commitments makes it essential for HMX-1 aircraft to deploy worldwide and operate in varying environmental and climate conditions.

The Global War on Terror has made it necessary to improve communications and survival capabilities beyond the current helicopter fleet's structural and performance characteristics. The navy has initiated a Presidential Helicopter Replacement Program (VXX), with two new vertical lift aircraft having improved safety and survivability features and the capability to provide improved and uninterrupted communications with all required agencies. The contract for the new VH-71A went to Lockheed Martin in January 2005 and completion is scheduled for October 2009. The new helicopter will have a 350 nautical mile range and a 140 knot maximum airspeed, and will be capable of carrying fourteen passengers.

ABOVE LEFT: An F/A-18C Hornet from Strike Fighter Squadron-146 launches from the flight deck of the carrier USS John C. Stennis, which is deployed in the Arabian Sea for operations in both Afghanistan and Iraq.

have a crew of two. Hornets are typically armed as follows: one M61A1.A2 Vulcan 20mm cannon; a mix of AIM-9 Sidewinder, AIM-7 Sparrow, AIM-120 AMRAAM, Harpoon, Harm, SLAM, SLAM-ER, and Maverick missiles; Joint Stand-Off Weapons; Joint Direct Attack Munitions (JDAM); and various general purpose bombs, mines, and rockets.

The McDonnell Douglas AV-8B V/STOL Harrier II has also been around for many years and is the principal strike aircraft on amphibious assault ships. The AV-8B performs both close and deep air support using conventional and guided weapons. Depending upon the mission, AV-8Bs carry MK-82 500-pound bombs, MK-83 series 1,000-pound bombs, GBU-12 500-pound laser guided bombs, GBU-16 1,000-pound laser guided bombs, AGM-65E infrared Maverick missiles, AGM-65E Laser Maverick missiles, CBU-99 cluster munitions, AIM-9M Sidewinders, and a Lightning II targeting POD to deliver GBU bombs with pinpoint accuracy.

The F-35B Joint Strike Fighter is being developed for the Marine Corps, navy, and air force as the nation's next generation strike fighter. The Lockheed Martin/Northrop Grumman aircraft will be a stealthy, supersonic strike-fighter, with a short takeoff, vertical landing (STOVL) variant for the Marine Corps, an aircraft carrier-capable variant for the navy, and a conventional takeoff and landing variant for the USAF. The F-35B will replace the AV-8B and F/A-18A/C/D in the Marine Corps, the F/A-18C in the navy, and the F-16C and A-10 in the air force. Marine F-35Bs will have a 450 nautical mile combat radius and be capable of 550-foot short takeoffs when fully loaded with the equivalent of two 1,000-pound bombs and two air-to-air missiles. British Aerospace Engineering is also involved in the project as a full partner. The Netherlands, Canada, Denmark, Norway, Turkey, and Australia also hold lesser partnerships in the project.

As a part of the F-35B's advanced mission systems, all radar, targeting, and distributed aperture electronics will be incorporated into the pilot's helmet-mounted display monitor, thereby eliminating the need for the traditional heads-up display in the cockpit.

The F-35B is still going through design review. Low rate initial production is scheduled for 2007, but the demonstration phase is not expected to finish until 2013.

TOP: The aging F/A-18 is constantly being improved with software and accessory enhancements.

ABOVE: AV-8B Harriers have recently been enhanced with new computer equipment, enabling them to employ bomb variants equipped with target-seeking Joint Direct Attack Munitions (JDAMs).

require a Vertical Unmanned Aircraft System (VUAS) to fill the complex mission requirements in the Global War on Terror and other area threats. Pioneers are constantly being upgraded to increase flight hours from 1,500 to 4,500 a year, with new engines, sensors, and communications systems, and every effort is being made to keep the UAVs operational until the VUAS comes on stream in the 2013–2015 timeframe.

The mission of the VUAS is to support JTF/MAGTF commanders with real-time reconnaissance, surveillance, targeting, and weapons employment. The aircraft fits neatly into the Marine corp's future doctrinal concepts of expeditionary maneuver warfare, Seabasing, and ship-to-objective tactics. VUAS will fly autonomously or under the control of ground-based or airborne commands. It will carry noise signature equipment, a payload of electro-optical infrared cameras, and an improved laser designator and radio relay. The aircraft will be able to employ a vertical takeoff and landing system that will enable it to be launched and recovered aboard ships or in hostile ground locations. When the VUAS becomes available during the next decade, on-board systems working with the interoperable communications suite in the Ground Control Station will make the unmanned aircraft a multi-mission force multiplier with limitless applicability across the spectrum of Marine Corps missions.

ABOVE: A "Night Owl" RQ-2A Pioneer surveillance Unmanned Aerial Vehicle (UAV) is launched from its dual-rail catapult mounted on a five-ton truck during trials at the Cherry Point Marine Base, North Carolina.

Unmanned Aerial Vehicles

The Marine Corps has employed unmanned aerial vehicles (UAVs), such as the Pioneer, since 1986 to provide near real-time reconnaissance, surveillance, and intelligence to tactical commanders. During Desert Storm, a battalion of Iraqi soldiers attempted to surrender to a UAV! The requirements of the MAGTF

The Dragon Eye UAV

The Dragon Eye is a family of reusable and expendable low-cost UAVs equipped with sensor systems designed to provide intelligence and situational awareness to small unit maneuver and support commanders. The aerial vehicle weighs six pounds, has a 45-inch wingspan, and is powered by two battery-operated motors that move the UAV at 35mph at 300 to 500 feet above the ground. The vehicle is bungee-launched by two Marines and flies its route by using Global Positioning Satellite data for navigation. The Dragon Eye can be assembled and launched in about ten minutes. It is preprogrammed from the ground, requires no other operator input, and has a range of about 10 kilometers (line of sight). The UAV has already been satisfactorily tested in Iraq and 342 systems are currently authorized for production.

LEFT: A Dragon Eye Unmanned Aerial Vehicle (UAV) being launched at Camp Ripper, Kuwait, during Operation Iraqi Freedom.

Ground Combat Equipment

Ground combat remains an integral part of the relationship between the navy and the Marine Corps. Every Marine is a rifleman and a warfighter, regardless of the spectrum of tasks to which he or she may be assigned. In order to meet the future objectives of the MAGTF, an entirely new arsenal of weapons and weapon systems will be emerging over the next several years.

In 2007, the Infantry Automatic Rifle program began replacing the current M249 Squad Automatic Weapon. The new 5.56mm automatic rifle will be lighter, more durable, and more reliable, thereby enhancing the rifleman's maneuverability and displacement speed. Full replacement of the M249 is scheduled for 2008.

The current Modular Weapon System (MWS) consists of an M16A4 rifle and an M4A1 carbine. Both weapons are being retrofitted with a mounting adapter for infrared target designators, optics, a modified M203 launching system, and other equipment, which together improves accuracy, target detection, and engagement capabilities day or night. The Rifle Combat Optic (RCO) is a fixed 4X optical sight attached to the rail adapter of M16/M4A1 rifles. The RCO uses dual illumination technology—fiber optics for daytime and tritium for night and low-light conditions.

The Marine Corps Sniper System consists of three primary weapon systems: the M40A3 Sniper Rifle, the Designated Marksman Rifle (DMR), and the M82A3 Special Application Scoped Rifle (SASR). The M40A3 is a bolt-action, extended range, anti-personnel weapon used for precision engagement of enemy targets out to 1,000 yards. The DMR is a semi-automatic, precision antipersonnel weapon designed primarily for security, explosive ordnance disposal, and anti-terrorism missions. The SASR is a semi-automatic, extended range, antimaterial weapon designed to fire a variety of .50 caliber ammunition at targets up to a mile. The M82A3 SASR was being replaced by the M107 SASR beginning in late 2007.

LEFT: Sergeant Anthony Viggianni of the 2nd Battalion, 6th Marines, 22nd MEU(SOC), carries his 5.56mm M16A4 rifle while returning from combat against Taliban insurgents in Afghanistan on June 3, 2004. Three Marines were wounded in a firefight that killed five Taliban.

BELOW: A Marine from Company "C", 1st Battalion, 7th Marines, patrols the streets of Qadawi, Baghdad, with a loaded SMAW (shoulder-launched multipurpose assault weapon) rocket launcher as he and fellow Marines from the 1st Tank Battalion root out insurgents lurking in buildings during the evening of April 11, 2003.

ABOVE: Lance Corporal Juan Vella, a sniper with the 1st Battalion, 4th Marines, Regimental Combat Team 1 (RCT-1), sights through the telescope mounted atop his 7.62mm M40A1 sniper rifle.

will also include night vision, laser range finding, variable magnification, and special capabilities for fighting in urban environments.

A new generation of lightweight night vision equipment is being made available to Marines on the ground: AN/PVS-7 night vision goggles and the AN/PVS-14 monocular night vision device. AN/PVS-7 goggles use prisms and lenses to provide the Marine with simulated binocular vision. The binocular device comes with a neck strap but can be mounted to the head or helmet. AN/PVS-14 monocular night vision devices use image intensifier technology. The unit can be used as a hand-held pocket scope or be fixed to the head, helmet, or weapon mount.

The MAGTF has established a Company and Battalion Mortars Program to meet the requirements of 24-hour, all-weather, offensive and defensive operations and maneuver on the battlefield. Improved systems on the drawing board will in 2008 replace the M224 60mm mortar currently used by companies and the M252 81mm mortars used by battalions.

A Scout Sniper Capability Set (SSCS), consisting of a shooter and a spotter, is currently being programmed for release from 2008. Replacements include the spotting scope, which has not been changed for fifty years, and the addition of day and night optical devices for the M40A3 and M82A3 sniper rifles. The SSCS

Expeditionary Fighting Vehicles

To support the role of the MAGTF, the Marine Corps has initiated an acquisition program to meet the requirements of Expeditionary Maneuver Warfare (EMW). By the 2020-2025 timeframe, the Corps plans to replace all the Light Armor Vehicles (LAVs) and main battle tanks now in service with vehicles of enhanced fighting capability. Another goal is to reduce vehicular weights, increase component commonality, and provide better fuel efficiency compatible with Seabasing objectives.

- The Expeditionary Fighting Vehicle (EFV) will become the primary means of tactical mobility for the Marine rifle squad during amphibious operations ashore. In 2010 the EFV will begin replacing the Assault Amphibious Vehicle (AAV7A1), which was fielded in 1972 and is now thirty-five years old. Fully tracked and armored, an EFV will be operated by a crew of three and be capable of transporting seventeen combat-equipped Marines ashore using any body of water available. An EFV will also have the speed and maneuverability to operate with main battle tanks on shore.

- As part of the Firepower Enhancement Program, the Corps' M1A1 main battle tank will receive the new second-generation thermal sight and a far-target location capability. The advanced thermal sight consists of infrared optics and an infrared focal plane array. Targeting accuracy will further be improved with laser rangefinders tied to a Global Positioning System Receiver capable of delivering munitions to targets within a 30-yard circle at a distance of 5,000 yards, day or night,

MAGTF Total Munitions Requirements		
	2006	2007
Small Arms Family	186,657,724	139,881,017
Mortar Family	77,070	104,766
Tank Family	5,091	11,833
Artillery	150,578	225,154
Rocket Family	0	4,000

FAR LEFT, TOP: Marine sniper systems include the M82A3 Special Application Scoped Rifle (SASR), a semi-automatic, extended range, anti-material weapon designed to fire .50-caliber ammunition to 1,600 meters.

ABOVE CENTER: Marines taking the Infantry Officer's Course lay down covering fire with an M224 60mm lightweight mortar during assault training at Twenty-nine Palms, California.

ABOVE: The new Expeditionary Fighting Vehicle (EFV) looks like an amphibious tank and an Assault Amphibious Vehicle rolled into one, which in short almost describes what it is. By 2010 it will begin replacing most amphibious assault vehicles, but not tanks.

ABOVE: The Assault Breacher Vehicle (ABV) is a tracked, armored engineer vehicle that provides deliberate or in-stride capability to breach minefields and problematic obstacles. The vehicle comes equipped with a full-width mine plow, two MK155 linear demolition charge systems, a remote control system, and a lane-marking system mounted on an M1A1 tank chassis.

through smoke, fog, or other battlefield obscurants.

- The development and retrofit of Light Armored Vehicles (LAVs) is actually a combination of a Service Life Extension Program (SLEP) in addition to developing new LAVs to replace those still in service. The SLEP program has already completed installation of upgrades in most of the fleet. These include new thermal sights with integrated laser rangefinders, updated computer capability, the latest command and control hardware and software systems, and improved ballistic protection and automatic fire suppression. New LAVs with all the fleet upgrades and others on the drawing board will begin to come on line in 2007. Light armored vehicles currently in use include the LAV-25, which carries a crew of two and seven troops; the LAV-AT (anti-tank), which has a crew of four; the LAV-C2 (command and control), which carries a

driver and six command personnel; the LAV-L (logistics), which carries a crew of three with replenishment supplies; the LAV-M (mortar), which carries a driver and mortar crew; and the LAV-R (recovery), which carries a crew of three to recover and support disabled vehicles.

- An Assault Breacher Vehicle (ABV) is a new tracked and armored engineer vehicle that provides the MAGTF with the capability to breach minefields and obstructions. The vehicle is equipped with a Full-Width Mine Plow, two MK 155 Linear Demolition Charge Systems, a Remote Control System, and a Lane Marking System mounted on an M1A1 tank chassis. The ABV can be operated either remotely or by a two-man crew and is fast enough to keep pace with the maneuver force. The first nineteen combat units were in the schedule for 2007.

Sergeant Major of the Marine Corps

Only one enlisted Marine bears the title "Sergeant Major of the Marine Corps," the highest enlisted grade in the Corps. In 1957 Sergeant Major Wilbur Bestwick became the first to hold the rank. His pay was $320 per month, compared with roughly $5,000 today.

On June 27, 2003, 48-year-old John L. Estrada became the fifteenth Sergeant Major of the Marine Corps. He works in the Office of the Commandant and represents the 159,292 active duty enlisted force, of which 24,000 are still teenagers and 107,000 are on their first enlistment. Estrada enlisted in the Marine Corps on September 5, 1973, and completed training as an F-4 aircraft mechanic. In August 1982 he became a drill instructor at Marine Corps Recruit Depot in San Diego, California, and two years later was meritoriously promoted to gunnery sergeant. His office is now in the Pentagon, some fifty feet from the commandant. He travels regularly with the commandant and meets frequently with generals. When he chats with senior enlisted men, they listen carefully. His recommendations to the commandant bear great weight, and his testimony before U.S. Senate committees is carefully considered because of his knowledge of everything from high-tech weapons to training requirements.

Like the commandant, the Sergeant Major of the Marine Corps serves a four-year term, and he is there to represent the enlisted Marine in the affairs of the Corps.

ABOVE: Sergeant Major of the Marine Corps is the highest ranking non-commissioned officer in the Corps. Carlton W. Kent replaced John L. Estrada (pictured) in the role, mid-2007.

LEFT: Commandant of the Marine Corps General James T. Conway speaks to Marines on March 21, 2007, at the Norfolk Naval Station in Virginia. Conway's tasks are particularly challenging because on November 13, 2006, he received the baton from Commandant General Hagee, who in 2006 was responsible for developing the Marine Corps' Concepts and Programs for the future, many of which still require implementation.

Changing of the Guard

On November 13, 2006, General James T. Conway became the 34th commandant of the Marine Corps. He said that his job, among other matters, was to "posture the Marine Corps for the future." Part of his role involved providing a right-sized force of special breed warriors "equal to every generation that has gone before them" and consisting of men and women who are "combat-tested, smart, tough, and rightfully proud." With such people, Conway intends to build a Corps of the future "on the solid foundation of the Marine Air Ground Task Force (MAGTF)," which has already demonstrated "uncommon versatility in combat environments" and will continue to do so in the future.

Wherever threats exist, Marines will be the first to respond. In the past, they have answered the nation's most urgent calls, and in the future they will always be ready to respond whenever the president calls. They are, as their motto states, always faithful.

BIBLIOGRAPHY

Alexander, Joseph H. and Bartlett, Merrill L.. *Sea Soldiers in the Cold War: Amphibious Warfare, 1945-1991.* Annapolis: Naval Institute Press, 1994.

_____. *Storm Landings: Epic Amphibious Battles in the Central Pacific.* Annapolis: Naval Institute Press, 1997.

Arthur, Robert A. and Cohlmia, Kenneth. *The Third Marine Division.* Washington: Infantry Journal Press, 1948.

Bayler, Walter J. *Last Man Off Wake Island.* Indianapolis: Bobbs-Merrill Company, 1943.

Belote, James H. and William, M. *Corregidor: The Saga of a Fortress.* New York: Harper & Row Publishers, 1967.

Berry, Henry. *Semper Fi, Mac: Living Memories of the U.S. Marines in World War II.* New York: Arbor House, 1982.

Butler, Smedley D. *Old Gimlet Eye: The Adventures of Smedley D. Butler.* New York: Farrar and Rinehart, 1933.

Cagle, Malcolm W. and Manson, Frank A. *The Sea War in Korea.* Annapolis: U.S. Naval Institute, 1957.

Catlin, Alburtus W. *With the Help of God and a Few Marines.* New York: Scribner's, 1918.

Chenelly, Joseph R. "Aviation Deck Operations," *Marine Corps News,* 20 June 2001.

_____. "15th MEU(SOC) Stands Ready," *Marine Corps News,* 11 October 2001.

_____. "Harrier Jets Conduct Airstrikes in Afghanistan," *Marine Corps News,* 4 November 2001.

Clifford, Kenneth J. *Progress and Purpose: A Developmental History of the U.S. Marine Corps, 1900-1970.* Washington: History and Museums Division, HQMC, 1973.

Coe, Charles. *Young Man in Vietnam.* New York: Scholastic, Inc., 1990.

Cohen, Roger and Gatti, Claudio. *In the Eye of the Storm.* New York: Berkley Publishing Co., 1991.

Collum, Richard S. *History of the United States Marine Corps.* Philadelphia: R. L. Hamersly and Company, 1890.

Conway, James T. "Farther and Faster in Iraq." *Proceedings,* 1233 (January 2005), 48-52.

_____. "Lethal, Scalable, & Responsive," *Proceedings,* 1,246 (December 2006), 20-121.

Cosmas, Graham A., ed. *Marine Flyer in France: The Diary of Captain Alfred A. Cunningham.* Washington: History and Museums Division, HQMC, 1974.

Daniels, Josephus. *The Wilson Era.* Chapel Hill, N.C.: University of North Carolina Press, 1946.

DeChant, John A. *Devilbirds.* Harper & Row Publishers, 1947.

De St. Jorre, John. *The Marines.* New York: Doubleday, 1989.

Ellsworth, Harry A. *One Hundred Eighty Landings of the United States Marines, 1800-1934.* Washington: History and Museums Division, HQMC, 1974.

Frank, Benis M. *Marines in Lebanon, 1982-84.* Washington, D.C.: Government Printing Office, 1987.

Franks, Tommy. *American Soldier.* New York: 10 Regan Books, 2004.

Geer, Andrew C. *The New Breed: The Story of the U.S. Marines in Korea.* New York: Harper and Brothers, 1952.

Gordon, Michael R. and Trainor. Bernard C. *The General's War.* Boston: Little, Brown, 1995.

Griffiths, D. N. "Waging Peace in Bosnia," *Naval Institute Proceedings,* No. 1,091, January, 1994.

Hagee, Michael W. *USMC Concepts + Programs.* USMC, 2006.

_____. "33rd Commandant of the Marine Corps – Guidance." http://www.marines.mil/cmc/33cmc.nsf/attachments/$File/33cpg.pdf

Halsey, William F. *Admiral Halsey's Story.* New York: Whittlesy House, 1947.

Harbord, James G. *The American Army in France.* Boston: Little, Brown and Company, 1936.

Heinl, Robert D., Jr. *Soldiers of the Sea: The U.S. Marine Corps, 1775-1962.* Annapolis: U.S. Naval Institute, 1962.

_____. *Victory at High Tide: The Inchon-Seoul Campaign.* Philadelphia: Lippincott, 1968.

Hewitt, Linda L. *Women Marines in World War I.* Washington: History and Museums Division, HQMC, 1974.

Hilburn, Matt. "The Rescuer," *Seapower,* 49:10 (October 2006), 48-50.

Hunt, George P. *Coral Comes High.* New York: Harper & Row Publishers, 1946.

Isely, Jeter A., and Crowl, Philip A., *The U.S. Marines and Amphibious War: Its Theory and Practice in the Pacific.* Princeton, N.J.: Princeton University Press, 1951.

Jones, James L., Jr. *Marine Corps Strategy 21.* http://www.usmc.mil/templateml.nsf/25241abbb036b230852569c400 4eff0e/$FILE/strategy.pdf

Kelly, Mary Pat, "Rescue: Out of Bosnia," *Naval Institute Proceedings,* No. 1,109, July, 1995.

Kent, Zachary. *The Persian Gulf War.* Hillside, N.J.: Enslow Publishers, Inc., 1994.

King, John. *The Gulf War.* New York: Macmillan Publishing Co., 1991.

Kosnik, Mark E. "The Military Response to Terrorism," *Naval War College Review,* Spring, 2000.

Kreisher, Otto, "Marines Passing the Torch in More Ways Than One," *Proceedings,* 1241 (July 2006), 15.

Krulak, Victor H. *First to Fight: An Inside View of the U.S. Marine Corps.* Annapolis: Naval Institute Press, 1984.

Lehrack, Otto J. *No Shining Armor: The Marines at War in Vietnam.* Lawrence, Kan.: University Press of Kansas, 1992.

Lejeune, John A. *The Reminiscences of a Marine.* Philadelphia: Dorrance and Company, 1930.

McClellan, Edwin N. *The United States Marine Corps in the World War.* Washington: Historical Section, HQMC, 1968.

_____. "A Brief History of the Fourth Brigade of Marines," *Marine Corps Gazette,* December, 1919.

McMillan, George. *The Old Breed: A History of the First Marine Division in World War II.* Washington: Infantry Journal Press, 1949.

Merrill, W. A. "This Is My Rifle," *Marine Corps Gazette,* December, 1960.

Metcalf, Clyde H. *A History of the United States Marine Corps.* New York: G. P. Putnam's Sons, 1939.

Miller, Nathan. *Sea of Glory: The Continental Navy Fights for Independence, 1775-1783.* New York: David McKay Company, 1974.

Millet, Allan R. *Semper Fidelis: The History of the United States Marine Corps.* New York: Macmillan Publishing Company, 1980.

Montross, Lynn. *U.S. Marine Corps Operations in Korea, 1950-1953.* 5 vols. Washington: Historical Branch, HQMC, 1954-1972.

Morison, Samuel Eliot. *History of United States Naval Operations in World War II.* 15 vols. Edison, N.J.: Castle Books, 2001.

Moskin, J. Robert. *The U.S. Marine Corps Story.* Boston: Little, Brown, 1992.

Nash, Howard P., Jr. *The Forgotten Wars.* New York: A.S. Barnes and Company, 1968.

Navy Department. *Naval Documents Related to the United States War with the Barbary Pirates.* Washington: Government Printing Office, 1939-45.

_____. *Naval Documents Related to the Quasi-War between the United States and France.* Washington: Government Printing Office, 1935-38.

_____. *Official Records of the Union and Confederate Navies in the War of the Rebellion.* Washington: Government Printing Office, 1894-1922.

Newcomb, Richard F. *Iwo Jima.* New York: Holt, Rinehart and Winston, Inc., 1965.

Parker, William D. *A Concise History Of the United States Marine Corps 1775-1969.* Washington: Historical Division Headquarters, U. S. Marine Corps, 1970.

Proehl, C. W. *The Fourth Marine Division in World War II.* Washington: Infantry Journal Press, 1946.

Quilter, Charles J. *U.S. Marines in the Persian Gulf: With the I Marine Expeditionary Force in Desert Shield and Desert Storm.* Washington: History and Museums Division, 1993.

Richards, T. A., "Marines in Somalia: 1992," *Naval Institute Proceedings,* No. 1,083, May 1993.

Russ, Martin. *The Last Parallel.* New York: Rinehart, 1957.

Schwarzkopf, H. Norman, with Petre, Peter. *It Doesn't Take a Hero.* New York: Bantam, 1992.

Sherrod, Robert. *History of Marine Corps Aviation in World War II.* Washington: Combat Forces Press, 1952.

_____. *On to Westward.* New York: Duell, Sloan and Pierce, 1945.

Simmons, Edwin H. *The United States Marines: The First Two Hundred Years, 1775-1976.* New York: Viking Press, 1974.

Simmons, Edwin H., et al. *The Marines in Vietnam, 1954-1973: An Anthology and Annotated Bibliography.* Washington: History and Museums Division, HQMC, 1974.

Sledge, Eugene B. *With the Old Breed at Peleliu and Okinawa.* Annapolis: Naval Institute Press, 1996.

Smith, Charles R. *Marines in the Revolution: A History of the Continental Marines in the American Revolution, 1775-1783.* Washington: History and Museums Division, HQMC, 1975.

Smith, Holland M. *Coral and Brass.* New York: Scribner's, 1949.

Smith, S. E., ed. *The United States Marine Corps in World War II.* New York: Random House, 1969.

Stockman, J. R. *The Battle for Tarawa.* Washington: Combat Forces Press, 1947.

Sweetman, Jack. *American Naval History: An Illustrated Chronology of the U.S. Navy and Marine Corps 1775-Present.* Annapolis: Naval Institute Press, 1984.

Thomason, John J., Jr. *Fix Bayonets! And Other Stories.* New York: Scribner's, 1926.

Toland, John. *But Not in Shame.* New York: Random House, Inc., 1961.

Trevett, John. "Journal of John Trevett," *Rhode Island Historical Magazine,* vol. 7 (1887), 30-48.

Twining, Merrill B. *No Bended Knee: The Battle for Guadalcanal.* Novato: Presidio, 1996.

Vandegrift, A. A. *Once a Marine: The Memoirs of a General.* New York: W. W. Norton & Company, 1964.

Westcott, Allan, ed. *American Sea Power Since 1775.* Philadelphia: J. B. Lippincott Company, 1947.

Wolfert, Ira. *Battle for the Solomons.* Boston: Houghton Mifflin Company, 1943.

Zimmerman, John L. *The Guadalcanal Campaign.* Washington: Combat Forces Press, 1949.

INDEX